Badiou and Deleuze Read Literature

Plateaus – New Directions in Deleuze Studies

'It's not a matter of bringing all sorts of things together under a single concept but rather of relating each concept to variables that explain its mutations.'
Gilles Deleuze, *Negotiations*

Series Editors

Ian Buchanan, University of Wollongong
Claire Colebrook, Penn State University

Editorial Advisory Board

Keith Ansell Pearson
Ronald Bogue
Constantin V. Boundas
Rosi Braidotti
Eugene Holland
Gregg Lambert
Dorothea Olkowski
Paul Patton
Daniel Smith
James Williams

Titles available in the series

Dorothea Olkowski, *The Universal (In the Realm of the Sensible): Beyond Continental Philosophy*
Christian Kerslake, *Immanence and the Vertigo of Philosophy: From Kant to Deleuze*
Jean-Clet Martin, *Variations: The Philosophy of Gilles Deleuze*, translated by Constantin V. Boundas and Susan Dyrkton
Simone Bignall, *Postcolonial Agency: Critique and Constructivism*
Miguel de Beistegui, *Immanence – Deleuze and Philosophy*
Jean-Jacques Lecercle, *Badiou and Deleuze Read Literature*
Ronald Bogue, *Deleuzian Fabulation and the Scars of History*
Sean Bowden, *The Priority of Events: Deleuze's Logic of Sense*
Craig Lundy, *History and Becoming: Deleuze's Philosophy of Creativity*
Aidan Tynan, *Deleuze's Literary Clinic: Criticism and the Politics of Symptoms*

Visit the Plateaus website at www.euppublishing.com/series/plat

BADIOU AND DELEUZE
READ LITERATURE

Jean-Jacques Lecercle

EDINBURGH UNIVERSITY PRESS

© Jean-Jacques Lecercle, 2010, 2012

First published in hardback by Edinburgh University Press 2010

Edinburgh University Press Ltd
22 George Square, Edinburgh EH8 9LF

www.euppublishing.com

Typeset in Sabon
by Servis Filmsetting Ltd, Stockport, Cheshire

A CIP record for this book is available from the British Library

ISBN 978 0 7486 3800 0 (hardback)
ISBN 978 0 7486 4905 1 (paperback)

The right of Jean-Jacques Lecercle
to be identified as author of this work
has been asserted in accordance with
the Copyright, Designs and Patents Act 1988.

Contents

Introduction		1
Chapter 1	Disjunctive Synthesis	6
Chapter 2	A Question of Style	38
Chapter 3	Deleuze Reads Proust	68
Chapter 4	Badiou Reads Mallarmé	92
Chapter 5	A Modernist Canon? Badiou and Deleuze Read Beckett	119
Chapter 6	Reading the Fantastic after Badiou and Deleuze	158
Conclusion: Aesthetics or Inaesthetics?		189
Bibliography		205
Index		211

Introduction

Tell me which literary texts you read and how you read them and I shall tell you what kind of philosopher you are and how important your philosophical contribution is.

Alain Badiou begins the introduction to his magnum opus *Being and Event* by positing three numbered theses, or 'assumptions', about the 'current general state of philosophy'.[1] In a pastiche of the philosopher's practice, I shall start by stating my own three assumptions, or theses.

Thesis one. Badiou and Deleuze are two of the most important contemporary philosophers. This is the weak version of the thesis, which, I am afraid, is trivially true. All you have to do in order to ascertain this is to browse among the philosophy section of any Waterstone's bookshop. A few years ago, the shelves were filled with books of philosophy of an impeccably analytic cast, where applied ethics vied with the philosophy of mind. Today, Wittgenstein and Cavell (who is not even an analytic philosopher) are lone survivors in a sea of translations from the French or German: Adorno, Barthes, Baudrillard, Blanchot and so on to the end of the alphabet. Badiou and Deleuze figure prominently in that glorious list. There is hardly a text by Deleuze that has not been translated into English and translations of Badiou are coming thick and fast (the massive second part of his magnum opus, *Logic of Worlds*, published in 2006, has already been translated).[2] The time of the research monograph devoted to a little known philosopher is already past – the time of readers, primers and assorted cribs is increasingly near. So the weak version of my first thesis is trivially true indeed. But I decided to write this book because I believe in a *strong* version of the thesis: Badiou and Deleuze are *the* two major contemporary philosophers. I am entirely aware of the highly contentious nature of this strong version, perhaps even of its outright falsity. How dare I ignore Derrida or Foucault, or even Lyotard? And what about, if we extend the field, Adorno and Heidegger? At this stage, the strong version can only be supported by a philosophical decision (a move that should please

Badiou). Whether this will induce effects of truth remains to be seen. But the fidelity, to use Badiou's term, is already there: I believe that the work of Badiou and Deleuze is there to stay, *aere perennius*. And this Pascalian wager on the future of philosophy is supported by an analysis of what Badiou himself calls the 'moment of French philosophy': an 'adventure' that for him begins with Sartre's *Being and Nothingness* and ends with Deleuze and Guattari's *What Is Philosophy?*, but also, Badiou claims with characteristic but understandable immodesty, with his own work: 'Time will tell; though if there has been such a French philosophical moment, my position would be as its last representative.' [3] A strange statement for a philosopher who claims that what he has in common with Deleuze is the rejection of all thought of the end (as in the phrases 'the end of philosophy' or 'the end of history') and of finitude, but a statement that must be understood in the light of his conception of history as a dotted line of 'historical sequences' that produce eternal truths but that are themselves deciduous. I happen to believe that Badiou's claim, large as it may seem, is justified – that there is such a thing as a moment in French philosophy and that Deleuze and Badiou are its major representatives. In saying this, I have already moved towards my second thesis.

Thesis two. Badiou and Deleuze form a pair, which is a form of unity, the unity of a set, and a pair of opposites, which is a form of distance or separation. We could describe this in the language of Deleuze: they share a plane of immanence, where their individual lines cross (in agonistic strife), then converge and are entangled (in a philosophical correspondence), while remaining entirely distinct and ultimately separate. We shall need a concept to describe this form of relation which is a non-relation (and certainly a non-relationship) – the Deleuzian concept of 'disjunctive synthesis' will do the philosophical work that is needed. But we can also, more traditionally but perhaps more perspicuously, describe this situation in the language of Bourdieu (which in this case is not incompatible with the language of Deleuze): contemporary French philosophy is a field of forces, in which Badiou and Deleuze occupy two opposite places that function as poles and, by acting as attractors, structure the field. As we can see, my second thesis is as strong, and potentially as unpalatable, as the first. But there is a third thesis, which is perhaps even worse but which actually impelled me to write this book.

Thesis three. The best way to enter the (non-)relation between Badiou and Deleuze is through the way they read literature. Again,

Introduction

a weak version of the thesis is trivially true. Their interventions in the field of literature are as numerous as they are notorious. Badiou is a novelist and playwright, a complete philosopher like Sartre his mentor, and he is the author of theses on drama and a 'handbook' of what he calls 'inaesthetics', in reality a collection of essays mostly on literary texts.[4] His philosophical works, from *Théorie du sujet* to *Logic of Worlds*, abound in 'readings' of poems and other texts. Deleuze, at a time when he was still a historian of philosophy in the French tradition, devoted a volume to a reading of Proust, and the last collection of essays published in his lifetime is largely devoted to literature – obviously a lifelong passion.[5] The weak version of the thesis is even more trivial than this: in showing an interest in art (Deleuze wrote extensively on painting and the cinema, Badiou has an essay on dance in his 'handbook') as well as literature, Deleuze and Badiou play the usual role of continental philosophers who, unlike their analytical counterparts, never hesitate to wander beyond the narrow limits of their favourite subjects: Heidegger and Adorno, Foucault and Derrida, as the French language has it, *ne sont pas en reste* (they, too, wrote extensively on literature).

But there is a strong version of the thesis. It can take two forms. The first states that literature plays a crucial role in the contents of our philosophers' respective positions. For Badiou, literature is a condition of philosophy. Sometimes it is included in the field of art, one of the four fields (science, politics, art and love) in which events occur and procedures of truth are conducted – literature is a source of truth, unlike philosophy, whose more modest task is to 'compossibilise', to think together the truths produced in other fields. Sometimes, the conditions are, through synecdoche, reduced to two: the matheme and the poem, mathematics and literature. In both cases thinking the poem is, for the philosopher, of the essence. For Deleuze, literature is a constant source of thought experiments, it is one of the fields in which thought is at work, perhaps even in an exemplary fashion, as the literary text is a locus where the shift between interpretation ('What does it mean?') and experiment ('How does it work? Let's put it to work!') is least expected and most fruitful. This is why Proust, Lewis Carroll and a host of American writers are as important to philosophy as Hume and Spinoza. The second form of the strong version of the thesis goes one step further. In a pastiche of Deleuze's attitude, it is not interested in the contents of the philosophical positions of the two philosophers, even where they directly concern literature: it seeks to ask their texts the wrong question, not 'What does it say?' but 'How is it written?', a type of question usually reserved for literary texts, in which we perceive the local version of Deleuze's question, 'How does it work?' So the second form of the strong version demands that we attempt to describe the authors' style, their use of rhetoric, their taste for metaphor and/or narrative (a kind of philosophical analysis which is also characteristic of deconstruction). In other words, the second form suggests that the task of our critical account of that (non-)relation is to treat the two philosophers as poets (which in a sense they are): not only to read them, or to read them reading, but to read them writing.[6]

In doing all this, I am not particularly original, at least as far as the first form of the strong version of my third thesis is concerned. Badiou, in his essay on the moment of French philosophy, has already trodden that path. In that essay, he describes what he calls 'the alliance between philosophy and literature' as 'one of the characteristics of contemporary French philosophy'.[7] He enthuses over the quality of writing to be found in those texts ('they wanted to be *writers*').[8] He identifies the 'one essential desire' of the French philosophical moment as 'turning philosophy into an active form of writing that would be a medium for the new subject'.[9] By which, of course, he means the subject of the historical sequence of French philosophy, whose concept it is the task of that philosophy to construct. That the construction of a new concept of the subject is an essential concern of contemporary French philosophy is a highly contentious thesis – not least for Deleuze, who deemed the concept exhausted and created a host of substitutes (haecceities, assemblages, etc.) among which the philosophical work of the concept was distributed. Nevertheless, Badiou's analysis comforts me in my attachment to the strong versions of my first and my second thesis. Badiou and Deleuze, those conceptual characters, embody the two aspects of the French philosophical moment. They are separated by their individual philosophical positions and conjoined by their belonging to the same field of forces, to the same moment of the conjuncture. They are conjoined by their common appraisal of literature as a source of thought and by their fascination for the act of writing, as they are separated by their singular ways of reading literature as well as by their idiosyncratic philosophical styles, which are also styles of writing.

I would like to end this introduction on a personal note. I do not claim to belong to the 'French philosophical moment'. But I was a student in its heyday, and one can never forget the sheer exhilaration of reading philosophy in France in the late 1960s and early 1970s, of discovering the philosophies of Badiou and Deleuze. Glory was it in that dawn to be alive, but to be a student was very heaven.

And I don't believe for a moment it was a sunset.

Notes

1. A. Badiou, *Being and Event*, London: Continuum, 2005, p. 1.
2. A. Badiou, *Logic of Worlds*, London: Continuum, 2009.
3. A. Badiou, 'The Adventure of French Philosophy', *New Left Review*, 35, 2005, p. 68.
4. A. Badiou, *Handbook of Inaesthetics*, Stanford, CA: Stanford University Press, 2005 (French edition: *Petit manuel d'inesthétique*, Paris: Seuil, 1998).
5. G. Deleuze, *Proust and Signs*, London: Continuum, 2008 (first English translation: New York: George Braziller, 1972; first French edition: *Proust et les signes*, Paris: PUF, 1964; definitive edition, 1972); *Essays Critical and Clinical*, London: Verso, 1998 (1993).
6. Badiou, 'The Adventure of French Philosophy', op. cit., p. 72.
7. Ibid., p. 73.
8. Ibid.
9. Ibid., p. 76.

1
Disjunctive Synthesis

Confrontation

In 1976, one called the other a fascist. The other replied by talking of intellectual suicide. Those were the heady days of the aftermath of May '68 at the University of Vincennes in Paris, when even the slightest political difference became a pretext for the exchange of what the French language poetically calls *noms d'oiseaux*, in other words insults. So in an article published in the theoretical journal of an obscure Maoist sect,[1] of which he was 'a leading member', Badiou called Deleuze a fascist, as he recalls, with a hint of nostalgic mischievousness, in the opening pages of his book on Deleuze.[2] In those days, Badiou was a young lecturer in the philosophy department, with no philosophical *oeuvre* to speak of behind him: two novels, one slim volume published in the celebrated *Théorie* series directed by Althusser, and two essays, which he himself classifies as 'political', not philosophical texts, in a short-lived series directed by Sylvain Lazarus and himself with the same left-wing publisher, François Maspéro.[3] But he had years of political militancy behind him, first in a small left-wing socialist party, the *Parti Socialiste Unifié* (*PSU*), then in a small Maoist group called UCF (m-l), where 'C' stands for 'Communist', of course, and 'm-l' for 'Marxist-Leninist'. Deleuze, on the other hand, was already a full professor in the same department. He had already published a considerable body of work, from *Empiricism and Subjectivity* (1953) to *Kafka* (with Félix Guattari, 1975), including two massive volumes (on difference and repetition, on Spinoza and the concept of expression) which constituted his *thèse d'Etat*, the double monstrosity then required from the prospective occupant of a chair. More importantly perhaps, he was, with Guattari, the best-selling author of *Anti-Oedipus*, and his classes were attended by a motley crowd of students and assorted eccentrics, in lecture rooms thick with the smoke of countless cigarettes, as the film of one of his lectures shows.

Badiou's article, with its provocative turn of phrase ('they can't be supposed to be illiterate, so it must be supposed they are crooks'[4] – he is talking about Deleuze and Guattari), was provoked by the success of *Anti-Oedipus* and the recent publication of *Rhizome*, which was later included as the introduction to *A Thousand Plateaus*. We can, I think, understand the rage (which is not the same think as condoning it): between the anarchic political philosophy of flows and desire and the strict Marxism-Leninism of the militant Maoist, no compromise was possible, and Badiou was putting into practice the Maoist injunction to 'shoot the leaders' (*feu sur les états-majors*) – he even went as far as organising and at least once leading expeditions of Maoist students into his colleague's classes, for an exercise of public criticism and self-criticism, in imitation of the Great Cultural Proletarian Revolution in China. Deleuze, it seems, was mildly annoyed by such aggressions – he was of a milder and less militant temper.[5] Badiou, in his book, recalls that Deleuze called him a 'bolshevik'. But that was hardly an insult, either for Badiou who *was* a bolshevik or for Deleuze who was a firm critic of Stalinism but an admirer of Lenin (a chapter of *A Thousand Plateaus* is devoted to his pamphlet on slogans). Badiou also recalls that Deleuze talked of 'intellectual suicide': a more serious form of dismissal, in which the established mandarin deplores the political activism of his promising young colleague, who is not only wasting his time and talent but is caught in a form of quasi-religious persuasion that makes individual thought impossible. Both insults, of course, turned out to be misguided: it is in the nature of insults to be blatantly false. Deleuze, unlike most of his contemporaries, never ceased to stand on the left of the left, and Badiou, while still a political militant, has become the major philosopher that we know.

The university of Vincennes (or Paris VIII) was a strange institution. It was erected in the summer of 1968, in three months, in the woods of Vincennes, immediately east of Paris. It was housed in prefabs, and was expropriated towards the end of the 1970s and relocated in Saint-Denis, a working-class suburb in the north of Paris, where it now stands. It was created by a politically astute Secretary for Education, who sought to provide a playground for leftist students and academics at a safe distance from the centre of Paris. But the academic founders of the institution were given complete freedom as to the appointment of their colleagues, the organisation of the curriculum and the type of students they wanted to teach (in an attempt to reach the common people, *le peuple*, the university took in students who did not have a *baccalauréat*, the usual requisite for university entrance). The result of such academic freedom was remarkable: Foucault was in charge of appointments, and he became the first head of the philosophy department. Among its members were Deleuze, Badiou, Rancière, Lyotard, Balibar and François Châtelet. The head of the English department was Hélène Cixous, who recruited Christine Brooke-Rose, and there was a department of psychoanalysis founded under the aegis of Lacan, where Jacques-Alain Miller, Lacan's son-in-law and editor of the seminars, reigned. Never was such academic brilliance so concentrated in a French university. The only competitor in the field was the Ecole Normale Supérieure, with Althusser and Derrida on the staff and Lacan giving his seminars for a few years.

Amid such intellectual ferment (the attempted normalisation of the institution co-occurrent with its transfer to Saint Denis did not quite work), Deleuze and Badiou spent most of their teaching careers (Badiou transferred to the Ecole Normale Supérieure at a late stage). But they hardly spoke to each other.

In the first chapter of Badiou's book on Deleuze, there is a nostalgic and sometimes touching account of this non-relationship. Although they taught in the same department in the same building, they hardly ever met (no dinner parties, Badiou regrets, no postprandial walks, no lengthy conversations on the telephone). And yet, more than a decade later, from 1992 to 1994, they entered into philosophical correspondence, on Badiou's insistence, Deleuze's persistent diffidence being shown by the fact that he forbade the publication of the letters and apparently destroyed them. But it seems that Badiou has kept them: in a corner of his study, there must lie some of the most important letters in contemporary philosophy . . .

By the early 1990s, the conjuncture had changed. Neither Badiou nor Deleuze renounced political commitment and intervention: Deleuze's texts on Palestine and various political subjects are collected in the last volume of his essays;[6] Badiou is still involved in a group called *L'Organisation politique*, and his first best-seller came late in 2007 with a book analysing the electoral success of Nicolas Sarkozy,[7] in which 'one of the points to be held', as he calls them, is 'the communist hypothesis'.[8] In a context of political and intellectual reaction, political abysses were bridged and differences gave way to proximity if not alliance. Badiou and Deleuze shared the same detestation of the *nouveaux philosophes*, those darlings of the media whose philosophical work was nil. And since Badiou had emerged as a considerable philosopher in his own right, the conditions for a real philosophical confrontation, perhaps even a dialogue, were ripe. It is doubtful whether this would ever have come to pass, Deleuze's hostility to dialogue being as notorious as his talent in practising it with Félix Guattari or Claire Parnet. But in 1996 he committed suicide, leaving Badiou alone in the field.

Conjunctures

Confrontation means divergence and, as we shall see, philosophical differences, both in concept and style, between Badiou and Deleuze are unbridgeable. But such differences, significant as they are, emerge on a background of convergence. For Badiou and Deleuze were not only members of the same academic institution, but also the products of the same historical conjuncture and the same philosophical tradition.

The historical conjuncture, that of postwar France, has its climax in the May events of 1968, a philosophical and political turning point for both of them. The May events may even be considered as an *event* in the technical sense of the concept in Badiou's system, the beginning of a historical sequence, albeit short, engaging the construction of a political truth and processes of fidelity and subjectivation. Both philosophers have remained faithful to that event — certainly a minority option. In one of his electoral speeches of 2007, the president-to-be, Nicolas Sarkozy, called for the eradication of the spirit of '68, while one of the leaders of the movement, André Glucksmann (who has become the most explicitly reactionary of the new philosophers), sat in the first row of the audience. For Badiou and Deleuze, fidelity to the revolutionary impetus of the May events, to what Deleuze used to call his 'common-or-garden leftism', was not a vain concept.

The philosophical tradition that they share goes back much further, even further than what Badiou calls the 'moment of French philosophy', which, as we saw, begins for him with Sartre's *Being and Nothingness* and the ideal of the philosopher as writer and political militant. Badiou and Deleuze had the same training in philosophy, they were both subjected to the same institutional hurdles, the competitive entrance exam to the Ecole Normale Supérieure (Badiou passed, Deleuze narrowly failed), the equally competitive *agrégation* in philosophy (in which both excelled). That training, which was not without a form of stifling scholasticism, was based on a thorough knowledge of canonical philosophy (Plato and Kant, but neither Nietzsche nor Marx), envisaged from the point of view of the history of philosophy (Deleuze's first books, on Hume, Bergson and Kant, bear witness to this), and on the two technical exercises of *dissertation* (in length, but not in spirit, comparable to the essay: strong rhetorical architecture and a gift for elegant expression were indispensable requirements, as anyone who has read Bergson will realise) and *explication de textes*, a form of close commentary which, again, required powers of synthesis and rhetorical skill. And it is interesting to note that both academic exercises were, and still are, common to the training of students of literature and of philosophy: the proximity of philosophy to literature is already inscribed in French institutions.

Such historical and institutional background explains one of the philosophical tenets Badiou and Deleuze have in common: their hostility to the analytic tradition in philosophy (which never really caught in France, Jacques Bouveresse being a lone exception).[9] Deleuze called Wittgenstein an 'assassin of philosophy' (this was in *Abécédaire*, that series of television programmes which he insisted was to be broadcast only after his death, in which, therefore, he dispensed with the usual precautions of politeness) and, as Badiou forcefully puts it, he hated logic[10] – at least the form of logic prevalent in Anglo-Saxon philosophy (we recall he wrote on the 'logic' of sense and of sensation). Badiou's affect is apparently milder: he indulges in deliberate misprisions of Wittgenstein (not least his concept of language-game), but he is strongly critical of philosophers that restrict their interest to logical or grammatical questions, and his recent book on Wittgenstein, the title of which sums up his position, is extremely critical.[11] In short, both philosophers strongly resist the 'linguistic turn' in philosophy, a position which happily coexists with their interest in literature and their attitude towards language.

Continental and analytic

A short excursus, to be taken tongue-in-cheek, will show what their styles in philosophy have in common, in contrast with the analytic way of doing things. I would like to suggest that the opposition between what is broadly (very broadly) known as 'continental' and 'analytic' philosophy develops along the following six contrasts.

1. Where analytic philosophy is dry, continental philosophy is copious. Paul Grice gained a worldwide reputation on the strength

of two essays.[12] Collections of essays by various hands on a given subject are, for analytic philosophers, a standard way of publishing their works. Continental philosophers, on the other hand, favour the thick treatise, like Sartre's *Being and Nothingness*, or at least the two hundred page volume. In France, this tendency was accentuated by the institution of *thèse d'Etat*, that academic pachyderm which ran to several hundred pages and took ten years to write: *Difference and repetition* and Foucault's *Histoire de la folie à l'âge classique* belong to that category, as does Gilbert Simondon's *L'Individu et sa genèse physico-biologique*,[13] which exerted considerable influence on Deleuze. And even if Badiou's two *summae* (that is how he himself, quite rightly, calls them) came too late to gain that sort of academic recognition, as the *thèse d'Etat* was abolished in 1984 and replaced by the equivalent of a PhD, they are typical of the genre, at least in length and scope.

2. Where analytic philosophy is argumentative, continental philosophy is thetic. There is nothing Anglo-Saxon philosophers like better than a good debate, and that Oxford Union type of philosophical practice influences their mode of writing. Austin's first article on performatives is characteristic: he starts by positing and defending the 'constative v. performative' contrast and ends up dissolving it.[14] Deleuze, on the other hand, openly despised discussion and preferred writing *à quatre mains*: for him, a debate was merely an opportunity to exhibit one's intellectual brilliance at a small cost and at the expense of serious thought – this is why he refused, with very few exceptions, to take part in colloquia, those forums for academic vanity. And if Badiou's texts are usually the site of an unremitting demonstration (in which he is close to the early Wittgenstein and the logical trend in analytic philosophy), he always starts, like Althusser, who was one of his masters, from a set of carefully numbered theses, which he uses as axioms (in the case of *Being and Event*, they are indeed axioms, the axioms of set theory): for him, there is always a moment of *decision*, which is the crucial moment.

3. Analytic philosophy is logicist, continental philosophy is literary. The ideal figure for the analytic philosopher is the logician, and the rationale for such degrees as PPE (Philosophy, Politics and Economics) in Oxford is the belief that the contribution of philosophy to the study of politics and economics is teaching the students to think and argue logically. This attitude towards logic often influences the shape of philosophical research in the

analytic tradition. We need only think of the relationship between Davidson and Tarski. Continental philosophers, in spite of what their opponents would like to think (remember the polemic between Derrida and Searle, and the infamous episode of the petition, signed by Quine and other distinguished philosophers, against Derrida being granted an honorary degree by Cambridge university), also practise the art of philosophical argument. In the case of Badiou, as we have seen, this takes the form of a quasi-mathematical demonstration. Readers of *Logic of Worlds*,[15] his second *summa*, can turn to the end of the volume and find a numbered list of the sixty-six propositions demonstrated in the book. But their relation to logic is entirely different: they do not treat it as the transcendent method that rules all forms of philosophy. In other words, they do not make a fetish of it, preferring to concentrate on the construction of concepts. And such construction does not avoid questions of form – what is now called 'philosophy as a kind of writing', the philosopher as stylist, is a characteristic of French as of all continental philosophy. This entails a different relationship to literature – this is what this book is about: where analytic philosophers hardly write on literature or the arts, practically all continental philosophers have devoted an important part of their work to literature, with the possible exception of Althusser (who, in a sense, delegated the task to Macherey). Deleuze and Badiou are not the least literary of such philosophers.

4. Where analytic philosophers believe that there is progress in philosophy as in science, continental philosophers enjoy revisiting their predecessors – this means not only that philosophers of old are like the old masters in the history of art, that their achievements must be revisited, their positions constantly rehearsed, but more importantly that their problems are still as vitally significant now as they were centuries ago. When Strawson writes about Kant or Ryle about Descartes,[16] it is to correct their mistakes and point out their limitations. And let us not even mention Hegel, who is beyond the pale. Continental philosophers, on the other hand, show considerable piety towards their forebears – that is why the history of philosophy is an integral part not only of their training but of their practice. So Althusser re-reads not only Marx but Montesquieu and Machiavelli; Derrida re-reads Rousseau and Hegel, Deleuze Hume, Nietzsche, Spinoza and Bergson and Badiou claims to be a Platonist philosopher and 'meditates' on a

host of his predecessors. For analytic philosophers, the tradition is as passé as Newtonian physics: something to be respected, even foraged for anticipations, but something largely alien to current problems. For continental philosophers, the urgent task is that of a return: to Freud, Marx or Plato.

5. Where analytic philosophy is technical, continental philosophy is of a generalist cast. A highly specialised subject, analytic philosophy makes no effort, when it defines the relevant questions and constructs the requisite concepts, to allow the non-specialist to take part in the holy mysteries. Continental philosophy, on the other hand, likes to address sixth-form students, and this difference is even institutionalised: whereas the A level in philosophy is a relatively recent invention and is taken by a tiny minority of students, all candidates for the French *baccalauréat* have to take a paper in philosophy – for a significant minority, it is even the most important paper. And continental philosophy likes to address the concerns of the general public: where the analytic philosopher is a shy and retiring creature, the continental philosopher is a man, or woman, of the world – his or her voice is heard on the *agora*, in the media, thus gaining a form of recognition. Thus, when Jacques Derrida died, president Chirac indulged in a few words of public condolence and a brief eulogy of the great man. Thus Deleuze, who writes in a highly specialised philosophical idiom (no one will claim that *Difference and Repetition* is as easy to read as a Jane Austen novel), gave public lectures on Spinoza that were followed by hundreds of people, most of whom were not philosophers in the strict sense. (Deleuze was duly proud of this and rejoiced in the fact that *The Fold* had been appreciated by Japanese paper folders and Australian surfers.) And at one time, in the carriages of the Paris metro, one could see impeccably dressed yuppies hurrying towards the business centre of La Défense while flicking through the pages of *What Is Philosophy?* (the title of the book is the very inscription of the desire to go beyond the boundaries of the specialised subject). Thus Badiou, whose philosophical work, although written with the utmost clarity, is of a highly technical nature (situation, count-for-one, state of the situation, edge of the void, evental site, presentation and representation, etc.: one has to enter the closed world of the system to make sense of these concepts), is also capable of writing for sixth-formers, and on exactly the same subject as he does in his *Ethics*, which indeed originally appeared in a series intended for that audience,[17] not to mention,

of course, his many interventions in current affairs, of which his best-seller on Sarkozy is the best example.[18]
6. Where analytic philosophy – this point is a consequence of the preceding one – is closed, continental philosophy is open. For analytic philosophers, philosophy is a subject unto itself: with the exception of 'applied ethics', it does not mix with other subjects, whereas nothing human is alien to the continental philosopher, especially the human sciences. Again, there is an institutional reason for this in the French context. For a long time, any student wishing to do research in psychology, sociology, anthropology or linguistics had to pass the *agrégation* in philosophy, as there was no equivalent exam in those subjects. Thus both Lévi-Strauss and Bourdieu were *agrégés de philosophie*, which means they underwent a thorough training in that subject before devoting their energies to their preferred field of research, a situation which naturally influenced their scientific practice. This openness of philosophy, or opening up towards other subjects, often to the point of invasion, but not without the inverse counter-movement, explains why French philosophers so confidently write about literature and art when they do not practise it themselves, like Sartre or Badiou, and why 'French Theory' met with such success in departments of comparative literature in the United States. And we understand why Badiou defines the task of philosophy (a modest but nevertheless an essential one) as the 'compossibilisation' of procedures of truth in the four fields (science, art, politics and love) where truths, in the emphatic plural, emerge, why philosophy is practised only 'under the conditions' of truths produced in other fields, the fields in which, unlike in philosophy, events occur.

If we restrict the field of continental philosophy to Deleuze and Badiou, the contrast takes another, massive, form: the focus on first philosophy, otherwise known as ontology, versus the dismissal of such interests as sheer metaphysics and the concentration on logical and grammatical problems. For Badiou and Deleuze, philosophical problems can never be merely grammatical: they have to be substantial. Hence their energetic rejection of the 'linguistic turn': in his first philosophical opus, *Théorie du sujet*, Badiou called this exclusive preoccupation with language, 'idéalinguisterie',[19] a coinage based on Lacan's coinage of 'linguisterie', which describes his idiosyncratic approach to language. The addition of 'idéal' insists on the gross idealism of all philosophies centred on language.

Metaphor or concept

I have, of course, caricatured the undeniable differences between two traditions, and I am aware that their very names, 'continental' and 'analytic', are gross oversimplifications. But Deleuze's and Badiou's common hostility to the analytic tradition is equally undeniable and goes some way towards explaining the convergence of their philosophical practices. For there are material conditions for philosophy, conditions of institution, of conjuncture and moment, of tradition, which explain why the differences between our two philosophers appear to have turned into similarities. They share the same historical conjuncture and they share a fidelity to its revolutionary component, the events of May 1968. They are products of the same institutional training, and their academic career took place in the same exceptional institution. They emerged from the same intellectual background, where the discipline of philosophy occupies a central place, and they share the same conception of the discipline: they are philosophers *in the same sense* (for both, ontology, not logic, is the core of the subject, and philosophical problems can never be mere grammatical problems – for them, too, art and literature are an integral part of philosophy's concerns). So the similarities are considerable and obvious. But equally considerable are the differences: it is clear that, as philosophers, they are poles apart, and their former political hostility turns out to have been the least of their differences.

To capture such conjunction of convergence and divergence, we need a metaphor, perhaps even, if we manage to reach that giddy height, a concept. The French language offers the hackneyed biblical metaphor of *frères ennemis*, but that would oblige us to decide which is Abel and which Cain. We might suggest, trusting the implicit wisdom of the English language, that their respective philosophies are at cross purposes, a potentially Deleuzian image of series diverging and lines crossing: but that would not be equal to the seriousness, and the quality, of their differend. And perhaps the last word is the name we are looking for. We remember that, in Lyotard,[20] it denotes a difference which cannot be resolved for lack of a language common to both parties. But even if Deleuze's and Badiou's philosophical positions are incompatible, even if their styles of doing philosophy, in spite of their shared background, diverge sharply, it cannot be said that they do not share a language, for reasons we have just described, least of all the French language in which they write (and writing is for them of no mean philosophical importance).

In an essay devoted to Badiou's place in French philosophy and centred round the question of a 'history of truth', Etienne Balibar suggests that the phrase in question 'circulates in the writings of a constellation of authors' and 'at the same time signals the differences between them'.[21] To name such mixture of similarity and difference, he uses three phrases in the same sentence: 'It constitutes, in other words, the index of a point of heresy that both unites and divides them, or brings them together in a "disjunctive synthesis" around their differend.' [22] 'Point of heresy', 'disjunctive synthesis' between inverted comas, 'differend': the choice is wide. The inverted commas around the second term inscribe a double allusion: to a Deleuzian concept of prime importance, and to the use Badiou makes of it in his reading of Deleuze. I think we have found the requisite metaphor, and it turns out to be a concept.

Disjunctive synthesis

The phrase is used as the title of the first essay Deleuze wrote with Félix Guattari.[23] It has been used by one critic to describe the type of writing, *écriture à quatre mains*, practised by Deleuze and Guattari. Here is Anne Sauvagnargues describing that text, devoted to the novelist and philosopher Pierre Klossowski, which found its way, in a modified version, into *Anti-Oedipus*:

> The text re-uses the notion of disjunctive synthesis that Deleuze introduced in *The Logic of Sense* – an important notion which here finds its point of application. Synthesis, for Deleuze, does not mean a return to the one, but a disjunctive differentiation that works through bifurcations and transformations, rather than through fusion and the identity of the same. Such differentiating synthesis, a synthesis without conjunction, is applied to the singular practice of writing with four hands, and changes not only the status of the text, but its construction.[24]

The concept of synthesis, it appears, plays a role both in *The Logic of Sense* and *Anti-Oedipus*. Its origin is to be found in Kant, where it plays an essential role, as it names the operations through which we make sense of the chaotic multiplicity of phenomena. There are three syntheses: of apprehension in intuition, of reproduction in imagination, of recognition in the concept. Kant is working his way from sense to intellect or understanding, and in each case the object of the exercise is to grasp together a multiplicity under a form of unity, be it an object of the senses, an image or a concept. In Deleuze,

Disjunctive Synthesis

where the phenomena are given in the form of series (in *The Logic of Sense* – series of things, of words, of thoughts, etc.) or flows of energy (in *Anti-Oedipus*), the function of synthesis is to capture and regulate the connection or intersection of such series or flows: to segment, to connect, to fuse, so that again the world of phenomena should acquire form. There are three syntheses in Deleuze as in Kant: of connection, of conjunction, of disjunction. The first two are easy to grasp: two series or lines connect together in a single sequence; two separate lines or series are conjoined in fusion, like rivers. The disjunctive synthesis, however, has a strong paradoxical flavour, as it seeks to connect and separate at the same time, to keep together what must ultimately remain apart. The phrase is, indeed, somewhat of an oxymoron, as the Latin prefix 'dis' contradicts the Greek prefix 'syn': you should not be able to separate and conjoin at the same time. A disjunctive synthesis, for traditional logic, is an impossibility. But it is precisely on this new concept, on this new 'logical' operation, which belongs to the logic of paradox, that Deleuze constructs his distinctive ontology of absolute difference, against the Aristotelian logic of subject and predicate and the Hegelian logic of contradiction.[25]

The concept first appears in the seventh series of *The Logic of Sense*, where Deleuze, reading Lewis Carroll, develops his theory of portmanteau words (the term is Carroll's own: Deleuze calls them 'esoteric words').[26] Portmanteau words, we remember, are the result of the contraction of two distinct words into one, as when a Victorian portmanteau, a kind of suitcase, was folded. Thus the word 'Snark', as in *The Hunting of the Snark*, is said to be a contraction of 'snail' and 'shark', and the creature it denotes is duly monstrous. Deleuze distinguishes between three types of portmanteau words. *Contracting* portmanteau words concern a single series (here a series of words); they coalesce successive elements, as we all do when we speak too fast, and all the words of a sentence may be contracted into one unintelligible word. Carroll's example comes from *Sylvie and Bruno*, where 'y'reince' represents the phrase 'your Royal Highness' reduced to a single syllable. *Circulating* portmanteau words concern two heterogeneous series which are made to coexist in them: this is the canonical case of the Snark, where two series of phonemes, but also of bodily parts, are made to converge in a linguistic monster and a monstrous creature. Lastly, *disjunctive* portmanteau words operate the ramification of two coexisting series, which they keep both at once together and apart. Deleuze's example comes from Carroll's preface to *The Hunting of the Snark*, where he quotes Pistol's injunction to Justice Shallow, in Shakespeare's *Henry the Fourth, Part Two*, 'Under which King, Besonian? Speak or die!' He comments on the scene in the following fashion:

> Supposing that [. . .] Justice Shallow had felt certain that it was either William or Richard, but had not been able to settle which, so that he could not possibly say either name before the other, can it be doubted that, rather than die, he would have gasped out 'Rilchiam!'[27]

This is no chimera, unlike the Snark or the Gryphon (both an eagle and a lion): the two elements are incompatible, as they belong to the same paradigm and cannot occupy a single syntagmatic position. And yet they must, as the choice of one rather than the other is too dangerous – a question of life and death. The disjunctive synthesis which produces the portmanteau word, the true esoteric word, allows Justice Shallow to do just that.

The three syntheses are more extensively described in the twenty-fourth series, 'Of the Communication of Events'.[28] The *connective synthesis* operates on one series only, and its linguistic marker is 'if . . . then': the connection is one of consecution and consequence. The *conjunctive synthesis* constructs two series in their convergence, and its linguistic marker, predictably, is 'and' (they are literally taken together). The *disjunctive synthesis* distributes two series through their divergence, and its linguistic marker is 'or', a connector that, in natural languages, has the useful property of being ambiguous between an inclusive interpretation ('p or q' is true if one of the propositions is true, which means that both may be true) and an exclusive one ('p or q' is true if one proposition is true and the other false). Perhaps this ambiguity of a linguistic marker which corresponds to two logical connectors is the best image we may hope to have of a disjunctive synthesis. The paradoxical nature of this synthesis is of course fully acknowledged by Deleuze: indeed that is its main interest for him (we remember that *The Logic of Sense* is not divided into chapters but into 'series of paradoxes'). His question is: under which conditions is that disjunction a true synthesis? His answer is that the disjunctive synthesis does not exclude any predicates (a simple ascription of identity, combined with the law of non-contradiction, means that certain predicates will be validated for the subject, and others excluded) but rather organises the circulation of events along the two series thus conjoined in their difference. Such disjunction does not deny or exclude, it is strongly affirmative (it is prepared to conjoin incompatible predicates): it affirms difference, makes

Disjunctive Synthesis

distance a positive characteristic, thus allowing the conjoining of two series that remain apart by the circulating event. The disjunctive synthesis is the logical operation that is needed by a philosophy of absolute or 'asymmetrical' difference, not the traditional philosophy of identity and representation.

The paradox of the disjunctive series is further developed in the thirty-second series, 'On the Different Kinds of Series'.[29] This chapter is devoted to a theory of the genesis of language through the stages of noise, voice, speech and language proper. This genesis is sexual and the solution to the paradox of the disjunctive synthesis is to be found in psychoanalytic theory (we must not forget that *The Logic of Sense* precedes *Anti-Oedipus* by several years, and that in the preface Deleuze describes his project as 'an attempt to develop a logical and psychoanalytic novel').[30] So, in the beginning, when the child is still in the womb or just born, there is only noise, what Deleuze calls 'the family rumour', which already speaks about the child, to the child, but which she does not yet perceive as speech addressed to her. In the second stage, the stage of the voice, the child realises that the flow of sounds in which she is immersed is made up of voices: she learns to do what we adults constantly do without any longer thinking about it, she cuts up the flow of sound into a series of discrete segments, phonemes, characterised by their differential values. Here, Deleuze follows Serge Leclaire, the psychoanalyst who theorised erogenous zones and their differential intensities.[31] When the child moves to the next stage, from voice to speech, a sexual position is reached: not only is the flow of sound turned into a series of linguistic signs, ready for communication and meaning (the last stage of this genesis of language), but the originary body-without-organs is now a sexual body, an articulation of erogenous zones. The famous portmanteau word of Leclaire's patient, 'pordjeli', inscribes the parallel genesis, through the three types of synthesis, of language and the sexual body. Thus the erogenous zones are brought together into a sexual body through a connective synthesis, they are articulated into *this* sexual body through the operation of conjunctive synthesis (Deleuze calls it 'the phallic coordination of zones' – *raccordement phallique*)[32] and the body of erogenous zones becomes the sexual body of the individual subject through the disjunctive synthesis that operates via the Oedipus complex. In other words, the role of disjunctive synthesis is to complete the genesis of the subject's sexual body and of her language at the same time: the three syntheses are linked to the three formative elements of language – phonemes (connective synthesis of sounds into distinctive elements), morphemes (articulation of such elements into a syntax, through conjunctive synthesis) and 'semantemes' or elements of meaning (the syntax now carries meaning, the two diverging series of words and things are held together and yet kept separate by the operation of disjunctive synthesis). The fourth stage, language proper, the stage of reference, enunciation and communication, is the surface consequence of the emergence of articulated meaning from the depths of the sexual body: only with designation, manifestation and signification will the business of meaning, common sense, good sense and sense proper be finally transacted.

The concept of disjunctive synthesis, therefore, is developed on two levels, the level of language, which provides the main illustration of the concept in the shape of its linguistic marker, and the level of the sexual body. In *The Logic of Sense*, where the two levels are articulated, the portmanteau or esoteric word, as operator of disjunctive synthesis, plays the same role as the empty square in Deleuze's structuralist theory of sense and meaning[33] – an element that glides along the two series of signifier and signified, itself devoid of meaning but achieving meaning in the synthesis it operates. Meaning is the result of the circulation of this floating signifier, the point of convergence of diverging series. In *Anti-Oedipus*, where neither language nor the sexual body of psychoanalysis any longer play a major role, the disjunctive synthesis, like the other two syntheses, is a productive operation of desire, reality and the unconscious. The various syntheses cut the flow of libidinal energy, they connect it (synthesis of connection), they register it into series and semiotic codes (disjunctive synthesis), they contract into a form of subject (synthesis of contraction) – as we can see, the order of syntheses has changed, and the disjunctive synthesis now occupies the middle place. The linguistic markers of the respective syntheses have also changed: to the synthesis of connection corresponds the 'and then . . . and then' of the connection of part objects; to the synthesis of disjunction corresponds the 'either . . . or' of the schizophrenic patient, whose disjunction distributes heterogeneous series and flows and achieves the unity of experience; to the synthesis of conjunction corresponds the 'so that was it!' of recognition and *prise de conscience*.[34] The disjunctive synthesis, Deleuze and Guattari add, is not a synthesis of contradictory terms as in Hegelian sublation (*Aufhebung*), it reaffirms the individual separate existence of the terms it conjoins, it remains open and not closed in the circularity of the dialectic.

20

I think we understand the importance of the concept for Deleuze. It haunted him all through his work, and it survived the stage of *The Logic of Sense*, the positions of which were largely abandoned when Deleuze met Guattari. It is connected with the main concepts of his ontology (series and empty square; flows and cuts; events) and of his philosophy of language (esoteric words and the stuttering of language, floating signifier and the distinction between meaning and sense). It provides a rationale for the practice of *écriture à deux* with Guattari. Above all, it is the very embodiment of Deleuze's notorious hostility to the Hegelian system: the three syntheses are Deleuze's answer to the Hegelian dialectic, and the function of the disjunctive synthesis, which is affirmative and resists closure, is to replace and deny the third moment of the dialectic, the moment of unity of the contradictory terms through sublation.

Badiou reads Deleuze

The concept of disjunctive synthesis, therefore, is not a mere metaphor, a short circuit to describe the philosophical relation between Deleuze and Badiou. It is a fully-fledged concept. There are two reasons for attempting to capture this (non-)relation under precisely this concept. First, the concept, if it is Deleuze's answer to the dialectic, is a major point of divergence. Badiou in his Marxist-Leninist phase was a strict Hegelian (in *Théorie du sujet* he uses a logic of contradiction, with due reference to Mao's disquisitions on the subject, not a logic of difference).[35] And if the dialectic seems to have disappeared from *Being and Event* (it is not strictly compatible with an ontology based on set theory), it makes an explicit reappearance in *Logic of Worlds*, where Badiou states that his position is not that of dialectical materialism (the infamous *diamat* of Stalinist fame) but of a materialist dialectic.[36] So, unlike Deleuze, Badiou consistently thinks of himself as a dialectician, even if it can be argued that the 'and' of *Being and Event* is not the 'and' of conjunctive synthesis but a marker of disjunctive synthesis: the event, being supplementary to the situation in which the multiple is presented, is outside being (the event is nothing, a nothing, a flash in the pan, captured only in retrospective truth procedures) and yet, it must have some sort of link with the situation in which it occurs at the point of an eventual site – this is a notorious difficulty in Badiou's system, the crux, for instance, of his divergence with the theory of hegemony in Laclau.[37]

The second reason, which is of more direct interest to us, is that the concept of disjunctive synthesis is the guiding thread of Badiou's reading of Deleuze, in the book he devoted to him. The relation between Deleuze and Badiou is not evenly balanced. Their discussion on equal terms, as we saw, cannot be published. And after Deleuze's death, Badiou's interventions on the work of his colleague were numerous to the point of obsession: there is a chapter on Deleuze's ontology in *Briefings on Existence. A Short Treatise on Transitory Ontology*,[38] a section on the event according to Deleuze in *Logic of Worlds*[39] and a short obituary in *Pocket Pantheon*.[40] His review of *The Fold*, which must be added to this list, pre-dates Deleuze's death by a few years.[41] But the main text is the book on Deleuze, *Deleuze: The Clamor of Being*,[42] published in a series of introductory texts, to which Badiou also contributed a volume on Beckett and Rancière a volume on Mallarmé.[43] Except, of course, that the book is hardly an introduction to Deleuze and can only be described as a strong and idiosyncratic reading, which duly incensed Deleuze's followers.[44] There is nothing particularly surprising in this: the books of Slavoj Žižek and Peter Hallward on Deleuze[45] fall within that category, for it would seem that Deleuze's thought, unlike Badiou's, is sufficiently fluid and open-ended to invite creative misprision, to speak like Harold Bloom. In strong contrast with Badiou's obsessive interest in Deleuze's work, the latter never seems to have been greatly interested in Badiou's work. This is partly due to the respective dates of publications of their books: *Being and Event* was published in 1988, by which time Deleuze had already published most of his work. *What Is Philosophy?*, published in 1991, is the only book by Deleuze in which Badiou is mentioned, on two pages only.[46] Badiou is 'example no. XII' in a chapter dealing with prospects and concepts. He is accused of reintroducing transcendence through the separation of the event from the ordinary multiple of the situation. He is also accused of entertaining an old-fashioned concept of philosophy as superior, as 'floating in empty transcendence', and his concept of multiplicity is called 'monist' ('any multiplicity' means *one* multiplicity) whereas Deleuze's theory of multiplicities in the plural demands that there should be at least two. This curt reading of Badiou, the force of conviction of which is limited, is not so much a mark of interest as an outright dismissal, and Deleuze has been accused of interpreting Badiou in a way that makes his work unrecognisable.

The same accusation has been levelled, more than once, at Badiou's reading of Deleuze.[47] But it can in no way be taken as a dismissal.

Disjunctive Synthesis

In his recently published obituary of Deleuze in *Pocket Pantheon*, Badiou draws up the five main 'motifs' of Deleuze's philosophy.

1. In Deleuze, we recognise the centrality of an affirmative posture, against any 'thought of the end', whether it be human finitude or the end of philosophy.
2. Deleuze's only real concept of a synthesis is the synthesis that separates (we recognise our disjunctive synthesis): this is linked to Deleuze's conception of thought as a form of violence imposed on the thinker – we are 'forced to think', or forced into thinking.
3. Deleuze's concept of time centres on eternity, not the usual temporal sequence: Badiou calls this the 'temporal intemporality' of Deleuze's event – this is an anti-phenomenological motif: we must abandon the 'consciousness of time' for good.
4. Deleuze does not share the general obsession with language, a sad characteristic of poststructuralism and postmodernism, and he does not consider that the judgement is the main form of thought – in so doing, he takes an anti-Kantian posture, in which he is close to Badiou.
5. Deleuze is hostile to the dialectic, which for him is 'exhausted', and he refuses to celebrate the power of the negative – this is coherent with the first motif of affirmation.

Points (1) and (4) in this list show the convergence between Badiou and Deleuze, points (3) and (5) their divergence. And point (2), the disjunctive synthesis, has been taken by Badiou as a point of entry into Deleuze's philosophy.

That the disjunctive synthesis is an essential concept for Deleuze is made explicit by Badiou in his book. In the chapter devoted to the univocity of being and the multiplicity of names, in a section dealing with 'Heidegger's limits', Badiou links the disjunctive synthesis to the conception of the One he ascribes to Deleuze:

> Being 'occurs' in the same way in all its modalities – in the visible and language, for example (one could cite others). Thus, in assuming that there is an intentional relation between nomination and the thing, or between consciousness and the object, one necessarily breaks with the expressive sovereignty of the One. Were the objection to be made that these modalities are at least minimally 'related' to each other in so far as they are all modalities of the One, one need but reply that the essence of this relation is nonrelation, for its only content is the neutral equality of the One. And it is, doubtlessly, in the exercise of this nonrelation that thought 'relates' most faithfully to the Being that constitutes it. This is what Deleuze calls

a 'disjunctive synthesis': one has to think of the nonrelation according to the One, which founds it by radically separating the terms involved. One has to steadfastly rest within the activity of separation, understood as a power of Being. One has to explain that 'the nonrelation is still a relation, and even a relation of a deeper sort' ([*Foucault*], p. 63; translation modified), insofar as it is thought in accordance with the divergent or disjoining movement that, incessantly separating, testifies to the infinite and egalitarian fecundity of the One. But this disjunctive synthesis is the ruin of intentionality.[48]

It is well-known that Badiou's reading of Deleuze, contrary to an established critical tradition, makes him a philosopher of the One (thus imposing on him a form of Platonism), rather than the thinker of anarchic multiplicities, processes of becoming, complex assemblages of machines or enunciations, lines of flight and all-pervading difference. That there is a case for such a reading, the above quotation makes clear: Deleuze appears to be a consistently Spinozist philosopher, the disjunctive synthesis being the name of the (non-)relation between the various modes of the one substance, a relation deeper than the intentional relation between name and thing, sign and referent. Such (non-)relation is best described through the Spinozist concept of expression, to which Deleuze devoted a volume of his thesis.[49] This, according to Badiou, is Deleuze's solution to the traditional problem of the mind–body relation: not through the intentional relation of phenomenology (one of Deleuze's ambitions is to discard phenomenology) but through the working of absolute difference – the operation which the disjunctive synthesis also names – except that – this is where Badiou's reading sharply differs from the critical *doxa* about Deleuze – such differences are always related to the One, to whose 'infinite fecundity' they testify. It is at this point, of course, that the reader of Deleuze tends not to recognise her favourite philosopher in Badiou's version.

Badiou links the concept of disjunctive synthesis to another Deleuzian concept, the concept of 'life', another name for the One Being. Disjunctive synthesis, in this context, is the centre of what Badiou calls 'Deleuze's other logic', not the Aristotelian logic of categories, the logic of exclusion and inclusion ('and', 'or', 'neither ... not'), but a paradoxical logic where all such relations are 'superimposed' in one relation of 'and-or-neither-nor': a logic where any conjunction is also a form of disjunction. Only such a logic can be faithful to the univocity and neutrality of being, and the disjunctive synthesis is the name for this superimposed nexus of relation:

Disjunctive Synthesis

'Deleuze called this neutrality "and-or-nor" connector, the *disjunctive synthesis*. It must be said that Being as a neutral power deserves the name "life" because it is, in terms of a relation, the "or-and-nor," or the disjunctive synthesis itself.'[50] So disjunctive synthesis is now the name of one of the modalities of Being, Being as relation.

We understand why Badiou chose the concept as his guiding thread through Deleuze's ontology. For him, it is the very embodiment of Deleuze's superficial because mistaken anti-Platonism ('Deleuzianism is fundamentally a Platonism with a different accentuation').[51] The disjunctive synthesis is what Deleuze opposes to Plato: 'beings are merely disjointed, divergent simulacra, that lack any internal relation between themselves or with any transcendent Idea whatsoever.'[52] The discussion turns around the Platonist concept of 'simulacrum' (the idea is the model; the actual realisation of the idea, the icon – the real bed made by the carpenter in accordance with the idea of the bed – is a good copy; the simulacrum or idol, the bed painted by the artist in imitation of the real, or rather phenomenal, bed is a second-order, bad copy). Deleuze's strategy is to free the simulacrum from its relation of subservience to both the icon and the idea:[53] the simulacrum is a positive power that dissolves the system of model and copy, original and representation. The simulacrum is the power that denies all foundation or grounding (*fondement*), in the joyous chaotic operation Deleuze calls *effondement* ('ungrounding'), and which he assimilates to the phantasm at work in the work of art. Badiou's strategy in discussing this passage is to fold Deleuze back on to Plato by claiming that the Platonist concept of the simulacrum, far from being purely derivative, a second-order copy, is a positive one: 'I am not sure that Plato is so far from this view of beings, even sensible beings, as immanent differentiation of the intelligible and as positivities of the simulacrum.'[54] In other words, the Deleuzian theory of the independence of the simulacrum is neutralised by being assimilated to another version of the ontological difference, between Being and being, the One and the simulacra in which it expresses itself.

As Badiou's interpretation of Deleuze unfolds, it becomes clear that the disjunctive synthesis is the master concept that unites all Deleuze's main concepts into a system. At the cost of reducing Deleuze's three syntheses to the one disjunctive synthesis (the 'and-or-neither-nor), Badiou accounts for Deleuze's vitalism, which, like all vitalisms, 'including Spinoza's version [. . .] (the philosophy of the power of being) requires the absolute unity of a relation'[55] – even if this relation is defined as a non-relation. When he analyses the virtual

25

as 'the principal name of Being in Deleuze's work',[56] and in this concept identifies the grounding of his philosophical system so that Deleuze's philosophy may be called a 'Platonism of the virtual',[57] Badiou distances Deleuze from the traditional concept of ground as mimetic (the model is the ground for its copies or imitations). In Deleuze, singular beings, produced by the dynamic power of Being as its expression, have no need to resemble anything: 'they are fortuitous modalities of the univocal and, being as far removed as possible from any mimetic hierarchy, can only be thought in their anarchic coexistence through disjunctive synthesis.'[58] But that relation between being and Being, in the paradoxical mode of disjunction, is, according to Badiou, Deleuze's version of grounding. And that Deleuzian ground is the virtual. The One, 'the virtual reservoir of dissimilar production' is 'the virtual totality'.[59] And this is where transcendence returns within Deleuzian immanence: the position of the virtual totality of the One is transcendent in relation to the multiplicity of beings that express it, whose chaotic proliferation is held together by disjunctive synthesis. It is no wonder, therefore, that we discover that the concept of the fold is Deleuze's solution to the paradoxes created by the relation which is no relation, disjunctive synthesis. The question that Deleuze's ontology asks is the following: 'Given that thought is set in motion by disjunctive syntheses, and that it is solicited by beings which are in nonrelation, how can it be in accordance with Being, which is essentially relation?'[60] The concept of fold is Deleuze's answer to this paradox. Badiou's deduction, which owes much to a reading of Deleuze's *Foucault*,[61] envisages a dual topology of exteriority and limit, and the folding of the limit into an inside. This process of the outside folding itself into an inside is the very process of subjectivation. The subject – the inside – is the result of the invagination of the outside – the world. Badiou concludes: 'We might as well say that we finally reach the point where the disjunction is intuited as a simple modality of the One: the common limit of the heterogeneous forces that absolutely externalize the objects, or forms, is the very action of the One as self-folding.'[62]

Capture

Badiou's reading has one considerable advantage. It is a strong reading (I shall return to this notion in the next chapter) in that it turns Deleuze's philosophy into a coherent system, an ontology of the One, a Platonism of the virtual. It has one considerable disadvantage – apart from the possibility that it might be a misreading: it turns Deleuze's philosophy into a mirror image of Badiou's, with the expected inversions produced by the need for symmetry. In other words, that strong reading, like many or most of its kin, is an attempt at capture.

The object of the strong reading of a philosopher is double. The first object is to establish or renew the critical position, to situate the philosopher by making his problem explicit and systematising it. This is how Deleuze read his predecessors; this is also how Hallward and Žižek read him. The second object, when the critic is also a philosopher in his own right, is an assessment of convergence and divergence. The strong reader places the work he reads in proximity to his own, which requires a minimal amount of empathy, but also at a distance, in order to remain within the ambit of his own problem. Where the strong reading is also an attempt at capture, a third object will appear: to place the philosopher thus read and criticised in a position of subservience.

Badiou's reading fulfils all three objects. As we have seen, the problem he identifies in Deleuze is ontological, and centres around the operation of the disjunctive synthesis. The second and third objects are reached in four different ways.

1. Badiou places Deleuze where he himself will not be placed, even if Deleuze has no taste for such placement. Badious's ontology is an ontology of the multiple, based on the mathematics of set theory (there is no One, there is no Whole). Therefore Deleuze's ontology must be an ontology of the One-Whole (call it Life, call it the Event, call it the one throw of the dice): 'Deleuze's fundamental problem is most certainly not to liberate the multiple but to submit thinking to a renewed concept of the One.' [63] So the critical *doxa* that interprets Deleuze as a thinker of multiplicity is wrong. And because Badiou's is a strong reading, it is clear that he has a point there, even if we decide, following Todd May, to describe Deleuze as a thinker of both the One and multiplicities.[64] His argument is that Deleuze's reference to the One is meant to bolster up the thought of immanence: the Deleuzian 'One' (call it Being as difference, Spinoza's substance, desire in *Anti-Oedipus*, memory in Bergson – the list is Todd May's) is whatever comforts immanence. One consequence of such placement in Badiou's reading – and one that goes against the grain of all previous interpretations – is that Deleuze's philosophy of life turns out to be a

philosophy of death ('The result is that this philosophy of life is essentially, just like Stoicism [. . .] a philosophy of death').[65] Such a paradoxical conclusion is understandable if the object of the reading is the placement of an opponent: Badiou wishes to occupy the pole of life (he likes to quote Lin Piao, 'The essence of revisionism is the fear of death'),[66] so Deleuze has to occupy the pole of death. There is, of course, a thought of death in Deleuze, but it does not contradict in any way his strong affirmation of life, it is in no way a melancholy or dolorous resignation to finitude.

2. Badiou's reading – this is a direct consequence of the previous placement – excludes Deleuze from the field he himself wishes to occupy. This is the case with claims of the reintroduction of transcendence within immanence. Badiou is of course entirely aware of the move he is making, as he is, as the French language picturesquely phrases it, merely 'returning the politeness' (*retourner la politesse*). As we saw, the accusation of a return to transcendence is exactly what Deleuze, in his only reference to his colleague's work, aims at Badiou. This is how Badiou puts it, with uncharacteristic precaution: 'The result is that Deleuze's virtual ground remains for me a transcendence, whereas for Deleuze it is my logic of the multiple that, in not being originally referred to the act of the One, fails to hold thought firmly within immanence'.[67] You will have noticed that he manages not to formulate Deleuze's accusation of transcendence explicitly. And the idea that the virtual is a 'ground' in Deleuze's philosophy is, of course, highly contentious, the usual image of the philosopher being one that privileges *effondement* over grounding. The same goes for Badiou's overturning of Deleuze's overturning of Platonism: for him, as we have seen, Deleuze's philosophy is a form of differently accented Platonism and it is 'organized around a metaphysics of the One'.[68] Deleuze finds himself excluded from the fields of immanence and of multiplicity, which Badiou emphatically wishes to occupy. There is an element of dramatic irony in this: in his first philosophical opus, *Théorie du sujet*, Badiou, who then based his philosophy on the Maoist axiom 'One divides into Two', accused Deleuze of practising an ultra-leftism of the multiple and stated that any thought of the multiple 'presupposes the One as substance and excludes the Two'.[69] But there is also an element of insight, of a correct reading, in this 'differently accented Platonism' that Badiou attributes to Deleuze: for the dialectic of the One and the Multiple can undoubtedly be said to be the core of the philosophical tradition we still call Platonism.[70]

3. When Badiou includes Deleuze in fields which he himself occupies, it is in a subordinate position, which turns Deleuze's philosophy into a weak version of Badiou's. And such inclusion is often a forcible one. Deleuze's lack of interest in, or even dislike of, the notion of truth is notorious (in *What Is Philosophy?* he states that philosophy does not consist in knowledge, nor is it inspired by truth, but by categories such as 'interesting' or 'remarkable').[71] But for Badiou this smacks of Freudian denial, so the concept is reintroduced within Deleuze's philosophy, under the paradoxical name of 'the power of the false': 'All in all, "power of the false" is exactly the Deleuzian name, borrowed from Nietzsche, for truth.'[72] The same could be said, as the third movement of Badiou's reading is inseparable from the second movement, of the ascription of Platonism. Badiou has always been explicit, forcefully so, about his Platonism. By contrast, Deleuze's unacknowledged Platonism of the virtual is a *platonisme honteux*: the overthrow of Platonism ultimately fails, Deleuze's anti-Platonism is just an instance of the modern *doxa* (another instance is Heidegger) and – Badiou's *Deleuze* ends on this – Deleuze is the last of the pre-Socratic philosophers, a great philosophical physicist, one of those 'thinkers of the All',[73] a position which Plato's critique made it impossible to hold. So Deleuze manages to be both an unwitting Platonist and a pre-Platonist philosopher.
4. Lastly, Badiou's reading proceeds by excision: he excludes from Deleuze a significant part of himself by avoiding any mention of a large proportion of his work – that part the name of which is 'Deleuze and Guattari'. That his reading operates a selection among Deleuze's works clearly appears in the extracts that are appended to the body of his text (this apparently bizarre practice is due to the series in which the book was published, a series of short introductions followed by even shorter extracts): *The Logic of Sense, Difference and Repetition, Cinema 1* and *2, Foucault*. Between the first two of these books and the last three, there is a gap of sixteen years, the years of Deleuze's collaboration with Guattari, of *Anti-Oedipus* and *A Thousand Plateaus* – hardly minor works. It would be a strange reading of Wittgenstein that ignored the *Philosophical Investigations* and concentrated on the *Tractatus* on the one hand and on *On Certainty* on the other. But such iconoclasm is entirely explicit: Badiou's aim is to overturn what he perceives as a critical *doxa*, what he calls 'the superficial *doxa* of an anarcho-desiring Deleuzianism',[74] which turns Deleuze

into 'the joyous thinker of the world's *confusion*'.[75] Badiou no longer calls Deleuze a fascist (as we have just seen, by *Théorie du sujet*, published in 1982, Deleuze is rather a left-deviationist),[76] but his judgement on *Anti-Oedipus* has not changed: it was not a matter of the politics being misguided as the philosophy was hardly any better. I am afraid, however, that, in doing this, Badiou is caught in another form of *doxa*, which deplores the association of Deleuze, a respectable philosopher, with Guattari, a mere charlatan, whose independent work is feeble, hardly worthy of critical notice. The revelation, in the recent biography, that *What Is Philosophy?* was written by Deleuze alone and that Guattari merely appended his signature to the finished manuscript has not helped.[77] The *doxa* is of course as unfair as it is prevalent – Anne Sauvagnargues's book on the aesthetics of Deleuze and Manola Antonioli's book on his 'geophilosophy' are welcome exceptions:[78] most of the concepts that have been put to work in the wake of Deleuze's work (concepts of nomadism, lines of flight, deterritorialisation, the critique of linguistics, etc.) belong to that period and that collaboration, which Badiou superbly ignores.

But I am being unjust to Badiou. I am turning a strong reading into a mere demolition, the annihilation of a philosophical opponent, whereas a strong reading is a construction whereby a philosopher constructs himself by constructing his Other. But there are two types of Other: the excluded Other, the philosopher whose positions are utterly incompatible with the strong reader's, and the included Other, whose positions the strong reader might have adopted, except that he decided to reject or deny them, which means he constructs himself in contradistinction with his included Other. This second Other is linked to the strong reader in a relation of disjunctive synthesis. If the conceptual character who for Badiou embodies the right path in philosophy is Plato, the excluded Other is, naturally, the Sophist, Badiou's or philosophy's eternal opponent. This is how Ray Brassier and Alberto Toscano, in their postface to a collection of essays by Badiou, describe 'modern sophistry', in contrast with the 'aleatory rationalism' which is their name for Badiou's philosophical stance:

> But to respond to the challenge of modern sophistry by expropriating philosophical intuition permits the truly contemporary philosopher to recognize that the sophistical schema only seems to be in favour of dissemination and multiplicity. From the standpoint of an aleatory realism, it is essential to perceive how the sophist, while seeming to sing the praises of

Disjunctive Synthesis

universal difference and exception and the inapplicability of any rational categorial schema, is still committed to the notion that the multiple can itself be characterised, that it can be given the quasi-transcendental lineaments of discourses, language-games, embodiments, strategies, and so on. Though sophistry abandons the immanence of thought to philosophical intuitions of the kind endorsed by critique and dialectics, it simply shifts the locus of unified transcendental legislation, to language in particular, thereby generating, beneath the gaudy appeal of discursive multiplicity, a new figure of the Whole and the One.[79]

It is tempting to read the name of Deleuze under that characterisation of the modern Sophist, or at least Badiou's Deleuze, the apparent philosopher of difference and multiplicity, two terms that barely conceal his commitment to the Whole and the One. But this might be a misreading, as the 'gaudy' multiplicities in question are primarily discursive ones, the multiplicities of language-games and strategies. So that even if the language used points at Deleuze ('intuition', 'universal difference', etc.) as much as at Derrida, the real Sophist is the philosopher who has taken the 'linguistic turn', from Wittgenstein to the poststructuralists, as exemplified by Lyotard, whereas Deleuze emphatically refused to take that turn (even if that refusal conceals a problem, as I have tried to argue elsewhere).[80] And here we must pay renewed attention to the last page of Badiou's *Deleuze*, where another figure of the philosophical Other appears, the included Other, not the Sophist but the pre-Socratic philosopher, not the philosopher the Platonist must struggle against in ever-renewed antagonism, but the philosopher he succeeds and supersedes. And such is the aim of the construction of Deleuze in Badiou's strong reading: a polarity in a field of forces where Badiou occupies the opposite pole – a conjunction (they share the same field, the same conception of philosophy, their respective planes of immanence have an intersection) which is also a disjunction, as they occupy opposite poles of attraction. Deleuze and Badiou AND Deleuze or Badiou AND neither Deleuze nor Badiou. No wonder the title of the introduction to Badiou's *Deleuze* is 'So Near! So Far!'

So near! So far!

The time has come to try and take a more distant view of that philosophical relation. We might do this by using the typical Deleuzian tool of a correlation, where Badiou is the first term, Deleuze the second:

1. a mathematical versus a vitalist ontology;
2. the focus on the real, in a sense similar to that of Lacan as well as in the traditional sense versus the couple of virtual and actual (both of which are, in Deleuze, equally real);
3. a mathematical, set-theory concept of the multiple versus a dual view of multiplicities as intensive or extensive, qualitative or quantitative;
4. two opposite concepts of the event: events as the rare and instantaneous supplements to the situation, introducing the radically new and originating procedures of truth versus events as actualisations of the one virtual Event, as the eternal non-occurring part of all that occurs;
5. truth in the plural, but not in philosophy (the four fields in which truth emerges and which condition philosophy are politics, science, art and love), versus a marked disinterest for the notion of truth (the 'remarkable' or the 'interesting' is what really matters, the true is only of secondary interest – the obsession with the question of truth is a characteristic of the image of thought Deleuze wishes to overturn);
6. a concept of the subject that is central to the system, the result of the advent of the event and the aleatory supplementation of the situation versus an explicit dismissal of the concept, whose philosophical work is distributed among a-subjective or pre-subjective concepts: haecceities, assemblages, singularities, etc.

Badiou is entirely clear as to the nature of this contrast. This is how, at the end of his essay on Deleuze's vitalist ontology, he formulates it:

> This is how, by seeking out to learn from this genius, I reached the conviction that the pure multiple, the generic form of Being, never itself greets the event as a virtual component. On the contrary, the event befalls unto it through a rare and incalculable supplementation.
>
> To achieve this, I had to sacrifice the Whole, sacrifice life and sacrifice the great cosmic animal; whose surface was enchanted by Deleuze. Thought's general topology is no longer 'carnal and vital,' as he used to declare. It is caught in the crossed grid of strict mathematics, as Lautréamont used to say, and the stellar poem, as Mallarmé would have said.[81]

I shall have more to say about the word 'genius', a form of praise that smacks of extravagance, and of course about that 'stellar poem' as one of the conditions of thought, for they indicate the boundaries of the common philosophical field where Deleuze and Badiou are poles apart, the field of the affirmative infinity of thought. As they went through the 1980s, that 'nightmare decade of reaction', in the words of its chronicler François Cusset,[82] the lineaments of that field became clearer to them, as they are to us now. According to Cusset, the decade was characterised by the general abandonment of any thought of emancipation (in Badiou's terms this marks the end of a historical sequence, the sequence opened by the events of May 1968), but equally by the end of any critical thought (of which the movement away from Marxism is a symptom). On this historical background we might describe the convergence of the thoughts of Deleuze and Badiou as situated, if not on a common plane of immanence, at least on two strata in sufficient proximity to have a strong intersection and form a *voisinage* (a neighbourhood – a concept which, incidentally, does not only belong to Deleuze, where it is used to describe the position of singularities, but also to *Théorie du sujet*, where it supports the analogy between the parallel themes of materialism and mathematics).[83] Such a *voisinage* involves a form of political philosophy, centring on a critique of representative democracy, a position they share with Rancière's extreme egalitarianism (Badiou has always rejected any participation in the electoral process, while Deleuze supported the comedian Coluche when he declared himself a candidate for the post of President of the Republic). And this anti-representative political philosophy is in turn dependent on an anti-representative conception of philosophy at large (for Deleuze, the corset of representation is characteristic of the dogmatic image of thought).[84] The *voisinage* also involves a common conception of philosophical practice, centred on the construction of an *oeuvre*, against the rising stars of French philosophy, the *nouveaux philosophes*, whose philosophical work was as negligible as their media impact was considerable. In the introduction to his book, Badiou nostalgically approves of Deleuze's pamphlet, that notorious denunciation of the new philosophers' non-works. It involves a common mistrust of the ideology of human rights, and of the replacement of political thinking by a return to morality and religion (Badiou's *Ethics* has nothing to do with this return to moral philosophy). And it also involves a common rejection of the poststructuralist cum analytic 'linguistic turn' in philosophy. Deleuze on this point is faithful to Bergson, whose mistrust for the traps language sets to thought is well-known and Badiou, as we have seen, inveighs against the linguistic sophists. Last but not least the intersection or *voisinage* involves not merely a common passion for literature, but the conviction that literature is a condition for philosophy, that the proposition 'literature thinks' is an object of crucial philosophical elucidation. On the disjunctive synthesis of Badiou and Deleuze, I shall leave the last word to Badiou, at the very end of his philosophical obituary of Deleuze:

> Yes, the front line [. . .], where he stands with us, and thus proves to be a considerable contemporary philosopher, is this: thought must be faithful to the infinite on which it depends. It must not make any concession to the detestable spirit of finitude.[85]

Notes

1. A. Badiou, 'Le flux et le parti', in 'La situation actuelle sur le front de la philosophie', *Cahiers Yenan*, 4, Paris: Maspéro, 1977. The same publication has a review of Deleuze and Guattari's *Rhizome*, entitled 'Le fascisme de la pomme de terre', signed by one Georges Peyrol, which Deleuze and Guattari's biographer, François Dosse, claims is a pseudonym for Badiou. The title of that piece needs no comment. It is in that piece that Deleuze and Guattari are called 'pre-fascist ideologists'. See F. Dosse, *Gilles Deleuze Félix Guattari*, Paris: La Découverte, 2007, p. 432.
2. A. Badiou, *Deleuze: The Clamor of Being*, trans. Louise Burchill, Minneapolis, MN: University of Minnesota Press, 1994, p. 2 (9). Whenever possible, I quote the English edition of the French text: the page of the French text is given in parentheses.
3. A. Badiou, *Almagestes*, Paris: Seuil, 1964; *Portulans*, Paris: Seuil, 1967; *Le concept de modèle*, Paris: Maspéro, 1969 (second edition, Paris: Fayard, 2007); *Théorie de la contradiction*, Paris: Maspéro, 1975; A. Badiou and F. Balmes, *De l'idéologie*, Paris: Maspéro, 1976.
4. Dosse, op. cit., p. 432.
5. He once said to one of his students, before going to take his class: 'I must go. Badiou's gang are coming today.' Dosse, op. cit., p. 432.
6. G.. Deleuze, *Two Regimes of Madness*, New York: Semiotext(e), 2007 (2001).
7. A. Badiou, *The Meaning of Sarkozy*, London: Verso, 2008 (2007).
8. Badiou has since devoted a book to such a 'hypothesis': A. Badiou, *L'Hypothèse communiste*, Paris: Lignes, 2009.
9. See, for instance, his recent book, *La connaissance de l'écrivain*, Paris: Agone, 2008, an exercise in the analytic philosophy of literature.
10. A. Badiou, 'Deleuze's Vitalist Ontology', in *Briefings on Existence. A Short Treatise on Transitory Ontology*, New York: State University of New York, 2006, p. 66 (65).
11. A. Badiou, *L'antiphilosophie de Wittgenstein*, Caen: Nous, 2009.

Disjunctive Synthesis

12. H. P. Grice, 'Meaning' and 'Logic and Conversation', in *Studies in the Way of Words*, Cambridge, MA: Harvard University Press, 1989, pp. 213–23 and 22–40.
13. G. Simondon, *L'Individu et sa genèse physico-biologique*, Paris: PUF, 1964.
14. J. L. Austin, *Philosophical Papers*, Oxford: Clarendon Press, 1970, pp. 233–52.
15. A. Badiou, *Logic of Worlds*, London: Continuum, 2009 (2006).
16. P. F. Strawson, *The Bounds of Sense*, London: Methuen, 1966; G. Ryle, *The Concept of Mind*, Harmondsworth: Penguin, 1963 (1949).
17. A. Badiou, *Ethics: An Essay on the Understanding of Evil*, trans. P. Hallward, London: Verso, 2001 (1993).
18. See the collection of essays: A. Badiou, *Polemics*, London: Verso, 2006.
19. A. Badiou, *Théorie du sujet*, Paris: Seuil, 1982, p. 204.
20. J.-F. Lyotard, *The Differend*, trans. G. Van den Abbeele, Manchester: Manchester University Press, 1988 (1983).
21. E. Balibar, 'Alain Badiou and French Philosophy', in P. Hallward (ed.), *Think Again: Alain Badiou and the Future of Philosophy*, London: Continuum, 2004, p. 23.
22. Ibid.
23. G. Deleuze and F. Guattari, 'La synthèse disjonctive', in *L'Arc*, 43, 1970, pp. 54–62.
24. A. Sauvagnargues, *Deleuze et l'art*, Paris: PUF, 2005, p. 17 (my translation).
25. On paradox as a path into Deleuze's philosophy, see P. Montebello, *Deleuze*, Paris: Vrin, 2008, where each of the seven chapters is devoted to a Deleuzian paradox.
26. G. Deleuze, *The Logic of Sense*, trans. M. Lester and C. Stivale, London: Athlone Press, 1990 (1969), pp. 42–7 (57–62).
27. L. Carroll, *The Annotated Snark*, ed. M. Gardner, Harmondsworth: Penguin, 1967, p. 42.
28. Deleuze, *The Logic of Sense*, op. cit., p. 174 (203–4).
29. Ibid., pp. 224–33 (261–7).
30. Ibid., p. xiv (translation modified) (7).
31. S. Leclaire, *Psychanalyser*, Paris: Seuil, 1968.
32. Deleuze, *The Logic of Sense*, op. cit., p. 232 (271).
33. G. Deleuze, 'How Do We Recognize Structuralism?', in *Desert Islands and Other Texts, 1953–1974*, New York: Semiotext(e), 2004, pp. 170–2. See also J.-J. Lecercle, *Deleuze and Language*, Basingstoke: Palgrave, 2002, ch. 3.
34. G. Deleuze and F. Guattari, *Anti-Oedipus*, London: Athlone Press, 1984, pp. 41 (49) and 76 (90). See also V. Bergen, *L'Ontologie de Gilles Deleuze*, Paris: L'Harmattan, 2001, pp. 352–4.

35. Badiou, *Théorie du sujet*, op. cit., pp. 43–4.
36. A. Badiou, *Logique des mondes*, Paris: Seuil, 2006, p. 12.
37. E. Laclau, 'An Ethics of Militant Engagement', in P. Hallward, *Think Again*, op. cit., pp. 120–37.
38. Badiou, *Briefings on Existence*, op. cit.
39. Badiou, *Logique des mondes*, op. cit., pp. 403–10.
40. A. Badiou, *Pocket Pantheon*, London: Verso, 2009 (*Petit Panthéon portatif*, Paris: La Fabrique, 2008, pp. 106–11).
41. A. Badiou, 'Gilles Deleuze, *The Fold: Leibniz and the Baroque*', in C. Boundas and D. Olkowski (eds), *Gilles Deleuze and the Theatre of Philosophy*, London: Routledge, 1994, pp. 51–69.
42. Badiou, *Deleuze: The Clamor of Being*, op. cit.
43. A. Badiou, *Beckett, l'increvable désir*, Paris: Hachette, 1995; J. Rancière, *Mallarmé, la politique de la sirène*, Paris: Hachette, 1996.
44. For an account and endorsement of those outraged reactions, see Dosse, op. cit., pp. 43–57.
45. S. Žižek, *Organs Without Bodies*, London: Routledge, 2004; P. Hallward, *Out of This World. Deleuze and the Philosophy of Creation*, London: Verso, 2006.
46. G. Deleuze and F. Guattari, *What Is Philosophy?*, London: Verso, 1994 (1991), pp. 151–3 (143–4).
47. See 'Badiou/Deleuze', in the journal, *Futur Antérieur*, 43, 1997, pp. 49–84.
48. Badiou, *Deleuze*, op. cit., p. 22 (15).
49. G. Deleuze, *Expressionism in Philosophy: Spinoza*, New York: Zone Books, 1990 (1968).
50. Badiou, 'Deleuze's vitalist ontology', op. cit., p. 66 (65).
51. Badiou, *Deleuze*, op. cit., p. 26 (42).
52. Ibid., pp. 26–7 (43).
53. G. Deleuze, 'Plato and the simulacrum', in *The Logic of Sense*, op. cit., pp. 253–65 (292–306).
54. Badiou, *Deleuze*, op. cit., p. 27 (43).
55. A. Badiou, 'Afterword', in Hallward (ed.), *Think Again*, op. cit., p. 235.
56. Badiou, *Deleuze*, op. cit., p. 43 (65).
57. Ibid., p. 46 (69).
58. Ibid., p. 49 (67).
59. Ibid., p. 46 (69).
60. Ibid., pp. 82–3 (132).
61. G. Deleuze, *Foucault*, London: Athlone Press, 1999 (1986).
62. Ibid., p. 89 (133).
63. Badiou, *Deleuze*, op. cit., p. 11 (20).
64. T. May, 'Badiou and Deleuze on the One and the Many', in Hallward (ed.), *Think Again*, op. cit., pp. 67–76.

65. Badiou, *Deleuze*, op. cit., p. 13 (23–4).
66. Badiou, 'Afterword', in Hallward (ed.), *Think Again*, op. cit., p. 237.
67. Badiou, *Deleuze*, op. cit., p. 46 (69).
68. Ibid., p. 17 (30).
69. Badiou, *Théorie du sujet*, op. cit., p. 40.
70. See V. Descombes, *Le platonisme*, Paris: PUF, 2007 (1971), pp. 89 ff.
71. Deleuze and Guattari, *What Is Philosophy?*, op. cit., p. 82 (80).
72. Badiou, *Deleuze*, op. cit., p. 59 (89).
73. Ibid., p. 102 (150).
74. Quoted in Louise Burchill's introduction to Badiou's *Deleuze*, op. cit., p. xii.
75. Ibid., p. 10 (21).
76. Badiou, *Théorie du sujet*, op. cit., p. 223.
77. Dosse, op. cit., p. 539.
78. Sauvagnargues, *Deleuze et l'art*, op. cit.; M. Antonioli, *Géophilosophie de Deleuze et Guattari*, Paris: L'Harmattan, 2003.
79. R. Brassier and A. Toscano, 'Postface', in A. Badiou, *Theoretical Writings*, London: Continuum, 2006, p. 278.
80. J.-J. Lecercle, *Deleuze and Language*, Basingstoke: Palgrave, 2002.
81. A. Badiou, 'Deleuze's vitalist ontology', op. cit., pp. 70–1 (71–2).
82. F. Cusset, *La décennie. Le grand cauchemar des années 1980*, Paris: La Découverte, 2006.
83. Badiou, *Théorie du sujet*, op. cit., pp. 237–9.
84. On this, see D. Olkowski, *Gilles Deleuze and the Ruin of Representation*, Berkeley, CA: University of California Press, 1998.
85. Badiou, *Pocket Pantheon*, op. cit. (*Petit Panthéon portatif*, op. cit., p. 110 (my translation)).

2

A Question of Style

A passion for literature

My first chapter was concerned with the first two theses stated in the introduction (Badiou and Deleuze are major contemporary philosophers and they form a strange pair). Three areas of interest have emerged:

1. Deleuze and Badiou are united by a paradoxical relation of disjunctive synthesis (this concept names not only Badiou's guiding thread through the philosophy of Deleuze but a description of the field of philosophy on which each of them draws his plane of immanence: an ontological stance, the affirmation of the infinity of thought, a close relationship between philosophy and other fields, mathematics and art).
2. The notion of a strong reading, as practised by Badiou on Deleuze, at Deleuze's expense, but not as unfairly as has been claimed, since, as we shall see, Badiou's reading is faithful to Deleuze's own description of his practice as reader of other philosophers.
3. A common passion for literature (which takes a more prevalent form in Badiou than in Deleuze, who is equally interested in other arts, like painting and the cinema).

The last term, 'a passion for literature', requires glossing, in order to avoid the triviality of its common-or-garden meaning. It is true that Badiou and Deleuze share a passionate, all-pervasive and persistent interest in literary texts, but that is not particularly original among continental philosophers and not necessarily relevant to a confrontation of their philosophical styles. So we must attempt to give a more precise content to that 'passion', in other words we must construct a concept of 'passion for literature'. Help may come from Badiou's *The Century*, where the century's main characteristic is defined as 'a passion for the real'.[1]

The phrase 'a passion for the real', which in English is innocuously unambiguous, in its original French, *la passion du réel*, is ambiguous

A Question of Style

between an objective and a subjective genitive: it captures both the twentieth-century's passionate attraction for the real, and the passion that a century of wars and massacres has inflicted on the real. Badiou's argument goes through a number of moves, which can be expressed in a number of propositions. The first proposition is that the *devoir de mémoire*, the moral duty not to forget the horrors the century has inflicted on various communities, does not dispense us from the more important duty to understand and explain what has happened: whatever the importance we ascribe to memory, thought is even more important. To state that certain events (for instance the Shoah) simply cannot be thought is to deprive ourselves of the capacity to prevent similar occurrences in the future. For even the policies of the Nazis must be analysed and explained. The second proposition is a critique of individualism. The only subject the century's passion for the real allows is a collective subject: every 'I' is intelligible as part of a 'we', the 'we' of collective action; for the century, the only reality is the reality of collective projects (there has always been a voluntarist aspect in Badiou's philosophy, not least in his political philosophy: this is the specific difference of Maoism from other brands of Marxism). The third proposition states the necessity of a shift from ethics to politics. Badiou belongs to a generation that suffered from a surfeit of politics and neglected ethics. But he has never given up the centrality of politics and his ethics, as in the eponymous book, is a political ethics of fidelity and betrayal, not a glorified form of common morality. Hence his description, which stops short of celebration, of the cruelty of the century, his opposition to the ideology of victimisation (he advocates a 'formalised anti-humanism' against the bad humanism of the victimised body).[2] In a conjuncture that suffers from a surfeit of ethics and a lack of politics, such a position is a breath of fresh air. The fourth proposition enables us to understand what he means by the 'cruelty' of the century (beyond the obvious fact that massacres occurred on a hitherto unheard of scale: the turning point, the moment of brutalisation of society being not the Shoah but the First World War). The concept of real evoked by the characterisation of the century is inspired by the Lacanian concept of the Real, but also by the Hegelian concept of the real of the Idea. As such, the real is that which escapes our grasp, that against which we clash, but also what we must extract from the surrounding reality, that which must be purified from the reality that occults it, even if our relation to it is never harmonious but a site of contradiction and violent break. We come to the fifth proposition: the Maoist philosopher of *Théorie du sujet* is still a philosophical Maoist in so far as the century is not characterised by the figure of the One (the harmonious whole to which we aspire, be it the classless society of achieved communism or the Reich of a thousand years), but the Two of division and antagonism (the division of the class struggle, but also of war). The last proposition rehearses the central concept of Badiou's philosophy, the event as encounter with the real. We understand what the thesis of the passion for/of the real as characteristic of the century means: the twentieth century was a century of unequalled violence and cruelty, but also a century of collective hope and commitment; it was a century of murder and systematic suspicion (the Stalinist trials were a good example of that), but also a century of hope in a better future and the construction of a new figure of humankind. A passion for collective endeavour and engagement with the future, which contrasts sadly with the soulless individualism of the present conjuncture, which is preoccupied only with money, sex and social success; and a passion inflicted on the world in an endless sequence of wars and massacres.

The most interesting aspect of that picture and the aspect which is most relevant to our concern is the role ascribed to art. For Badiou, thinking the century is first and foremost thinking its art: hence the fact that the book is constructed around the reading of poetic or literary texts (by Mandelstam, Pessoa or Brecht), for a poem says more about the real of the century than a speech, famous and influential as it may be, by Martin Luther King. The reason is given in the development of a Hegelian contrast between manifestation (in which the subject is impelled to open up to the exteriority of the real) and representation (which acts as a means of legitimation): in a proposition that is inextricably philosophical and aesthetic, Badiou states that the real cannot be represented, but only presented.[3] And the real, being as fragile as it is cruel, can only be presented in its violent contradictions: it is the historical function of avant-gardes, with their artistic cum political manifestoes, with their insistence on the radical novelty of the event, with their conception of art as struggle, to achieve such presentation which is no representation.[4]

I believe we can derive a non-trivial concept of the passion for/ of literature from this. We understand why, for both Deleuze and Badiou, there is no philosophy which is not intimately linked to art in general and the art of language in particular. For Deleuze, literature is one of the practices that forces us to think; for Badiou, it is one of the conditions for philosophy, one of the sites in which the event is

A Question of Style

captured and procedures of truth may be conducted. Inversely, there is no literature without an intimate connection with philosophy: its internal philosophy, not always an explicit one, is what moves the artist into thinking, hence the necessity of a strong reading of literary, as of philosophical, texts, a reading which matches the violence of the thinking that occurs in both fields.

The phrase 'the passion for literature' carries two affects. It carries an affect of violence, a passion in the sense of Spinoza, that is a passive affect which reflects the violence that turns out to have been an unavoidable component of the century's worldview, and as such threatens to find its way into literary texts which it will fill with the melancholy of oppressive finitude, lack of freedom and historical despair. Such affect is more characteristic of postmodernism than of modernism, the literary conjuncture in which both Badiou and Deleuze select their canon. But the main affect carried by the century and expressed in its literature is a positive affect, an affect of desire and joy, one that increases the subject's power, expressing as it does the hope for a better future, the decision to militate for the emancipation of humankind, the desire to break out of the limits of language. Literature, for both our philosophers, is a vector of joyful affect, its 'passion' one that increases our power instead of decreasing it like the melancholy passions. Neither Deleuze nor Badiou have that dolorist, melancholy, post-Romantic attitude to literature which thrives on finitude and the absurd. Their passion for literature takes the shape of a philosophical style that is as passionate and joyful as its object. Hence the at first sight surprising subtitle to Badiou's book on Beckett, *L'increvable désir* (*Desire Unstoppable*): his reading is aimed at reclaiming Beckett from the mire of absurdist literature.

This passion for literature, in a more precise sense than the common-or-garden one, which is both the passionate affect of joy that literature carries and the passionate affect of joy both philosophers bring to thinking literature, enables us to move towards our third thesis. Analysing the passion for literature as an affect of joy allows us to invert the usual critical stance. It allows us to go beyond the reconstruction of two systems (Badiou is explicitly systematic; Deleuze's philosophy is entirely coherent, but better represented as a plane of consistency and a multiplicity of lines of flight). It allows us not to be content with extracting the relevant theses (as we saw, the formulation of relevant theses is at the heart of Badiou's practice of philosophy) or with formulating the relevant problem (which varies with each of Deleuze's philosophical projects), but to ask the apparently irrelevant question of the materiality of their philosophical practice, the question of the expression of that joyful affect in the practice of *writing* philosophy rather than simply formulating theses or constructing concepts. Only by asking what is philosophically speaking the *wrong* question will the necessary distance or displacement be achieved – the distance necessary to assess not what our philosophers want to do or claim to do, but simply what they do when they talk about literature: the continental philosopher is not merely a reader of texts (all philosophers are) but a *writer*, with a taste for literature both in the active and in the passive sense, a tradition that goes back to Parmenides, whose philosophy took the form of a poem, and to Plato, whose Platonism is concealed beneath a veil of irony and the labyrinth of dialogues that are also literary games. The wrong question, of course, turns out to be the right question, in so far as it places literature at the heart of Badiou's and Deleuze's philosophical undertaking. The price to pay for this shift of value can best be expressed in the fortunate paradox of philosophers who resist the linguistic turn but turn out to be not only lovers of literature but writers in their own right. The following is an outline of our answer to the now relevant question of their style of philosophy:

1. We find in both Deleuze and Badiou a militant conception of philosophy (philosophy not as interpretation of the world and of texts, but as experiment or intervention in the world and therefore in texts) which involves an interventionist form of writing. Writing philosophy is an aesthetic act (I borrow this concept from the work of the French philosopher of the sublime, Baldine Saint-Girons),[5] it involves an image of thought in which art and philosophy interfere with each other. It is not merely a form of aesthetics (Rancière discusses Deleuze's complex relationship to aesthetics,[6] and Badiou calls his essays on various arts 'essays in inaesthetics'), in other words there is no distinct philosophy of art but rather a disjunctive synthesis of art and philosophy, involving the capture and expression of strong affects. To say it in Deleuzian terms, the planes of consistency of Deleuze's and Badiou's philosophies is stratified with the plane of composition of art.
2. Writing philosophy involves the strong reading of other philosophers, a reading which is already a form of intervention and implies another, concomitant practice, that of strong writing. Or again, to put it briefly, our question is the question of the style (of philosophy, of writing) of Badiou and Deleuze.

A Question of Style

A bearded Hegel, a clean-shaven Marx

> In the history of philosophy, a commentary should act as a veritable double and bear the maximal modification appropriate to the double. (One imagines a *philosophically* bearded Hegel, a *philosophically* clean-shaven Marx, in the same way as a moustached Mona Lisa.).[7]

What Deleuze is describing here is his own method of reading texts, with a mixture of flippancy (a clean-shaven Marx), travesty (he alludes to the celebrated version of the Mona Lisa by Marcel Duchamp) and violence (the hapless philosophers are *philosophically* deprived of one of their striking characteristics). This is what I have called, in a phrase that needs explanation, a 'strong reading'.

Perhaps we should begin by wondering what a 'weak reading' of a text might be. Is it a reading that fails to convince its readers? Is it a reading that is too traditional to establish its right to exist, as we expect of a reading, as indeed of any research project, a modicum of originality? There are so-called Marxist readings that can be described as Marx and water. By way of contrast, a strong reading will thrive on the connotations of the adjective: it will involve force rather than form (if there is such a thing as a Deleuzian aesthetics, this will be its first proposition), it will involve a violence imposed on the text – forcing thought, as we have seen, is a Deleuzian theme, one with which Badiou would not disagree (the Lacanian concept of *forçage* plays a part in his theory of the subject).[8] As a matter of fact, the theory of strong readings was provided by Deleuze himself, at an early stage, in the first text of his *Negotiations*. The theory is encapsulated in a now famous phrase, when Deleuze describes his method of reading his philosophical predecessors: 'I saw myself as taking an author from behind and giving him a child that would be his own offspring, yet monstrous.'[9] That reading is a form of sexual violence, even of rape, is made entirely explicit in the text: 'I suppose the main way I coped with it at the time was to see the history of philosophy as a form of buggery or (it comes to the same thing) immaculate conception',[10] where it appears that this form of sexual violence is also an impossible one, short of a miracle. And here we may remember that Badiou justifies his own reading of Deleuze, in the face of the outrage it caused among Deleuze's followers, by suggesting he had been faithful to the theory of reading outlined in this passage.

The letter to a harsh critic was addressed to Michel Cressole, a student of Deleuze who had written the first book ever devoted to his work.[11] The book, the first but not the best in what is now a crowded field, was written in the flippant style of post-68 Paris, when the admiration one felt for one's masters was best expressed through insults.[12] Much is made in the book of the length of Deleuze's nails and similar irrelevancies. Deleuze's answer barely conceals his irritation, and it is written, tit for tat, in the same vein, with the same mixture of aggressiveness and vulgarity, which accounts for the sexual metaphors. So, the famous phrase does not do justice to the theory of reading thus adumbrated. The offspring, the strong reading, is not only monstrous, it is necessary, and the rape turns out to be an expression of love ('This intensive way of reading [. . .] is reading with love').[13] Otherwise, of course, we would be faced with the paradox that, with the exception of the book on Kant, Deleuze has always read philosophers whom he loved and defended against the mainstream tradition in the history of philosophy: he never wrote at length, if at all, on Plato, Aristotle or Hegel, so that the exclusive victims of his affectionate rapes were also the victims of the dominant image of thought in the history of philosophy. I am of course aware that claiming to have acted out of love would be a weak defence for a rapist, and that the metaphor goes against the grain of current political correctness: but those were the heady 1970s, when strong language was compulsory.

The time has come to move away from what now appears to us as an unfortunate metaphor – but we must keep the connotations of violence, intensity of affect and the paradox of the necessary impossibility or miracle. In fact the text provides a further description of the method of reading I have called 'strong', inspired by Deleuze's reading of Nietzsche. It may be usefully contrasted with Badiou's own reading method, which is also based on a form of violence, the violence of engagement and antagonism, for the one of unity must always give way to the two of separation and contradiction. On the same page, Deleuze opposes two ways of reading a text:

> There are, you see, two ways of reading a book: you either see it as a box with something inside and start looking for what it signifies, and then if you're even more perverse or depraved you set off after signifiers. And you treat the next book like a box contained in the box or containing it. And you annotate and interpret and question and write a book about the book, and so on and on. Or there's the other way: you see the book as a little non-signifying machine, and the only question is 'Does it work, and how does it work?' How does it work for you? If it doesn't work, if nothing comes through, you try another book. This second way of reading's intensive: something comes through or it doesn't. There is nothing

to explain, nothing to understand, nothing to interpret. It's like plugging in to an electric circuit.[14]

So either one unpacks the contents of a text, one reorganises and clarifies (which suggests the author was not clear-headed enough to do it himself), or one treats it as a machine, both small and a-signifying (we recognise in that term the language of *Capitalism and Schizophrenia*, with its non-signifying semiotics, and the distinction between the machinic and the merely mechanical: the text is a machine, the body is a machine, but they do not require the services of a skilled mechanic to be serviced). What we have here is a materialist conception of reading as production of meaning, as intervention, not interpretation of an already fixed meaning. The main question is indeed 'What can I do with this text?', hence the recourse to a-signifying semiotics. The text is full of signs, but not Saussurian signs, inducing signification through the cohesion of structured semantic fields and the coherence of syntactic organisation, designation through accurate reference, and manifestation as the presence of a subject of enunciation is felt through the requisite markers. We remember that in *Logic of Sense*, Deleuze defines doxic meaning, as opposed to sense, as the composition of signification, designation and manifestation.[15] Asking the 'wrong' question, 'How does it work?' takes us away from *doxa* into the realm of the machinic: pottering with those little machines, experimenting with them means reading for intensity rather than meaning (At what speed does the text move? Which bifurcations does it take in its rhizomatic proliferation? Which affects are involved? Are they melancholy or joyful?). We understand the paradoxical conclusion of the passage: there is nothing to explain, nothing to understand, nothing to interpret; the text is not a box, a receptacle of meaning, but an installation, if we use the artistic metaphor, or an electrical circuit, as the circulation of intensities and affects is what the text is about. Such is the passionate form of violent reading that Deleuze advocates, and it has nothing to do with a 'truth' of the text ('I believe in secrecy, that is, the power of falsity, rather than representing things in a way that manifests a lamentable faith in accuracy and truth').[16] With this phrase, 'the power of falsity', we are back to Badiou's reading of Deleuze, since we remember that such is, according to Badiou, the version of the unavoidable concept of truth that is to be found in Deleuze's philosophy – an excellent example of a strong reading, since it unblushingly inverts what Deleuze's text, with its emphatic rejection of accuracy and truth, seems to be saying.

Style

Let us take this last episode as an incentive to read both philosophers as they read each other, as well as other philosophers: asking the wrong questions, extracting the wrong problems, which will of course turn out to be the right ones. Not: how are the concepts articulated into a system? (the local equivalent of 'what does it mean?') but rather: how does it work? In other words, what is the philosopher's style?

Let us start not with the philosopher's writing style, his *écriture*, for we know that philosophy is a form of writing, but with his philosophical style. We are justified in doing this by Deleuze's extended concept of style, which does not cover just language but also life. (Henry James has his inimitable style, but Mods and Rockers had style too.) In Deleuze the concept of style covers not only the writers' practice of writing but her existential experience: '[Style] is a modality of becoming that forbids any form of separation between living and speaking, thought and the literary quest'.[17] But this absence of separation, which is a form of synthesis, is disjunctive; the work of art is autonomous with regard to its author, and 'style is never a matter of the man':[18] style is not a function of the author but of the text as part of a collective assemblage of enunciation.

So there is a Badiou assemblage of enunciation, which is not to be ascribed to the author's likes and dislikes or to his political positions (which are etymologically eccentric), but is a function of the texts which are remarkably coherent and yet entirely different as the system changes and develops all the time. Between *Théorie du sujet* and *Being and Event* there is a gap, which may be interpreted as a change of mind: the extreme Marxism-Leninism, of a Maoist and Lacanian cast (which remains perhaps the most important attempt to elaborate a Marxist philosophy for the late twentieth century), has given way to an ascetic ontology. And the relationship between *Being and Event* and *Logic of Worlds*, which ought to be of division of labour (the latter is supposed to be to the former what the *Phenomenology of Mind* was to the great *Logic*) can also be described as a movement away from strict ontology (which may account for the limited impact the second opus has had so far). But the three texts are united by a similar philosophical style. The apparatus of *Théorie du sujet*, an array of theses, always carefully numbered, principles and diagrams (the seminars are punctuated by 'at the blackboard' sequences, where diagrams, often of Byzantine complexity, out-Lacaning Lacan, are carefully drawn) has left traces in the later works. For the later work is equally systematic, and such systematicity brings with it a form of explicitness and perspicuity. Badiou is consistently a complex philosopher, but he is also entirely clear: there is a Badiou matheme, which calls for pedagogic exposition. Thus the three-page preface Badiou wrote for the English collection of his theoretical writings spells out the string of concepts that make up the skeleton of *Being and Event*.[19] You can 'do' Badiou in one paragraph, a paragraph repeatedly rehearsed in commentaries. Here is Bruno Bosteels, quoted by Žižek:

> Setting out from the void which prior to the event remains indiscernible in the language of established knowledge, a subjective intervention names the event which disappears no sooner than it appears; it faithfully connects as many elements of the situation as possible to this name which is the only trace of the vanished event, and subsequently forces the extended situation from the bias of the new truth as if the latter were indeed already generally applicable.[20]

I do not want to deny the talent of the commentator, who is a specialist of Badiou's political thought: I just want to note that the explicitness of the system makes such summary possible, without gross betrayal. And it would be impossible to do the same thing for Deleuze, for more than one reason. The first reason is that the historical determination of his concepts is greater. Some of the main concepts of his early work (the concept of essence in *Proust and Signs*, the concept of sense in *Logic of Sense*) have been abandoned or replaced in later works. One has the impression, explicitly acknowledged by Deleuze, that each new book is a new beginning. It can be argued that with *Being and Event*, Badiou's system has reached a stable state: with Deleuze, although some concepts are present throughout the *oeuvre* (the concepts of virtuality or of event), there is no stable state, only lines of flight, some of which are long and uninterrupted. The second reason is that, within a single work or period (for instance, the Deleuze and Guattari period), Deleuze's philosophical style is hardly systematic. A philosophical system can be described as a form of arborescence. Drawing on the preface to *Theoretical Writings* or on Bosteel's paragraph, one can represent the logical framework of *Being and Event*, if not as a tree, at least as a chain of logically articulated concepts: inconsistent multiplicity (without either a One or a Whole) → count for one →

presentation (of the elements counted for one) → situation → structure of the situation (its subsets) → representation (where the subsets are counted for one) → state of the situation (language, knowledge) → void of the situation (the null set) → edge of the void → evental site → event → generic procedure (generic set) → enquiry → truth through forcing → fidelity → subject. A list of similar concepts in Deleuze could be produced, but it would not have the structure of a chain, where each concept is linked to the preceding one by a logical or quasi-logical relation. In order to describe the plane of consistency on which Deleuze's concepts are deployed, one would have to use the Deleuzian concepts of rhizome, lines of flight, infinite speed, deterritorialisation and reterritorialisation. There is a sense in which the best metaphor to describe Deleuze's style of philosophy is the metaphor of the fold. As Tom Conley puts it:

> The passage of the fold from one work to the other attests to a style of writing that in itself is always folding, unfolding and refolding. Some concepts and figures shift emphasis or are metamorphosed when they migrate from one work to another. They show that in Deleuze's world everything is folded and folds, in and out of everything else.[21]

The very number of metaphors available in Deleuze's books for the description of his philosophical style is a good index of the proliferating aspect of that style. Indeed, one of the most convincing critiques of Badiou's reading of Deleuze is that he forces back the rhizome into a tree, that he systematises the unsystematic. For instance, the concept of simulacrum, which is at the heart of Deleuze's anti-Platonist stance in *Logic of Sense*, belongs to the pre-Guattari period and afterwards disappears. But Badiou's reading projects it, for the needs of overturning Deleuze's overturning of Platonism, on to the whole of his work. And by systematising Deleuze's philosophy, he dehistoricises it: there is a constant becoming in Deleuze's work – witness the three stages of the work on Proust, the last of which, belonging as it does to a much later period, is not entirely compatible with the first.

Theses and correlation

It is only too easy to express the different styles of the two philosophers in Deleuzian terms: by contrasting Badiou's striated with Deleuze's smooth style; or by opposing a plane of reference in Badiou to Deleuze's plane of immanence or of consistency; or again, by

A Question of Style

opposing Badiou's fixed concepts to the Deleuzian lines of flight, as concepts diverge and merge. That would be unfair to Badiou, so I shall attempt to express the difference by contrasting Badiou's taste for the positing of theses and Deleuze's chronic use of the device of a correlation.

Badiou, as we have seen, is a thetic philosopher: the matheme is a conceptual architecture and consists of a number of carefully articulated theses (each of the concepts in the chain of concepts quoted above is the core of a number of propositions or theses). The origin of this practice is probably to be found in Marx's theses on Feuerbach, although the result is entirely dissimilar, as Marx's theses were jotted down on a piece of paper without thought of publication or construction of a systematic argument.[22] The second origin, itself determined by the first, is Althusser's celebrated essay on Ideological State Apparatuses, where the argument proceeds through a number of carefully articulated theses.[23] In Badiou, however, the model is not only philosophical but also mathematical: we have not only propositions (as in *Logic of Worlds*) and theses, but axioms, theorems and lemmas. The thetic method has obvious advantages, which we have already glimpsed: the text enjoys all the advantages of clarity and explicitness, which means the system can be expounded, discussed and refuted. What we have is a philosophy under the condition of (mathematical) science. But since that philosophy also operates under the condition of poetry, the thetic philosopher meditates in an assertive mode, often against the grain of common sense, hence the strong feelings Badiou sometimes provokes. The subtitles of Badiou's texts (*Desire Unstoppable*,[24] *The Clamor of Being*) often illustrate that strongly assertive position: there is little place for uncertainty and doubt in this style of philosophy, a characteristic that becomes particularly obvious when Badiou talks about literary texts, where interpretation is usually more open and less affirmative. Thus, in *Pocket Pantheon*, Deleuze's philosophy is summarised around five 'motifs', a fine instance of pedagogic simplification, and in his *Beckett*, we find three types of subject in the text (the subjects of enunciation, of passivity and of the question),[25] as well as four 'functions' isolated by the text (movement and rest, being, language and the Other).[26] Somehow, the assertiveness of strict numbering is less congenial to the literary critic, used to the openness and multiplicity of interpretations (a possibility Badiou strongly denies in his readings of Mallarmé) than it is to the philosopher.

Deleuze, on the other hand, is, if I may say so, a correlative philosopher. Even if he rarely uses diagrams and never tables, he constantly uses the stylistic expository device whereby two objects are contrasted, along a line of flight, by two series of determinations which might be tabulated into a correlation. Thus, at the end of his introduction to the work of Sacher Masoch, sadism and masochism are jointly characterised along the following lines, where they are correlated in that order through a number of contrasts: (1) a speculative and demonstrative mode of thought versus a dialectical and imaginative mode; (2) a negative attitude based on direct negation versus a suspensive one based on denial; (3) a sadistic form of masochism versus a masochistic form of sadism; (4) a negation of the character of the mother and an exaggerated importance ascribed to the character of the father versus the denial of the mother and the annihilation of the father; (5) different roles and meanings ascribed to both phantasy and fetish; (6) a rejection of aestheticism versus a revelling in it; (7) an overall meaning provided by institutions versus an overall meaning provided by contract. I pass over one or two further contrasts and come to the last, which is presented as the summing up and totalisation of the preceding ones: (11) apathy versus coldness. Those contrasts are supposed to operate between the two forms of sexual perversion but also between the literary techniques and styles of Sade and Sacher Masoch.

This expository stylistic device is coherent with Deleuze's ontology: it involves the development of two series joined by a form of disjunctive synthesis. The series, organised as a sequence of juxtaposed elements, is a much more plastic form of ordering than the articulated tree, like the tree of Porphyry, based as it is on the twin principles of linearity and progression.[27] Indeed the correlation as used by Deleuze is incompatible with the dogmatic image of thought he wishes to overturn: what we have is not two lines, one representing the other (as in the classic case of the systematic parallelism between signifiers and signified in the linguistic chain of utterance), but a series of contrasts along a line of flight. The main aspect of the correlation, which is also its main philosophical interest, is that *there is always another column*: its principle of organisation is indeed a line of flight, there is no teleology in the correlation, as the passage from one column to the next does not mean one step further towards the exhaustion of a fixed number of possibilities within a system.

There are two possible sources for the device, the first of which

A Question of Style

is fully acknowledged by Deleuze, in his essay on structuralism:[28] the linguistic chain is organised in two parallel series (of words and things, of signifier and signified), along which the empty square circulates, producing meaning. The two series are endless, and endlessly diverging, only joined at irregular intervals by the *point de capiton*, the upholstery button or quilting point of Lacanian fame. From such series, which provide the structure of language, it is a short step to the correlation proper, the best instance of which is to be found in Jakobson's celebrated correlation of two types of aphasia, two types of organisation of language, two figures of speech and two literary genres:

	1	2	3	4	5	6	7
	Linguistic units	Linguistic operations	Types of aphasia	Figures of speech	Literary genres	Styles of art	Operations of the dream-work
1	Paradigm	Selection	Contiguity trouble	Metaphor	Romanticism	Surrealism	Condensation
2	Syntagma	Combination	Similarity trouble	Metonymy	Realism	Cubism	Displacement

The conceptual jump that allows the eminent linguist to go from figures of speech (their relation to linguistic operations and units, and therefore with types of aphasia is fairly straightforward) to literary genres and styles of art is staggering: this is following a line of flight with a vengeance.

The second source for the device of the correlation is – if it is indeed a source – unacknowledged: the reader of Wittgenstein (which Deleuze claimed he wasn't, going as far as calling Wittgenstein, in *Abécédaire*, an assassin of philosophy) cannot help being reminded of the famous family resemblance sequence, where A resembles B, which resembles C, and so on to N, which has no resemblance to A, the resemblance having drifted, as it does from sibling to sibling or from generation to generation.

We can now give a more precise description of the correlation, using Deleuze's own concepts (to the best of my knowledge he does not use the term itself):

1. A correlation is a rhizome – it can be entered at any point, so why not in the middle? (There is no beginning nor end, only a middle: the correlation, like a rhizome, grows at both ends.)

2. A correlation is a line of flight. It has no *telos* because it has no *arche* – again, there is always another column.
3. The correlation is organised by two forms of AND of addition, one vertical and one horizontal. (Jakobson's correlation has seven columns and two lines, but a correlation with more than two lines is entirely possible: there is always another line.)
4. The correlation always tends towards a diagram that complexifies it. (The famous spiral diagram in *A Thousand Plateaus* immediately comes to mind: its centre is the Signifier, and the spiral escapes, along its line of flight, with the figure of the Scapegoat – the potential signifier versus signified correlation has acquired spatial and conceptual dynamism.)[29]

We can summarise this description by providing the correlation of the correlation, contrasting the device with its Deleuzian antonym, the Hegelian dialectic:

	1	2	3	4	5	6	7	8	9
A	Correlation	Multiple	Anarchic	Open-ended	Relational	Line	Rhizome	Map	Rhythm
B	Dialectic	Single	Fixed origin	Teleological	Essential	Spiral	Tree	Triangulation	Closure

The correlation diagram reads thus: where a correlation involves a proliferation of concepts, the dialectic involves a single one; where a correlation is anarchic in the etymological sense, the dialectic involves a fixed origin or principle; the correlation is open-ended, which means that it always begins in the middle, whereas the dialectic is teleological; the correlation is relational (everything lies in the relation of disjunctive synthesis that (dis)unites the lines, whereas the dialectic develops an essence); the correlation can be mapped as a line, not a spiral like the dialectic, or a rhizome, not a tree: there is no triangulation, no determination of coordinates in the correlation, only open-ended mapping, which contrasts the rhythm of the correlation with the closure of the dialectic. This is of course unfair to the Hegelian dialectic, to which Badiou has remained, with due qualifications, faithful (it is, as we saw, central in *Théorie du sujet*, absent but not denied in *Being and Event*, and it makes a comeback in *Logic of Worlds*) but it reflects Deleuze's deep-seated hostility to it.

A Question of Style

Two modes of reading

We have described two styles of philosophy. Their difference implies a different mode of reading texts, beyond the Deleuzian 'taking the author from behind' approach. The Badiou mode of reading texts is assertive and critical: the object of the reading is a mixture of celebration (especially of poetic texts) and placement. Badiou's typical operation is separation through the recognition of antagonism (one is divided into two), which explains his frequent indulgence in sharp polemics ('I have never tempered my polemics; *consensus* is not my strong point').[30] The style has mellowed with age: we might compare *Pocket Pantheon*, where praise for his predecessors, including Deleuze, is lavish, with *Théorie du sujet*, where Deleuze is presented as a left-wing deviationist and the limitations of both Mallarmé and Lacan are made explicit. Deleuze's mode of reading is more difficult to pin down: he doesn't place the authors he reads, he tends to ignore his opponents and he rarely indulges in polemics (with the large exception of psychoanalysis, but even then the criticism is generic): there is, for instance, hardly a word on Hegel in all his works. Nor is his style appreciative and empathetic, it is rather an opening up of the text he reads, the identification and following of lines of flight. The best way of characterising such a mode of reading is to call it problematic: he forces out a problem, but he is little interested in solutions, unlike Badiou, whose system is a set of solutions. Hence, when they mourn a predecessor, two different forms of a grief may be observed. This is how Louise Burchill, in the introduction to her translation of Badiou's *Deleuze*, describes the difference between their two modes of reading:

> At no moment does Deleuze, in his text [on Foucault], play his philosophy off against the philosophy he assigns to Foucault; nor does he ever adopt the point of view of his system to isolate the failures of the other. On the other hand Badiou engages from the outset in a polemical dialogue with Deleuze's conceptualization, in which, if he elaborates – much as Deleuze does in *Foucault* – what he views as the underlying logic and movement of Deleuze's metaphysics, the aim is nevertheless to counter the conceptual coordinates so delineated with arguments that draw on a philosophical tendency opposed to Deleuze's own.[31]

The contrast appears to be between a mode of reading based on a principle of charity and one based on the operation of placement of the opponent. We can find an example of this in Juliette Simont's essay on Deleuze's and Badiou's critiques of representation, where she analyses Badiou's rhetoric in his Deleuze book, especially his use of adjectives. Badiou's reading, she claims, is 'strongly rhetorical', especially in his use of patronising laudatory adjectives and insinuating pejorative adjectives.[32] Badiou wishes to free philosophy from grammatical and linguistic constraints (so he claims in his *Briefings on Existence*: *l'emprise grammaticale et linguistique*, 'the dominion of grammar and linguistics'),[33] but the question of the type of language he writes must be nevertheless asked. Thus we noticed Badiou's use of the word 'genius' with reference to Deleuze in his essay 'Deleuze's Vitalist Ontology':[34] since the essay is devoted to a systematic account of Deleuze's mistakes in the field of ontology, mistakes that Badiou himself skilfully avoided, the term is either an example of irony, or a form of praise, extravagant if indirect, of Badiou himself.

Two styles of writing and yet another correlation

We have moved from a style of philosophy to a style of writing: the question of the philosopher's language is unavoidable, and we have entered the realm of stylistics. The object of stylistics, at least since the work of the founding father of the discipline, Leo Spitzer, is the description of the 'X-sentence', where X is the name of the author. Thus there will be a recognisable Proust sentence or a Hemingway sentence as worthy of parody as a picture by Cézanne is prone to be faked, for style is indeed what allows parody, pastiche and fakes. So we shall postulate that there is a Badiou sentence and a Deleuze sentence.

There are two types of Badiou sentences (at least). In *Théorie du sujet*, which collects seminars given from 1975 to 1979, the stylistic model is still Lacan and sometimes even Mallarmé: neither is known for the perspicuity of their style, so that this attempt at a Marxist-Leninist philosophy is still often couched in the syntactically complex idiom of *préciosité*. In the later works, however, and most notably in the major opus, the style has become as perspicuous as it is explicit. Badiou, who has a sense of humour, even gives a fictional account of this in the introduction to his latest novel, *Calme bloc ici-bas*. The novel, set in the fictional country of Prémontré (a child's dream: a whole new country, complete with imaginary geography and even a map, and an imaginary history of war and revolution – but a country which, of course, is startlingly reminiscent of modern France), describes the three styles of that nation's literature, all exemplified

A Question of Style

in the novel and distinguished by three different typographic characters: the classical style is clear and simple; the romantic style is metaphorical and syntactically complex; the modernist or sarcastic style is a-grammatical and laconic.[35] This could be a description of the evolution of Badiou's philosophical style, from the Romanticism of *Théorie du sujet* to the classicism of the later work. It remains to be seen whether we shall ever have a work of philosophy written in the sarcastic and ungrammatical style of modernism. For an instance of the Badiou sentence, we may quote the incipit to the first 'meditation' in *Being and Event*: 'Since its Parmenidean organization, ontology has built the portico of its ruined temple out of the following experience: what *presents* itself is essentially multiple; *what* presents itself is essentially one.'[36] Admire the rhetorical balance between the last two clauses; admire the classical simplicity of the syntax; admire the rhythm the skilful use of punctuation gives the sentence. Note also the remains of the Romantic style, in the metaphor of the ruined temple and its portico, with reminiscences of Claude and Hubert Robert rather than Poussin.

The Deleuze sentence is a different matter: it does not have the classical grandeur of the Badiou sentence. It is more sinuous, less skilfully balanced, it meanders, it follows the intensive line of syntax, it runs along its line of flight, it indulges in endless correlations. Not to choose the incipit to *Anti-Oedipus* once again, a fine instance of provocation, moved by the obvious pleasure there is in *épater le bourgeois* (shocking respectable readers),[37] I shall quote the opening words of *The Fold*:

> The Baroque refers not to an essence but rather to an operative function, to a trait. It endlessly produces folds. It does not invent things: there are all kinds of folds coming from the East, Greek, Roman, Romanesque, Gothic, Classical folds ... Yet the Baroque trait twists and turns its folds, pushing them to infinity, fold over fold, one upon the other. The Baroque fold unfurls all the way to infinity.[38]

The Deleuze sentence is syntactically simple (it is an excellent example of what is known as hypotactic style), but it has rhythm, a different rhythm from the Badiou sentence: it moves by twists and turns, along a line, or rather two lines in contrast (what the baroque is not, what it is), it proceeds by potentially endless accumulation, the line of flight running towards infinity (note the three dots at the end of the second sentence) and by syntagmatic accretion (note the number of appositions at the end of the third sentence). In other word, the Deleuze sentence is a fold and a fold upon a fold – here it is iconic of its referent. Nor is it simply a matter of the adequacy of the style to the subject matter: an analysis of the opening to the first chapter of *Difference and Repetition*, 'Difference in Itself', will yield the same stylistic results. I shall merely quote it here, as the reader will be immediately aware of the similarity of stylistic quality:

> Difference has two aspects: the undifferentiated abyss, the black nothingness, the indeterminate animal in which everything is dissolved – but also the white nothingness, the once more calm surface upon which float with unconnected determinations like scattered members: a head without a neck, an arm without a shoulder, eyes without brows.[39]

Deleuze's style is not metaphorical (the fold is not a metaphor), but it eschews the classicism of the Badiou sentence (without falling into the rhetorical weight of the Romantic style or the ungrammaticality of the sarcastic style): it is a baroque literary style, in his acceptation of the term. It has a poetic quality that Badiou refuses to allow himself (but in which he too indulges in his novels).

The comparison between Badiou's and Deleuze's styles of philosophy and writing styles can be summarised in yet another correlation:

	1	2	3	4	5	6
Badiou	Explorer of heights	System	Assertive and critical reading	Theses	Badiou sentence	Classical style
Deleuze	Pottering artisan	Plane of immanence	Taking the author from behind	Correlation	Deleuze sentence	Baroque style

The system gives its author a vantage point on the world. Even if there is neither One nor Whole and the philosopher is not in the position of Jupiter above, the system allows the stability and exhaustiveness of its articulated concepts: it is the rock on which the philosopher, like the King of the castle, firmly stands. The artisan, on the other hand, bent on the creation of his concepts, is not in this stable position: the concepts shift from work to work, they seem to acquire a life of their own, like characters in a novel, and the pottering goes on indefinitely, for the plane of immanence is only a fragile protection from the original chaos. Hence a mode of reading which is less assertive but in a way more violent: not so much the violence of decision

A Question of Style

(there is a strong form of decisionism in Badiou, and not only in his political philosophy) as of deliberate misprision, the price to pay for genuine creation (that there is a form of creationism – but not in the usual meaning among biologists – is at the centre of Peter Hallward's reading of Deleuze).[40] From those philosophical contrasts we can derive the opposition between thesis and correlation (one is certainly more systematic and assertive than the other), the Badiou sentence and the Deleuze sentence and the classical versus the Baroque style.

But perhaps the correlation could take one more column (there is always another column):

	7
Badiou	Literature as condition for philosophy
Deleuze	Literature as machine

Reading literature

That literature is a condition for philosophy, like art in general, is an essential tenet of Badiou's system. This explains why the elaboration of a Marxist-Leninist philosophy in *Théorie du sujet* takes the paradoxical detour of a reading of a Mallarmé sonnet, or why the analysis of 'the century' is conducted mostly through the reading of literary texts, from Mandelstam to Saint-John Perse. And nobody will accuse Badiou of neglecting the importance of literature. For him, it is a practice before it is an object of analysis. His first published books were two novels, *Almagestes* and *Portulans*.[41] *Calme bloc ici-bas*, his third novel, was published eleven years after *Being and Event*, and there is a sense in which it is informed by the system: it reads like a yarn, complete with disappearances, pursuits and *coups de théâtre*, but the 'events' narrated are, more often than not, events in the sense of Badiou, radically new occurrences in the fields of politics, science and love (for instance, we meet a mathematician who is trying to improve on Cantor). And several of his plays were staged in France in the late 1990s: they come complete with a theory of drama, in which, unexpectedly, the essence of drama is comedy. (Have I said that Badiou has a sense of humour?) And when Badiou appeals to literature as a condition for his philosophy, it is to defend a canon which is limited (his favourite, should I say his only, authors are Beckett, Mallarmé, Rimbaud, Pessoa and Mandelstam – Deleuze's taste is much more catholic), limited to poetry, as we have just noted

(Beckett, for instance, is treated more as a poet than a playwright) and typically high modernist: you don't catch Badiou mentioning Gaston Leroux, that ancestor of the closed-room whodunit, as Deleuze does in his essay of 1966, 'Philosophie de la série noire'.[42]

With Deleuze, on the other hand, we find no explicitly literary writing – philosophy is an obsession, and there is no leaving it, even for art – but a proliferation of literary references, as well as a more general interest in other arts. There is a sense in which the development of his interest in art goes from literature to a more general form of artistic semiosis: such is Anne Sauvagnargues's thesis in her *Deleuze et l'art*.[43] But she immediately concedes that the interest in literature was a lifelong passion in Deleuze (the last book he published in his lifetime, *Essays Critical and Clinical*,[44] is largely devoted to literature). Thus, in contrast with Badiou's, Deleuze's canon is (1) without bounds (someone has produced a concordance of literary allusions in Deleuze's works: there are 279 entries);[45] (2) without generic bounds, as Deleuze can philosophise about any type of literature, from the detective story, as we have seen, to avant-garde poets like Gherasim Luca, taking in the classical novel of the nineteenth century (Dickens, Zola) as well as contemporary drama from Beckett to Carmelo Bene; (3) with a national slant, as Deleuze is particularly keen on Anglo-American literature, having devoted most of his *Logic of Sense* to Lewis Carroll, and entitled a section of his *Dialogues* with Claire Parnet 'On the superiority of Anglo-American literature' – Crane, Lawrence, Melville, Kerouac, Fitzgerald are among his favourite authors; (4) with the same high modernist slant as Badiou: the entries on Artaud and Lawrence are among the longest in the index, and the longer books are devoted to Proust, Kafka and Beckett.

Now that we know which literary texts Badiou and Deleuze read, the time has come to watch them reading.

Badiou reads Mandelstam, Deleuze reads Kafka

The second chapter of *The Century* is entitled 'The Beast'. It is devoted to a poem by Mandelstam, of which this is the title, and which Badiou uses as a point of entry into the thought of the century: access to the century does not occur by way of history or sociology, and only by way of philosophy in so far as it is conditioned by poetry. As we remember, the central thesis of the book is that the century is characterised by 'the passion for the real'. Mandelstam is treated as one of the century's heroes as he experienced that passion not only in his flesh (he fell victim to Stalinist terror) but in his poetry (and here the term 'passion' recovers its ambiguity, as Mandelstam's passion must be understood in both senses of the term). Badiou reads the text, a poem of thirty-two lines which he begins by quoting in full, by extracting from it five fragments, in which he identifies five figures of the century: the Beast, the face-to-face-stare, the beast's 'vertebration' (its skeleton), the 'blood glued together' (a phrase borrowed from the poem) and finally the poem itself. These five figures are immediately translated into five philosophical questions that the century asks: the questions of vitalism, of voluntarism, of consistency, of the relation to the past, and of art as 'installed in the wait' (*dans l'attente*)[46] – art is the expectation of the unpredictable event. This reading, or translation, is preceded by a page on the historical context of Mandelstam's poem (the celebrated poem on Stalin, which cost him so much, is duly mentioned) and followed by three other poetic 'punctuations' of the century, by Breton, Heidegger and Yves Bonnefoy. From this brief summary it appears that the poem is a source for the thinking of the century by the philosopher: it allows the translation that makes the truth of the century explicit, a truth which the poem itself cannot formulate clearly either because it is written in Aesopic language (this may well have been the case with Mandelstam), or because its own path to truth is not propositional (and Badiou has a taste for hermetic poetry, as appears in *Calme bloc ici-bas*, where one of the characters is writing an interminable poem of resolute, but somewhat tongue-in-cheek, hermeticism, and the hero is a disciple of Mallarmé). The outcome of the reading is the formulation of a number of philosophical theses on the century, the last and perhaps the most important of which is that the century was a century of the poetics of the wait and of the threshold: what the poem does achieve is that it enables us to think the century anew, by being a source of further theses.

I shall not here rehearse Deleuze and Guattari's reading of Kafka. I shall only evoke that famous reading as an instance of creative misprision, a strong reading that 'forces' the text, in other words that forces a number of concepts or theses out of the text. And indeed, the importance of this reading for Deleuze's aesthetics cannot be undervalued: there is a sense in which such aesthetics is based on the concept of minority, which lies at the heart of the book on Kafka. In his essay, 'De la littérature en général, et de Beckett en particulier, selon Deleuze', Jean-François Louette formulates Deleuze's aesthetics in four theses.[47] The first thesis is that for Deleuze the task of literature is not the creation of forms: rather, literature is the unceasing genesis of a flow of life, an expression of desire. The second thesis is that literature has an impersonal quality: it is a site for welcoming pre-individual haecceities rather than the expression of a self, the self of the author or of the character. The third thesis is that literature is the expression of 'great health', a phrase Deleuze has borrowed from Nietzsche: that literature has to do with the clinical as well as the critical is inscribed in the very title of Deleuze's last book – what literature is about is, again, the power of life. The reason for this insistence on the link between literature and 'life' (a danger word for literary critics) will, I hope, appear in the next section. The last thesis is that literature implies a minorisation of the major use of language. And here, the reference is, of course, Kafka, a Jewish author writing in German in the Czech environment of the city of Prague – the concept of minority is attributed to him, as it is said to come from a passage of his diaries. From this passage Deleuze and Guattari have evolved a whole theory of literature around the three characteristics of a minor literature: a minor literature is not written in a minor language, it deterritorialises a major language; in a minor literature everything is immediately political: it is the very embodiment of the 1968 slogan 'the personal is also political'; a minor literature is not an individual affair, it is always produced by a collective assemblage of enunciation.[48] The importance of such a view of literature is not in doubt. The problem is that Kafka specialists strongly deny it originates in Kafka. In her essay, 'Deleuze et Kafka: l'invention de la littérature mineure',[49] Marie-Odile Thirouin points out that the text on which such analysis is based is not Kafka's own, but a collage of fragments from the diaries by Max Brod; that the concept of *littérature mineure* comes from a translation of the phrase *kleine Literatur* by Marthe Robert, which introduces a pejorative connotation absent in the original German (and duly inverted by Deleuze and Guattari); and that the position Kafka takes on the subject is not what Deleuze and Guattari claim: he is not dealing with the situation of a Jewish writer in Prague, but of authors writing in Yiddish, not German, in Warsaw, not Prague, or of Czech authors writing in Czech, and for him Jewish literature in Prague, being written in German, belongs to the great German literature, not to a minorisation of it. Hence we find the twin illusions that Kafka is the author of a text on minor literature and that his is a deterritorialising text. Yet the efficacy and creativity of what appears to be a gross misreading is not in doubt:

A Question of Style

for this is what a strong reading is, not so much an interpretation (interpretation there is in their reading, but it is incorrect) as a form of interference, an intervention, a forcing of the text. Violence is needed, Deleuze keeps saying, in order for us to think. The question remains, of course, of the limits of such violence, of whether anything goes in the matter of intervention as of interpretation. In the case of Deleuze and Guattari's strong misreading of Kafka, the answer to the questions 'Does it work? Does it produce interesting results?' is firmly positive.

Deleuze reads Dickens

The last words of a great philosopher have a duly touching quality. No doubt the brevity of Deleuze's last text and the enigmatic quality of its title, 'Immanence: A Life . . .' have helped to increase such emotional weight and to make it a cult text. In that title we note the colon of equivalence (how can immanence, an abstract concept, be equivalent not even to life but to *a* life?) and the three dots that seem to announce the end of a life (the essay was published only weeks before Deleuze committed suicide). And we note the interplay between the zero article, which refers to a notion or concept, and the indefinite article, which refers to a singularity. The essay reads like a summary of Deleuze's first philosophy as it once again stages the typical Deleuzian chain of concepts: the *ET* (AND) of the series versus the *EST* (IS) of identity; the transcendental field versus the empirical representation; an a-subjective, pre-reflexive, impersonal form of consciousness, a consciousness without subject or object (Deleuze obsessively comes back to Sartre's essay on the transcendence of ego); a plane of immanence. At this point in the essay, before the chain goes on to the event, to becoming, to singularities to the virtual (the essay is a fragment of a projected longer text on the concept of the virtual), a literary illustration is introduced, and Deleuze reads Dickens.

Chapter 3 of the third book of *Our Mutual Friend* is a strange chapter, as it seems to be a moment of stasis in the plot (its only relation to the main thread of the narrative is that it anticipates the death by drowning of the main villain who, in this chapter, almost drowns but is saved, which causes him to entertain the illusion, based on proverbial stupidity, that he can never drown). So Riderhood, the scoundrel, almost drowns when his small boat is sunk by a steamer on the Thames: he is brought ashore and, with difficulty, revived.

This is how Dickens accounts for the scene: Riderhood, between life and death, is no longer a character, only a life, and the other characters, who despise Riderhood, treat this life with the tenderness and care it deserves, which has nothing to do with the 'person' that bears it. For this is indeed an in-between moment: before, Riderhood was a villain, considered as such by the community (he had been forbidden to enter the pub where he is now lying in the hands of the doctor); after, when he has been revived, he is again a villain and behaves as such: he insults the people who have just saved his life and goes on with his life of nefarious deeds. In this in-between moment, we are no longer in space and time, even fictional ones: we are in a transcendental field, marked by the indefinite pronoun – not *the* life (of Riderhood), but *a* life: an indeterminate person but a determinate singularity. (This apparent paradox of indeterminate determinacy is carried by the two grammatical values of the indefinite article in English: generic extraction – 'a cat is an independent beast' – and singular extraction – 'there's a cat on the window sill'). Suddenly, in this in-between moment, a life has emerged, and that is what is worth struggling for, that is why the people in the pub fight to save someone who does not deserve to live. Such a life has the following characteristics: it is impersonal, singular, freed from the accidents of internal and external life (it knows neither subject nor object), it is a haecceity, singular but not individual (the bearer of a life has temporarily lost his name and all his personal characteristics), it is neutral, beyond good and evil, no longer the life of an individual, but 'the singular immanent life of a man who no longer has a name'.[50]

We could treat this reading as a forcing of the text, imposing on it a host of abstruse concepts (haecceity, plane of immanence, transcendental field, etc.) that stifle it: we could decide that Dickens is merely preparing the end of his plot (in which Riderhood will drown, in the embrace of the criminal schoolmaster), or that he is making his usual moral point, to show that Riderhood, who is not in the least grateful for having been saved, is beyond redemption. But that would be a mistake, as the philosopher who ignores such trivial reading is aware of aspects of the text no one has noticed before (and which, once noticed, become as obvious as a finally understood joke, when the quilting point of achieved meaning has been reached) – aspects of the text that account for the apparent irrelevance of the chapter with regard to the narrative as a whole (for my trivial reading is not merely trivial, it is also rather unconvincing). This is how Dickens describes the scene:

> The doctor-seeking messenger meets the doctor halfway, coming under a convoy of police. Doctor examines the dank carcase, and pronounces, not hopefully, that it is worth while trying to reanimate the same. All the best means are at once in action, and everybody present lends a hand, and heart and soul. No one has the least regard for the man; with them all, he has been an object of avoidance, suspicion, and aversion; but the spark of life within him is curiously separable from himself now, and they have a deep interest in it, probably because it *is* life, and they are living and must die.[51]

There is a contrast between the usual sarcastic tone of the beginning of the passage and the last sentence, where the text acquires a form of ethical seriousness. It is on this last sentence that Deleuze's reading is based: you have noted the appearance of 'a life . . .' in the italicised 'is' in the last sentence, as you have also noted the Frankensteinian 'spark of life', the naked life that is 'separable' from the person who bears it (a 'spark of life' is what Victor Frankenstein instils in the yet lifeless form of his creature).

I believe that this type of reading, although it is more of a translation and an intervention than an interpretation, is deeply faithful to the text. All we have to do to understand this is to compare it with another famous reading of *Our Mutual Friend*, by Henry James, a famous assassination of Dickens in general and this novel in particular, in the shape of a review of the novel. Here are the famous first words of that text: '*Our Mutual Friend* is, to our perception, the poorest of Mr Dickens's works. And it is poor with the poverty not of momentary embarrassment, but of permanent exhaustion.'[52] The criticisms addressed to the novel are systematic and far-reaching: there is no feeling in the writing (p. 32), no principle of nature, but only 'mere bundles of eccentricities' (p. 32), no humanity, as no single character can be said to refer to an existing type (p. 32): 'the people [. . .] have nothing in common with each other, except the fact that they have nothing in common with mankind at large' (p. 33). As a result of this, Dickens appears as a superficial writer (p. 34) and, a point that we read with special interest, he is not a philosopher: 'Mr Dickens is a great observer and a great humorist, but he is nothing of a philosopher' (p. 35). The task of the true novelist, who is also a philosopher, is to 'know *man*, as well as men' (p. 35): the greatness of a work of art lies in such a capacity to generalise.

In contradistinction to this analysis, Deleuze's reading makes it obvious that Dickens in this chapter is more of a philosopher than Henry James, in so far precisely as he escapes from the dogmatic image of thought to which James's account of the philosopher (and of the novelist) belongs. Against the novel as a canonical form of representation (of Nature, of Man), with its consequent generalisations (the italicised *man*), Dickens appears to be a philosopher of singularities, one who captures haecceities and events, an explorer of surfaces, not of the depths of human nature. In Deleuze's own terms, we might oppose Dickens's humour, a matter of surfaces, to the irony of Henry James, who considers mankind from the height of moral and philosophical abstractions (the choice of the indefinite article in '*a* life' does not only refer to the concept of singularity, but also to Deleuze's adherence to a form of empiricism), and reading the novel from such abstract heights, from that high moral ground, can only lead to the pointless assassination we find in his review.

And the objection that Deleuze is reading a short passage, not even a whole chapter, whereas James is reading the whole novel is not valid, as the page chosen by Deleuze is an excellent point of entry to the novel, and it enables us to perceive the grandeur of the text which Henry James has missed: the novel is not a matter of grotesque caricature and satire as James claims (p. 33), but of humour, the literary mode that captures the circulation of the event, the impersonal force of virtuality that produces actualisations in the shape of characters and accidents. Only from this point of view can we understand the grandeur of the celebrated opening of the novel, where the river, the Thames, that impersonal flow of life, is more important than the human characters that are caught in its current.

Conclusion

Reading those three readings may have given the impression that the contrast expressed in my last correlation is somewhat blurred. For there are similarities in the ways Badiou and Deleuze read literature. In both cases, they read for the content of the text, and show no interest in the signifiers: what we have in both cases is a philosophical, not a literary, reading. But there are differences as well in which the contrast is maintained. Contrary to expectations, treating literature as a condition for philosophy rather than a machine (how does it work?) means a closer attention to the text under analysis: Badiou quotes the entire poem and his commentary follows the flow of the text, providing as it goes philosophical translations of the truths the text produces. On the one hand we are closer to traditional literary analysis, and Badiou believes in syntax as the guarantee of the meaning of the text (in his essay on Mallarmé's 'method', in *Conditions*, he claims that the 'guiding thread for clarification' of the poem is syntactic;[53] in *Calme bloc ici-bas*, he has one of the characters, a faintly ridiculous grammarian, exclaim: 'syntax is the only protection [*garde-fou*] when we are seized with poetic fury').[54] We have a mixture of fidelity and exploitation, which Badiou describes in the following terms: the poem thinks, but it does not know – it requires philosophy to reach the knowledge the poem provokes but does not master; on the other hand, of course, it is such thinking, and such thinking only, that produces truths. There is something of a paradox here, which will be developed in Chapter 4.

Deleuze's account, on the other hand, is further from the literal aspect of the text, which he never even quotes. And yet in an important sense, it is much closer to its workings, as he sees aspects of the text which the professional critic, Henry James, utterly ignores, so that the inevitable translation of the thought of the text into philosophical concepts actually remains closer to the text than Badiou's analysis does: with Deleuze, at least in the case we analysed, one does not get the impression the text is a mere pretext or illustration, even if it is presented as such. The life in question is not only the life that Riderhood bears, it is also the life of the text, which Deleuze's commentary respects and makes present to us. But perhaps the time has come to watch the reading practices of our two philosophers in much more detail.

Notes

1. A. Badiou, *The Century*, London: Polity, 2007 (2005).
2. Ibid., p. 178 (251).
3. Ibid., p. 107 (153–4).
4. On this, see S. Rinzler's book on the discourse of twentieth-century manifestos, *La Passion du discours* (forthcoming).
5. B. Saint-Girons, *L'Acte esthétique*, Paris: Klincksieck, 2007.
6. J. Rancière, 'Existe-t-il une esthétique deleuzienne?', in E. Alliez (ed.), *Gilles Deleuze, une vie philosophique*, Paris: Les Empêcheurs de penser en rond, 1998, pp. 525–36.
7. G. Deleuze, *Difference and Repetition*, London: Continuum, 2004 (1968), p. xx (4).
8. A. Badiou, *Conditions*, Paris: Seuil, 1992, p. 193.
9. G. Deleuze, *Negotiations*, New York: Columbia University Press, 1995, p. 6 (15).
10. Ibid.

11. M. Cressole, *Deleuze*, Paris: Editions Universitaires, 1973.
12. For a brief portrait of Michel Cressole, see F. Dosse, *Gilles Deleuze Félix Guattari*, Paris: La Découverte, 2007, pp. 260–1.
13. Deleuze, *Negotiations*, op. cit., pp. 8–9 (18).
14. Ibid., pp. 7–8 (18).
15. G. Deleuze, *Logic of Sense*, London: Athlone Press, 1990, ch. 34. See also J.-J. Lecercle, *Deleuze and Language*, Basingstoke: Palgrave, 2002, ch. 3.
16. Deleuze, *Negotiations*, op. cit., p. 11 (21).
17. D. Carlat, 'Portrait de l'écrivain selon Gilles Deleuze', in B. Gelas and H. Micolet (eds), *Deleuze et les écrivains*, Nantes: Cécile Defaut, 2007, p. 183.
18. G. Deleuze, *Proust and Signs*, London: Continuum, 2008, p. 108 (201).
19. A. Badiou, *Theoretical Writings*, London: Continuum, 2006, pp. xiv–xvii.
20. B. Bosteels, quoted in S. Žižek, 'From Purification to Subtraction', in P. Hallward (ed.), *Think Again*, London: Continuum, 2004, p. 173.
21. T. Conley, 'Folds and Folding', in C. Stivale (ed.), *Gilles Deleuze. Key Concepts*, Stocksfield: Acumen, 2005, p. 180.
22. See P. Macherey, *Marx 1845*, Paris: Amsterdam, 2008.
23. L. Althusser, 'Idéologie et appareils idéologiques d'Etat', in *Positions*, Paris: Editions Sociales, 1976, pp. 67–126.
24. The French for this is 'l'increvable désir'. The English translation, in A. Badiou, *On Beckett*, eds N. Power and A. Toscano, Manchester: Clinamen Press, 2003, has 'tireless desire': although more accurate, that translation does not do justice to the register of the phrase (it belongs to popular language) and to its energy or even violence.
25. A. Badiou, *Beckett*, Paris: Hachette, 1995, pp. 35–6; *On Beckett*, op. cit., pp. 53–4.
26. Badiou, *Beckett*, op. cit., pp. 19–20 and 22–3; *On Beckett*, op. cit., pp. 45–7.
27. On the series in Deleuze, see M. Buydens, *Sahara. L'esthétique de Gilles Deleuze*. Paris: Vrin, 1990, pp. 24–5.
28. G. Deleuze, 'How do we recognize structuralism?', in *Desert Islands and Other Texts*, New York: Semiotext(e), 2003, pp. (238–69).
29. G. Deleuze and F. Guattari, *A Thousand Plateaus*, London: Athlone Press, 1988, p. 135 (169).
30. A. Badiou, *Deleuze*, Minneapolis, MN: University of Minnesota Press, 2000, p. 2 (8).
31. L. Burchill, 'Translator's Preface', in Badiou, *Deleuze*, op. cit., p. xii.
32. J. Simont, 'Critique de la représentation et ontologie chez Deleuze et Badiou', in C. Ramond (ed.), *Alain Badiou. Penser le multiple*, Paris: L'Harmattan, 2002, pp. 457–76.

A Question of Style

33. Badiou, *Briefings on Existence*, op. cit., p. 110 (124).
34. Ibid., p. 70 (71).
35. A. Badiou, *Calme bloc ici-bas*, Paris: POL, 1997, pp. 11–12.
36. A. Badiou, *Being and Event*, trans. Oliver Feltham, London: Continuum, 2006, p. 23 (31).
37. I indulged in a close analysis of this incipit in J.-J. Lecercle, *Deleuze and Language*, Basingstoke: Palgrave, 2002, pp. 8–12.
38. G. Deleuze, *The Fold*, trans. Tom Conley, London: Continuum, 2001, p. 3 (5).
39. G. Deleuze, *Difference and Repetition*, trans. Paul Patton, London: Continuum, 1994, p. 36 (43).
40. P. Hallward, *Out of This World*, London: Verso, 2006.
41. A. Badiou, *Almagestes*, Paris: Seuil, 1964; *Portulans*, Paris: Seuil, 1967.
42. G. Deleuze, 'Philosophie de la série noire', in *L'Ile déserte et autres textes*, Paris: Minuit, 2002, pp. 114–19.
43. A. Sauvagnargues, *Deleuze et l'art*, Paris: PUF, 2005.
44. G. Deleuze, *Essays Critical and Clinical*, London: Verso, 1998 (1993).
45. D. Drouet, 'Index des références littéraires dans l'œuvre de Gilles Deleuze', in Gelas and Micolet, op. cit., pp. 547–81.
46. A. Badiou, *The Century*, London: Polity, 2007, p. 21 (39).
47. J. F. Louette, 'De la littérature en général, et de Beckett en particulier, selon Deleuze', in Gelas and Micolet, op. cit., pp. 73–84.
48. G. Deleuze and F. Guattari, *Kafka*, Paris: Minuit, 1975, pp. 28–31.
49. M.-O. Thirouin, 'Deleuze et Kafka: l'invention de la littérature mineure', in Gelas and Micolet, op. cit., pp. 293–305. See also, for a similar argument, S. Korngold, 'Kafka and the dialect of minor literature', in C. Prendergast (ed.), *Debating World Literature*, London: Verso, 2004, pp. 272–90.
50. G. Deleuze, 'Immanence: A Life', in *Two Regimes of Madness*, New York: Semiotext(e), 2007 (2001), p. 391 (361–2).
51. C. Dickens, *Our Mutual Friend*, London: Penguin, 1971 (1864–5), p. 503.
52. H. James, '*Our Mutual Friend*', in *Selected Literary Criticism*, London: Penguin, 1968, pp. 31–5.
53. A. Badiou, *Conditions*, London: Continuum, 2008, p. 49 (109).
54. Badiou, *Calme bloc ici-bas*, op. cit., pp. 389–90.

3

Deleuze Reads Proust

What's in a strong reading

The importance of Proust for Deleuze, throughout his work, cannot be overestimated. In the concordance of literary allusions in his works, the Proust entry is the longest, and allusions are present in practically all his books, from *Proust and Signs* to *Essays Critical and Clinical*.[1] To the end, Deleuze kept quoting the celebrated Proustian description of the writer writing as if his maternal language were a foreign tongue – for him, this was the best description of style as the stuttering of language.[2] What better entry, therefore, into the world of Deleuze as a reader of literary texts than a close study of his Proust book?

But we do not come to this reading of Deleuze reading Proust empty-handed. The preceding chapter has described both Badiou and Deleuze as strong readers and sought to construct a concept of *strong reading*. The time has come to summarise this process of construction by stating the determinations of the concept. I suggest there are six such determinations – the determinations of the *philosophical* concept of strong reading, or perhaps of the concept of the strong philosophical reading, for this is how philosophers read literature.

The first characteristic of a strong reading is that it goes against the grain of received *doxa*. Its aim is to force the reader into thinking. The insistence here is on the violence of the practice. This is not merely the rather trivial practice of reading the object of the strong reading anew, with different eyes, from another point of view, for that is true of any interpretation worthy of the name: this involves a form of violence done to the text as to the reader, and the practice has been called 'an active dismantling of the text'.[3] Thus we shall learn that Proust's novel is about neither memory nor the past, but about learning and the future.

The second characteristic inscribes this forcing of thought in the shape of the extraction of a problem. Traditionally, the definition of philosophy is centred on the capacity of the philosopher for *étonnement*, for being astonished at what common opinion takes for granted. Such *étonnement* is expressed by formulating a problem in the very site where solutions have long been accepted. Although the Deleuzian definition of a problem is somewhat more complex, it is faithful to this traditional intuition. Reading Proust's *Recherche*, therefore, will centre on the extraction of a problem which pervades the text but is not explicitly formulated, the problem of learning.

The third characteristic goes from the extraction of a problem to the construction of the concept that grasps it. The creation of concepts is notoriously the task ascribed to the philosopher by Deleuze. In *What Is Philosophy?* such construction goes through the drawing of a plane of consistency, the description of a conceptual character and the formulation of a number of determinations of the concept. That such a construction is central to Deleuze's reading of Proust is made apparent in the very title of the book, where the concept – the concept of sign – is named. That such a concept has to be constructed and cannot be merely borrowed ready-made from the philosopher's predecessors will appear in the fact that Deleuze's concept of sign in this book has nothing to do with what we usually mean by sign, namely Saussurian sign.

The fourth characteristic of a strong reading is its persistence. The right problem, and the correct concept that grasps it, do not vanish once they have been respectively extracted and constructed: they persist (witness the fact that this early book was added to on two occasions, at a time when Deleuze's philosophical position had shifted considerably, so that the book in its final version contains two different layers of thought, if not three); but they also insist, as the problematic of the sign is taken up again, twenty years after the first publication of the Proust book and considerably expanded in the *Cinema* books, where the semiotics of Peirce is exploited through the usual form of Deleuzian *bricolage* and where the Saussurian concept of sign, based on the dichotomy of signifier and signified, is the object of an explicit critique.

The fifth characteristic is that the consequence of such extraction, construction, persistence and insistence is an intervention rather than an interpretation. Here we encounter a slight difficulty, as the rejection of interpretation (the question, as we saw, is not 'what is the meaning of the text? but 'how does it work?') is a central tenet of Deleuze's later philosophy, but in *Proust and Signs*, signs are meant to be interpreted and we find a positive theory of interpretation. But apart from the deciduous character of such a theory, we already find in the book all the aspects of reading as an intervention, most explicitly of course in the second and later section, 'The Literary Machine'. The best test of the intervention that the reading enacts is its capacity to shock the critical tradition of readings of Proust, although I am afraid we are not in the same situation as with the reading of Kafka evoked in the last chapter, as Deleuze's reading of Proust seems to have acquired canonical status.

There is a sixth characteristic of a strong reading: its very strength is a provocation for readers, in other words it calls for a *counter-reading*. We saw that such was the effect Badiou's reading of Deleuze had on its readers. The remainder of the chapter will move from the reading of Deleuze's reading of Proust towards a form of counter-reading, where it will be suggested that Deleuze *reads for style*.

Enonçable et énoncé: *pre-linguistic matters*

To illustrate the notion of a counter-reading, I shall do a modicum of violence to Deleuze's text and start reading it anachronically, against the current, starting with a passage in *Cinéma 2*,[4] a text written twenty years after the first publication of the Proust book. The passage can be found in the first section of the second chapter, a chapter devoted to the relationship between the cine-image and language (the title of the chapter is: 'Recapitulation of images and signs'). The section is devoted to a strongly polemical attack against the moment of structuralism in film studies, incarnated in the early work of Christian Metz, who defended the idea that there was a language of film, that images were utterances, to be analysed in terms of double articulation, of paradigm and syntagm. This, of course, tends to treat a film as a narrative, with a story line analogous to a linguistic chain.

But Deleuze will have none of this. For him, narration is never a *datum*, it is an effect of the organic composition of movement-images, hence his strong statement: 'the cine-image is not an utterance.'[5] He develops this by quoting Pasolini, on whose theoretical texts he often relies: the cine-image partakes of an idiom of reality (*langue de la réalité*) which is not a language. In that idiom, rather than the two axes (paradigm and syntagm) that define the structure of language, together with the discrete units that are selected or combined in them, we find processes of differentiation and specification, continuous variations and intensities (a description strongly reminiscent of Deleuze's own account of language as a system of continuous variations and intensities, an account totally opposed to that of mainstream linguistics). So what we have with the cine-image is what he calls a *matière signalétique*, sign-matter or sign-material, with 'modulation features' that are sensory, kinesic, intensive, affective, rhythmic, tonal and even (why not?) verbal (that long list is, of course, a quotation). If we look at this list of the modulation features that make up the cine-image, we note (1) that linguistic features come last, as an afterthought; (2) that the general tonality of the list is organic – it concerns the affects of the body, not the abstract ideality of the linguistic system: the cine-image has more to do with what Deleuze, in his Bacon book, calls 'the logic of sensation' (this phrase is used as the subtitle of the book) than with a logic of representation – the cine-image is sensory and organic, it does not represent or narrate; (3) if another art form is evoked in the list, as a point of comparison with the visual art form of the cinema, it is music rather than poetry: those modulation features are rhythmic and tonal, not articulated; (4) the most important term in the list is 'intensive', and intensities are what the structure of language, which is concerned with positions and differential values, cannot capture; (5) lastly, we finally understand what Deleuze means by 'modulation': the world itself is a dynamic entity, in a state of constant and continuous variation – the cine-image captures such variations directly without having to go through the screen of language and representation. Hence the apparent paradox of Deleuze's conception of the cinema: the cine-image, apparently a kind of photograph endowed with movement, is not a representation, and the cinema is not a representational art, and only contingently a narrative art. Exit Hollywood, pursued by a Deleuzian bear.

Deleuze has recourse to another authority on film theory, and Pasolini is supplemented by Eisenstein (this is not surprising if we remember the impact Eisenstein's texts, which were widely available in paperback, had on the French *intelligentsia* in the late 1960s and early 1970s). Thus Pasolini's 'idiom of reality', that which the cine-image spells out, works on materials which Deleuze describes in the terms of Eisenstein's theory of 'interior monologue'. For Eisenstein, the cinema, not the novel, is the site where we get a glimpse of an externalisation of our inner speech, the old *logos endiathetos*, the nature of which preoccupied the Greek and medieval philosophers, from Aristotle onwards.[6] Except that, for Eisenstein, and for Deleuze after him, *logos endiathetos* is not a form of mentalese or language of thought (the prevalent solution to the problem of inner speech in the philosophical tradition), nor is it internalised natural language (the minority solution), but an accretion of non-linguistic matter or material: a *masse plastique*, a shapeless but informable and deformable mass of a-signifying and a-syntactic material, not yet linguistically formed (although already formed semiotically, aesthetically and pragmatically). In other words, Eisenstein's interior monologue, as practised in the cinema, is a mass of material that emits signs (but not *linguistic* signs: we remember the Peircean efflorescence and multiplication of types of signs that is at the heart of *Cinema 1*: in the first chapter of *Cinema 2*, five more types have already been introduced). Those multiple and various signs produce aesthetic affects and induce action (hence the idea that the material is already 'semiotically, aesthetically and pragmatically' formed). The general lesson of this (a recurrent theme in Deleuze's work) is that *there is more to signs than merely linguistic or Saussurian signs*: Saussurian semiology, or the semiotics of languages, is not the model or base of all semiotics, nor is it the climax of their progression; it is only one among many, and does not enjoy any privileged position. More on this anon.

Deleuze sums up his analysis of what cine-images are made of by stating that their a-linguistic matter is a *pre*-linguistic matter: *pas une énonciation, pas des énoncés, un énonçable* ('It is not an enunciation, and these are not utterances. It is an *utterable*').[7] Such matters are liable to be uttered in a process of enunciation, they may give rise to utterances. It is only when language appropriates them, when narrative, for instance, is introduced, that utterances come to replace images and non-linguistic or pre-linguistic signs. The relationship between Saussurian semiology and more general semiotics is not only diluted but inverted: semiology is merely a secondary or belated form of semiotics. 'The language system, Deleuze claims, only exists in its reaction to a non-language material that it transforms'.[8] Hence the deliberate ambiguity of the title of this section: there are 'pre-linguistic matters', a rich source of all types of signs, and the material which the cine-image is made of; and such 'pre-linguistic matters' actually matter – the 'utterable' is not yet an utterance, and it does not necessarily have to become one. A whole theory of signs, and a strong reading of Proust, derive from this.

A problem

There is, however, a problem. Deleuze's formulation, which the title of the last section quotes, is bizarre. Far from offering a *solution* to the question of the relationship between cine-image and language, as he claims (an anti-structuralist solution, one that contradicts Metz), he makes such a relationship highly problematic because of the terms he selects to formulate it. If the matter, or material, that cine-images are made of is *pre-linguistic*, this means that it is waiting for language to shape or inform it. If such material is called 'utterable' (*énonçable*), such utterability sounds like Aristotelian *potentia* expecting to be actualised in utterances, in a process of enunciation. Even if it is claimed to be a-signifying, a-syntaxic and generally a-linguistic, the material is still, at least virtually, determined by language. There appears to be no independent way of talking about images (even if in his Bacon book Deleuze attempts to construct a series of concepts to do just that). So language in Deleuze is a *problem*. Let us spell it out.

Were Deleuze a Hegelian philosopher (which he emphatically is not), there would be a natural progression hailed as progress. From mute and inglorious pre-linguistic matters he would proceed to their appropriation by language and their metamorphosis into glorious utterances. We would thus move from etymological infancy to fluency. But it is a short way from fluency to empty garrulousness, and Deleuze, not being a Hegelian, rejects this narrative as too pat. His object is not to make language the apex or climax of an inevitable progression, but to put it in its place, a humble and dependent one. His object is to treat language as a sequel or epiphenomenon to images.

This, however, is not an easy task. (The paradox of the language hater who can only vent his hostility to language and distrust of eloquence through the eloquence of his words immediately crops up.) Hence the semantic tension that is felt in the word *énonçable*: a movement towards actualisation in *énoncé* or *énonciation*, and its immediate freezing or even retreat. Except that Deleuze, who is not a Hegelian, is hardly an Aristotelian philosopher either: he follows Bergson in ascribing a central place to *virtuality*. This *énonçable* is not merely possible: it is virtual, which makes it as real as an actual *énoncé*. We have indeed moved into a realm other than the realm of language: the realm of the virtual.

This move has drastic consequences for a philosophy of language always in part inherited from structuralism. The inversion of the customary relationship between semiology and semiotics is merely the symptom of a sea change. What we have is in fact a *dissolution* of the Saussurian sign on which the science of linguistics was founded:

both a *dilution*, as semiotics multiply because types of signs proliferate, and a *destruction*, as double articulation, the arbitrary character of the sign and the principle of immanence (which states that the science of language is constructed out of linguistic phenomena alone, carefully separated from the rest of reality) go by the board. Thus is the tyranny or imperialism of the signifier (a central theme in *A Thousand Plateaus*) finally overcome. Thus also is another philosophy of language, duly called pragmatics, born, one which at a fell swoop discards both Chomsky and Saussure and the heavy metaphysical weight their conceptions of language involve. (This is particularly obvious in the case of Chomsky, with his innate ideas and physical reductionism –in an important sense, Deleuze's new philosophy of language is anti-Chomskyan.) Lastly, thus is the logic of representation, the dominant image of thought in modern Western philosophy, also overcome. And this is no mean feat.

As an example of this achievement, I shall briefly consider what Deleuze and Guattari call 'non-signifying semiotics'. At first sight, the phrase appears to be an oxymoron: semiotics is the science of signs, and it is of the essence of signs that they should signify. But here is the definition I borrow from the Glossary, written by Guattari as an appendix to the English edition of his book *Molecular Revolution*:

> We distinguish signifying semiologies – those which articulate signifying chains and signifying contents – from non-signifying semiotics, which work from syntagmatic chains which do not produce effects of meaning and which are capable of entering into direct contact with their referents. Examples of non-signifying semiotics would be musical notation, the mathematical corpus, information or robotic syntaxes, etc.[9]

The central phrase of this definition is probably 'capable of entering into direct contact with their referents'. By this phrase, Guattari is leaving the position of structuralism, which rejects designation (or the relation between word and thing) and devalues denotation (or the relation between signified and referent), in favour of signification (or the relation between signifier and signified). The definition operates a return to designation, a relation of ontological mixture where words cohabit with things and utterances intervene in the midst of the world, *à même les choses*. In the moment of structuralism we have two series, of signifier and signified, separated but parallel, and sparks of meaning emitted at their infrequent conjunction by quilting points (*points de capiton*): this is the structure described in Deleuze's most structuralist text *How Do We Recognize Structuralism?* and put to work in *The Logic of Sense,* where it yields a theory of sense in contrast with meaning, that is with good sense and common sense. After the moment of structuralism, that is from *Anti-Oedipus* onwards, syntagmatic chains are not only in direct contact with their referents, but they interact with them, 'in diagrammatic interaction', as the French version of the Glossary says (so we have not only a mixture of bodies but a form of abstraction). The passage from one moment to the other, from one position to the other involves a denial of the ideality of meaning and an affirmation of the materiality of language. (Deleuze has always strongly admired the pan-somatism of the Stoics and is fond of quoting the pseudo-paradox, or sophism, attributed to Chrysippus, which goes: 'If you speak of a chariot, a chariot goes through your mouth' – not so much a blatant piece of sophistry as an evocation of the Stoic theory of causation, according to which physical bodies are causes of incorporeal effects.) And if we want to find an example illustrating that otherwise obscure statement, words are in direct contact and interaction with their referents, we only have to think of the semiotics of faces: faces signify (they emit signs of affect, etc.) but not through discrete units and double articulation. We are simply moving back from a digital to an analogic concept of sign: hence the development of a semiotics of 'facialities' (*visagéités* – as horrible a word in French as it is in English), to be found in the work of Guattari and in *A Thousand Plateaus.*

Let us take our bearings and consider our progress so far. It is a paradoxical, if not chaotic, sort of progress. We understand that language has been demoted from the central position it enjoyed in the moment of structuralism. (*The Logic of Sense,* the most structuralist of Deleuze's books, is where he comes nearest to offering a fully-fledged theory of language.) But the concept of sign escapes this general demotion: the Saussurian sign, that is the linguistic sign, is dissolved, but other signs increase and multiply. There are as many signs, and more, as there are regimes of signs, or semiotics. Yet the whole process of demotion and dilution is affected by ambiguity. The semantic tension in the term *énonçable* is not a chance occurrence. It is also present in *A Thousand Plateaus,* where those non-signifying semiotics are evoked. They belong to various types, which Deleuze and Guattari call 'pre-signifying', 'signifying', 'counter-signifying' and 'post-signifying'. The compulsive recourse to prefixes cannot but appear as an instance of Freudian denial: the centrality of language returns, like Banquo's ghost, in the inevitability of the term 'signifying', at the very moment when it is denied. It appears, therefore, that for Deleuze language is, paradoxically, something to be firmly put in its place and a constant source of fascination. This dialectics of repulsion and desire works through Deleuze's *oeuvre* and explains why at the same time he aims to subvert mainstream linguistics (*la linguistique a fait beaucoup de mal*, 'linguistics has done a lot of harm', he exclaims in *L'Abécédaire*) and he constructs, book after book, more than a sketch of a new philosophy of language. Language is indeed a *problem* for Deleuze: it is denounced, yet the question of the sign remains central.

The position Deleuze adopts towards the question of the sign can be summarised in the following diagram:

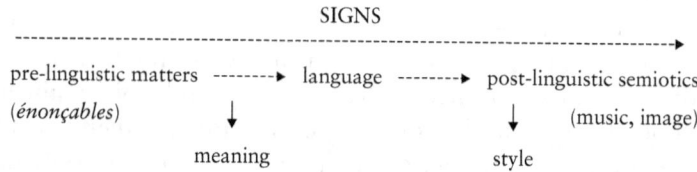

My contention is that this diagram is at work in Deleuze's reading of Proust's *Recherche* and that it will enable us to understand why and how, when Deleuze reads a literary text, he reads for style.

Signs and Proust

A brief word about *Proust and Signs*:[10] a very early book, his fourth (1964), but one he never quite abandoned, as its history shows. A second part, 'The literary machine', was added for the second edition in 1970, and a conclusion, 'Presence and function of madness: the spider', for the third edition in 1977. The fact that he added new material to the book, without rewriting it, is significant. The first part, written before he met Guattari, that is before he became interested in linguistics, belongs to a different problematic from the second, written shortly after *Anti-Oedipus* and bearing marks of this (the very title, 'The Literary Machine', seems to belong to the world of *Capitalism and Schizophrenia*). In spite of this complete change of problematic, there is a common thread that gives the book its unity: the centrality of the concept of sign and its relation to style.

The book starts, in typical Deleuzian fashion, with the violent extraction of a problem which carefully avoids traditional or commonsensical interpretations and provokes a shock in the reader. (It is not, therefore, exactly an interpretation: the description just given also applies to the cine-image and its affects in *Cinema 2*.) The object of the extraction and of the shock is the identification of a problem and the beginning of the construction of its concept. Now, a trivial reading of *In Search of Lost Time* (*La Recherche*) will, unavoidably so, tell us that the novel is about memory. Not so, of course, Deleuze. Here are the first lines of the book:

> What constitutes the unity of *In Search of Lost Time*? We know, at least, what it does not. It is not recollection, memory, even involuntary memory. What is essential to the Search is not the madeleine or the cobblestones.[11]

We may, I think, admire the bluntness of that incipit. In one brisk sentence or two, Deleuze dismisses the commonsensical view of *La Recherche* we have inherited from the critical *doxa*. Having thus duly shocked us, jogged us into thinking anew, he can formulate his problem, which he does on the second page:

> But however important its role, memory intervenes only as the means of an apprenticeship that transcends recollection both by its goals and by its principles. The Search is oriented to the future, not the past.
> Learning is essentially learning *signs*. Signs are the object of a temporal apprenticeship, not of an abstract knowledge.[12]

So it appears that Deleuze's reading, an intervention rather than an interpretation, consists of a shift of focus: we move from memory to apprenticeship, that is to learning (as the real object of *La Recherche*) and from learning to signs (as the objects of the process of learning). 'Learning' is in fact here a better translation of the French word *apprentissage* than the literal 'apprenticeship', as the French word evokes not only the figure of one who is apprenticed to an artisan, but also the concepts of *Bildungsroman* (or *roman d'apprentissage* in French). This shift in focus entails consequences about the conception of time: learning takes time, and it is not exclusively concerned with the past, far from it – the focus shifts from the past to the present and the future. *La Recherche* is not only about time vanished or lost, but also about time wasted (another meaning of the French phrase, *le temps perdu*). So, by stating that *La Recherche* does not so much look towards the past as towards the future, Deleuze practises his usual game of reading the text against the grain. The problem *La Recherche* evokes is not the problem of the passing of time, but of the time necessary for learning. And the concept that corresponds to this problem, that names it, is not memory but sign.

This of course implies the construction of a concept of sign. The beginnings will not be all that different from Saussure's construction: a sign is the sign of something. Apparently, we are still in the realm of representation. And what are the signs in Proust signs of? Deleuze eventually answers this question, but only after a while, as for him it is a secondary question. The essential question is different. What defines signs in Proust is not their referents, but the site of their emission: not what they are signs of, but who or what emits them, and in which context. The important thing about a Proustian sign is not what it denotes, but what it evokes.

Even as in Badiou's system there are events and truths in four fields (the fields of politics, of love, of science and of art), in Deleuze's Proust there are signs in four worlds: the world of *mondanité*, of worldliness, of aristocratic snobbery; the world of love, of falling in love and the pangs of jealousy; the world of sensible qualities, of perceptions and their affects, evoked for instance by a *madeleine* or a paving stone in Venice; and the world of art, Vinteuil's 'little phrase', *le petit pan de mur jaune* in a picture by Vermeer, and, *en abyme*, the novel itself.[13] We may note, incidentally, the proximity between this quadripartition and Badiou's four types of events, with the revolutions they foster.

In Deleuze's Proust, the encounter with the sign occurs in a context from which signs derive their significance and where learning is practised, as the aim of learning is the capacity to interpret signs. In this early book, which is totally indifferent to psychoanalysis and to Deleuze's emphatic rejection of it, he is not shy of talking in terms of interpretation. So our conceptual drift can be captured in the following diagram:

memory (less important than) → learning (about) → signs (in need of) → interpretation

Memory is less important than the process of learning, learning is about signs, and signs are constitutively in need of interpretation.

So interpretation is not only a possibility, but a necessity. In Deleuze's Proust, the world in which we live is full of mystery, a site for encounters, where the subject becomes who she is by learning her way through a maze of signs, which are not merely to be taken for wonders but must be interpreted. *La Recherche* is not content with exploring one human faculty, memory: it explores the essential activity of all human faculties, how the human being becomes a subject by learning signs, by constructing herself in the four regions that form the human world (or at least the world of Proust). So the *Recherche* is not only a search but a quest, but not simply a quest for self: it is the noblest of quests, a quest for truth. Here is Deleuze:

> The worlds are unified by their formation of sign systems emitted by persons, objects, substances; we discover no truth, we learn nothing, except by deciphering and interpreting.[14]

The interest of this is that it sets up another chain of concepts, which can be represented in a diagram:

signs → encounter → deciphering → truth

The encounter with signs jogs us into thinking, engages a process of deciphering, that is a process of thought (deciphering signs is what thought is about, it is the highest exertion of human intelligence) and the deciphering quest enables the subject to construct a truth. For Proust's position towards truth (or rather Deleuze's Proust) is neither relativist (there is no truth, only a multiplication of interpretations) nor naturalistic (there is something out there, namely objective truth). Truth has to be invented in both senses of the term: it has to be creatively imagined, and it has to be found where it always was, as an archaeological site is invented. This is why Deleuze calls every apprentice, every decipherer of signs, an Egyptologist.

So we have four worlds of signs, and consequently four types of signs, with specific characteristics. The *first world*, the world of *mondanité*, is a natural world of signs. For what is worldliness, if not an exchange, an emission and reception, of signs? But those signs are neither discrete nor articulated. Their characteristics are vastly different. For they are (1) *caught up in rituals* (the rituals of *etiquette*, of snobbery); (2) *ontologically heterogeneous* (signs of worldliness are indifferently elements of dress, gestures, utterances, even external implements: there are all sorts of ways of making what is known as a 'statement' of fashion); (3) *local* (they depend on a small group, a *milieu* or a *coterie*, outside of which they are meaningless: so that the same objects or features may be entirely different signs in different *milieus*); (4) *unstable* (in that they are subject to the accelerated time of fashion – one day they are in, the next they are passé); (5) (this is their main characteristic) they are *not* representations. A sign of worldliness does not represent its referent in its absence, it does not refer, it directly expresses. Why does it not refer? Because, Deleuze says, such signs are vacuous and stupid – signs of fatuousness, not of emotional depth or intellectual content. In the terms of Barthes, such signs have no denotation but only connotation: they directly connote, without denoting, a situation that Hjelmslev's semiotics (which Deleuze mentions in *A Thousand Plateaus*) cannot contemplate.

The *second world* of signs is the world of love. In the universe of Proust's novel, the loved one 'implicates' a world that must be 'explicated', that is deciphered by the lover. To love is to interpret the world folded in one's beloved. Hence another set of characteristics, again vastly different from those of the linguistic sign. Signs of love are: (1) *elusive* (how can I be sure that my interpretation is correct, that she reciprocates my love?); (2) *mysterious* (an aura of mystery surrounds the loved one: the very elusiveness of the signs she emits creates an atmosphere of anxiety bordering on awe: I am fully engaged in the process of loving, that is of deciphering, and I am under the impression, or illusion, that my life is at stake); (3) (this is the main characteristic) they are *mendacious*. For I, the lover, can never reach the truth: there is every possibility that the beloved is lying to me, for it is easier to lie than to utter the blunt truth; and there is every possibility that I am lying to myself, indulging in wishful thinking. As you can see, Deleuze's Proust is a pessimist: love is not described in terms of the communion of souls and the fusion of two bodies into one but in terms of solipsism and agonistic encounter. Take the first moments of falling in love, moments of maximal uncertainty (she loves me, she loves me not, or the petty bourgeois version: if the light goes green before I reach the kerb, he will leave his wife for me). The difference with Badiou's treatment of love, centred on the *coup de foudre* and its consequences, is obvious: in Deleuze's Proust, the main affect of love is not a passionate yearning for the other, but jealousy. The 'first law of love' in Proust is that jealousy is stronger than love. When signs have been explicated they prove to be mendacious, so that the lover, far from being welcomed into the fold, is excluded. So the signs of love, like the signs of worldliness, are not Saussurian signs, not representational signs, because they are pragmatic: each sign is a call for the calculus of implicit meaning, what Grice calls implicatures (she says this, but she cannot mean it literally, so she must mean that).[15] And this call for the calculus of meaning is a call for action: there is no interpretation without an intervention. The sign itself is not content with marking a situation: it intervenes in it.

The *third world* of signs concerns the signs of sensible qualities (the impression created by the *madeleine*, etc.). We are closer to the philosophical tradition. It has always been the case that the passage from sense impressions to perceptions involves construction, that is a synthesis of sense impressions (there are various versions of this, from Kant to phenomenology), and it also involves interpretation. And there is a moment of decision, the moment of recognition, when I decide that the mark on the wall is a snail, not a nail, as in Virginia Woolf's story, 'The mark on the wall',[16] or that what I see is a light effect rather than the ghost of my grandfather. This world, of course, is not merely the third world of signs, it is everywhere around us, it is *our* world, the *whole* of our world, so that Marcel moves in a world of signs, a receptacle for potential epiphanies.

Those signs also have characteristics that are not Saussurian. (1) They are *assertive*: they undoubtedly are, they are not projections, like the signs of love, not figments of our imagination. (2) They are *truthful*: they are not mendacious, like the signs of love, since perception, to speak like Wittgenstein, is a language-game where a notion of truth is necessary: the signs of sensible qualities must be carefully distinguished from dream and hallucination. (3) They are *material*, since they begin with the impression, a word to be taken literally, that they make on our senses. This materiality, however, is a limitation: as we shall soon see, a sign is nothing if it does not embody an immaterial essence. Hence the ambivalence of those signs: they are everywhere, they constitute our lived world, but they are disappointing. Although he is moving away from the logic of representation, Deleuze, at this stage, has not yet reached the logic of sensation that he constructs in the Bacon book. And is he not perhaps, in expressing disappointment in sensible signs and yearning for essence, abandoning the professed empiricism of his first book, the book on Hume?[17] The answer to this is that he is describing the world of Proust, whose instinctive Platonism will have to be overcome.

The *fourth world* is the world of the signs of art, with their specific list of characteristics. (1) They are *dematerialised*. This is an old preoccupation of aesthetic theory, one which Anglo-Saxon aesthetics has thoroughly explored: the sonata is distinguished from its various materialisations, either in its interpretation or in the manuscripts that transcribe it. (2) They are *all-embracing*: they have the capacity to launder, if you pardon me the bathetic metaphor, all other types of signs, to metamorphose them into signs of art. *La Recherche*, where the other types of signs are staged, turns them, *en abyme*, into signs of art: thus with the baron de Charlus, that paragon of worldliness, thus with Swann in love, thus with the cobblestones of Venice. (3)

They are *climactic*: the sequence of the four worlds of signs involves a progression, as all signs converge towards the signs of art, which incarnate the perfection of signs. This is due to the fact that (4) they are *essential*, that they express essences, and this is their essential characteristic, what all signs strive for.

From such an array of diverse characteristics, we may nevertheless derive a general theory of signs: this is what Deleuze duly does. In the world of Saussure, signs are dual. So they are, too, in the world of Deleuze's Proust, but the duality is situated elsewhere. A sign *designates* an object (remember that designation involves direct contact with the object: the sign is an object, the object is directly a sign – we live in a world of sensible qualities), but it also *signifies* something else (what I have called a connotation: this is why the best signs, the signs of art, are immaterial – they do not let themselves be enmeshed in the carnality of designation, but go straight for essences). We can therefore formulate the conception of the sign in Deleuze's Proust in the following diagram, which takes the usual Deleuzian form of a correlation:

1	2	3	4	5	6	7	8
Designation	Object	Pleasure	Recognition	Intelligence	Conversation	Friendship	Philosophy
Signification	Subject	Truth	Cognition (encounter)	Thought	Interpretation	Love	Art

This correlation occurs in a chapter entitled 'Apprenticeship': it describes the effect of signs, what they achieve. At one level, signs, or certain types of signs, involve friendly conversation, appealing to the human faculty of intelligence, which the Greeks called philosophy (a similar account of philosophy is to be found in *What Is Philosophy?*). On the other hand, they also, when they are true signs, the signs of art, engage thought, the passion of love and a process of interpretation or deciphering. And we note that truth is on the bottom line of the correlation, which seems to make recognition, or *doxa*, the realm of philosophy – an unkind thought, but one that is typical of the artist that Proust is. For, of course, there is a hierarchy in the correlation (the bottom line is more valuable than the top line), or at least a dynamism, whereby the top part of the correlation is always striving towards the bottom, where it finds its achievement. This might be a description of the very process of learning, of the passage from the objectivism that characterises the top row of the correlation (pleasure, not truth, recognition, not cognition, intelligence, not thought: this may make for a type of philosophy of a slightly dubious kind; this certainly makes for bad literature). The central point of the contrast is that, for Deleuze's Proust, philosophy is based on communication (conversation as the exchange of information) and art is based on interpretation.

But perhaps the most important column in the correlation is column 2, which contrasts subject and object. It is this contrast that constitutes the sign even as, conversely, the sign institutes the opposition between subject and object. In a world of signs, the object emits a sign, and the subject is subjectified in the process of recognising the sign as sign of the object and of interpreting it. So that the sign is deeper than the object to which it is still attached (it is a sign of the object) and than the subject that interprets it. The diagram below encapsulates this state of affairs:

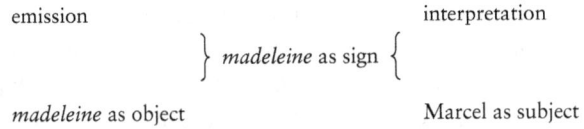

The *madeleine*, qua sign, is a triple or three-tiered entity. It is a bundle of sensible qualities, still attached to the object by their materiality; it is the site of an encounter, of an epiphany, a sign that must be interpreted, for signs must indeed be taken for wonders: it is, at this stage, already immaterial, but still attached to the subject that interprets it and which it makes a subject; and it is the expression of an immaterial essence, a sign of art, not *a madeleine*, but *the madeleine*, Proust's madeleine.

This account of the sign has, for anyone who has read the rest of Deleuze's work, two puzzling consequences. The first has already been evoked: in *Proust and Signs*, interpretation plays a central role. A sign is in need of interpretation, a sign inhabits an object in that the object needs a subject to interpret the sign it virtually emits. The interesting point, however, is that Deleuze describes interpretation as a subjectifying, but not a subjective process: it is always a 'we', never an 'I', even Marcel, that interprets. Or, rather, there is a pure impersonal interpreting that selects both object and subject. This is not quite the interpretation as representation that Deleuze will strongly reject later.

The second consequence is the centrality of essence. For our last diagram must be improved, and give way to this diagram:

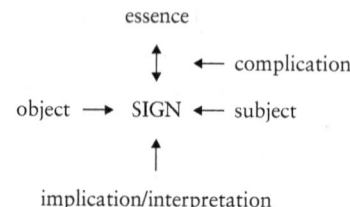

Meaning is implicated in the sign: the sign is a kind of monad, in the folds of which an entire world is contained. Interpretation etymologically explicates those folds. But the function of the essence is even more important: it holds the whole structure together by complicating both the object and the subject within the sign. The sign is folded, but the active enfolding is the work of the essence. In this description we recognise two constant themes in Deleuze's philosophy: the theme of expression, which he explores in his first book on Spinoza; and the theme of the fold, at the heart of his book on Leibniz. But we also recognise a problem: for the essence, as active enfolder, is placed in a position of transcendence, a fact duly noted in the diagram. And our philosopher is notorious for being a philosopher of immanence. So was *Proust and Signs* a Platonist book, which means that he changed his position afterwards, or can there be such a thing as an immanent essence? I shall plump for the second solution, but this involves a reconsideration of the signs of art.

What allows signs of art to express essences is that they are immaterial. This does not mean that they have no material existence (*le petit pan de mur jaune* – the patch of yellow wall – in the Vermeer painting is a coloured fragment of canvas), but that such existence envelops an immaterial entity (what identifies that patch of yellow wall as a specific fragment, not as an indistinct region of a larger canvas, or again, the musical note as opposed to the sound it makes and we hear). This is where we have a potential difference between Deleuze's Proust and Deleuze *tout court*. Proust's spontaneous philosophy (a philosophy unable to reach truth and consequently inferior to art) is Platonism whereas Deleuze has always opted, most explicitly in *The Logic of Sense*, for the Stoics against Plato. The problem of essences, therefore, is how to divest Proust of his instinctive Platonism. This operation takes the form of the construction by Deleuze of a concept of essence that is not transcendent, that is not a Platonist idea, but that is defined as *absolute difference*. Deleuze's solution is to treat the essence, and not only the sign, as a monad. More specifically, he insists on one characteristic of Leibniz's monad: that it is a unique point of view on the world. Each essence enfolds an entire world, complicates objects and subjects. This is what in literature we call an original voice, or more generally what in art we describe under the name of style. Thus the Proustian sentence or Cézanne's brush stroke encapsulates a point of view on the world, a unique way of viewing the world. So the essence is concerned with style, but not with a subject (the author or the artist): it is a point of view that complicates subject and object in a sign, or a work, of art. The central dimension in my last diagram is the vertical axis, the axis that goes from sign to essence.

Although we are no longer in Platonist transcendence (the essence is not a form, it is immanent in the sign it complicates – the sign is no longer a copy, the essence is not a model), there is more than residual idealism in Leibniz's doctrine of monads. This is discarded in the second part of *Proust and Signs*, where the essence is described in terms of materiality and machines: the title of this section, we remember, is 'The Literary Machine'. This occurs through the production of a new correlation, contrasting the image of thought of Greek philosophy, called *logos* for short (the character that incarnates it is of course Plato), and the *antilogos* of Proust's art. Here is the correlation:

1	2	3	4	5	6
Observation	Philosophy	Reflection	Explicit meaning	Conversation	Word
Sensibility	Thought	Translation	Implicit (implicated) signs	Silent interpretation	Name

The proximity of this correlation to the correlation formulated earlier is clear. But the differences are equally obvious. This is an anti-philosophical correlation where philosophy is demoted to the status of *doxa* and opposed to thought, where philosophical conversation (Deleuze, as we know, hated dialogue, including academic conferences, all through his life) induces the garrulous communication of explicit meaning, not the silent interpretation of the signification implicated in the signs of art. We are moving away from a logic of representation characterised by observation and reflection (an apt word), into something closer to an etymologically aesthetic logic of sensation (where the subject is in the world, acting and acted upon) where signs are sites for intervention, here called translation. So it is art, not philosophy, that thinks. It is art, not philosophy, that instead of being content with mere words, is capable of the highest operation, the operation of naming that calls into being and does not merely represent the given (a whole poetics is implied here). This new world, which the bottom line of the correlation defines, is the world of *antilogos*, the world of signs.

The two lines of the correlation can be contrasted as describing two different forms of language: the language of *logos*, of conversation, is opposed to the language of signs, of translation and interpretation. In the terms of our first diagram (p. 76), the first type of language is the one that yields meaning, the second is characterised by style. For this is the main characteristic of style: *it is of the essence*. It is essential to the theory of art implicit in Deleuze's Proust, and it belongs not to the individual author, but to the essence.

So the essence links the subject and the object, as in our last diagram, by imposing the monadic point of view of style. This is the first answer, still tainted with idealism, to the question of the essence. The second answer, where the essence becomes thoroughly immanent, is materialist: the point of view of the essence is embodied in *the treatment of the materials of art*, of sounds, images and words. Style is the acting out of the essence, the incarnation of an incorporeal quality. This paradox of the incarnation of the immaterial occurs, Deleuze claims, in the process of *metaphor* – a surprising choice again, as Deleuze is widely known as the philosopher who hates metaphors, who is fond of quoting Kafka's pronouncement, 'Metaphors are one of the things that make me despair of literature'. But here metaphor is the expression of the essence, of the incorporeal quality that achieves a link between different objects. When Deleuze claims that in Proust 'style is essentially metaphor', he means that style acts out, or captures, the essence by establishing a creative or imaginative equivalence between two objects. But there is a materialist twist to this: metaphor does not represent an ideal link between two objects, it materially makes them touch and coalesce. In other words, if style is 'essentially' metaphor, metaphor is 'essentially' *metamorphosis*. Two objects united by metaphor exchange their determinations, even their names. Thus (remember we are dealing with essences, with the world of art), Picasso's handlebar and saddle become the head of a bull, and the cine-metaphor fuses the two objects it convokes, even as

Daphne becomes a laurel in countless Italian paintings and sculptures of the Renaissance. We understand why we must take style not as a representational operation but as a form of intervention. And the Stoic theory of causality later expounded in *A Logic of Sense* enables us to understand how an immaterial and incorporeal essence can be an immanent effect of material causes. This is how style creates a world: a world of essences incarnated in the material metamorphoses of the object, in the capture of the interpreting subject's gaze. We have, therefore, a new chain of concepts:

Signs	Signs of art	Materials	Style	Metaphor	Metamorphosis	Essence
	(climax)	(immanence)	(work on materials)	(brings together objects)	(intervention)	(point of view)

Essence is the immanent point of view in the world created by style.

Lastly, we understand Deleuze's strangest pronouncement about style (one which he repeats at the very end of his *oeuvre*, in *Essays Critical and Clinical*): that style is equivalent to non-style. How can he say this of Proust, how can Proust's highly characteristic style be equated with an absence of style? The answer is that the concept of style is the site of a paradox: it is both highly individual (recognisable, likely to be imitated and parodied, etc.) *and* entirely non-subjective. Style is pure capture of the essence, which distributes both subject and object. Style is never 'the man' (*le style, c'est l'homme*), always of the essence. There is non-subjective style in the same way as there is non-subjective interpretation.

An illustration of the concept of style: Boldini's portrait

Because this is all too abstract, here is an illustration. In 1897, the Italian painter Boldini painted a portrait of Count Robert de Montesquiou, the model of the Proustian aristocratic aesthete (Monsieur de Norpois, etc.). The count, complete with handlebar moustache, goatee and loosely tied cravat, cuts a dashing figure, a worthy representative of the world of *mondanité*, the world of the vacuous signs of fashion. He looks with an interest mingled with reverence at an elaborately adorned cane which he holds in his right hand, no doubt the cane that he flaunts as he struts in the park.

That the portrait is rich in signs, that it gives forth all sorts of signs, is obvious. And it is equally obvious that the world of those signs is the world of worldliness. For the painting is indeed pervaded with vacuous signs: everything in it signifies, but only its own vacuity. The sitter's posture, his dress, his haircut, his cane – each of these is a statement of fashion. And all these signs have the specific characteristics of signs of worldliness. They are neither discrete nor articulated (they connote more than they denote, or rather they do denote, but their denotation is irrelevant: any other object might have replaced the cane, provided it was a pretext for a fashionable statement). They are caught up in ritual (the ritual of daily dressing; the ritual of partying in Faubourg St Honoré). They are ontologically heterogeneous (the cane is inextricably mixed up with the hand that holds it and the exaggerated gesture it expresses). They are local (such a portrait today makes us smile: it is dated and outdated; *our* statements of fashion take other forms, and our appreciation of the portrait is purely nostalgic). And they are, consequently, unstable: the posture and look of the sitter expresses a structure of feeling which is alien to us and has only survived thanks to Proust.

Can we go further in the analysis of signs? We must. So far, I have conformed to the logic of representation and talked of the person of the sitter and his statements, forgetting the rather conspicuous fact that this is a portrait, that those signs of worldliness are also signs of art. (We remember that one of the characteristics of signs of art is that they are all-embracing: they include signs of worldliness, and can be constructed out of them.) So we do find the other characteristics of signs of art in the portrait. The fact that we are looking at a reproduction makes the first characteristic (that signs of art are immaterial) trivially true: the portrait has material existence, it is unique and monumental, and can be seen in the Musée d'Orsay in Paris: but it is also a type, reproduced in endless tokens. The second characteristic of signs of art is their climactic nature: they are the best signs, or signs par excellence. And indeed our sitter, the Comte de Montesquiou, who thought very highly of himself as a writer, is today completely forgotten, and only remembered through the signs of art in whose excellence he survives, Boldini's portrait and a few pages in *La Recherche*: only through the signs of art has he acquired a modicum of eternity. The last, and main, characteristic is that signs of art express essences. But the painting is remarkable not so much for the fashionable statement made by the sitter as for the aesthetic statement made by the painter. Thus we notice a certain irony in the exaggerated pose of the sitter, captured in a careful and deliberate composition; thus, when we see the actual painting, we are struck by the treatment of the materials: the top of the cane, for instance, provides a dash of vivid blue in a portrait otherwise dominated by black, grey and brown tones; and the creamy white of the gloves – which Montesquiou had specially made for the sitting – is a way of making them appear *plus vrais que nature* (in this proverbial phrase, 'truer than nature', the French language pays homage to the power of the false, which is central to Deleuze's aesthetic). And the portrait obviously belongs to a long and glorious tradition (we could compare it to Lotto's *Portrait of a Young Man Reading a Book*, which is in Venice). So, in the portrait, there is every sign of the presence of style. That cane, of which Montesquiou was so inordinately proud because it had belonged to Louis XV, is typical of this: it fixes the beholder's gaze; it acts, in its dash of vivid colour, as a deliberate *punctum*. It is a sign of worldliness, a metaphor, but one that is metamorphosed into an object of aesthetic gaze, an aesthetic object – the cane of an aristocratic fop, and yet far more than a cane, the sign of the appearance of the essence.

Reading for style

I have tried to read Deleuze reading Proust in order to illustrate his version of a strong reading. And the conclusion I have reached is that Deleuze's strong reading reads for style: the emergence of style and the capture of essences is its objective. Deleuze does read Proust for style, even if he is paradoxically inclined to maintain that Proust has no style: he constructs a concept of style out of Proust, a concept that concerns the problem Deleuze extracts from Proust, the problem of signs. My own contention, which was developed in my own reading of Deleuze,[18] is that in the rest of his work the concept of style (the presence of which is constant) names Deleuze's own problem, the problem of language.

There is indeed a history of the concept of style in Deleuze. We have caught it, in *Proust et les signes*, at its very beginning (hence its strange associates: interpretation, essence, metaphor). But the concept persists, and it is always associated with the name of Proust, especially with the famous statement, 'The poet speaks a foreign tongue in his own language'. At the other end of the *oeuvre*, in *Essays Critical and Clinical*, we catch a final glimpse of the concept, now defined through the twin characteristics of a-grammaticality, or stuttering, and the striving of language towards its limits in silence or in non-linguistic media, images or sounds. We are again back to my first diagram, where style is opposed, within language, to meaning, that is to good sense and common sense. And we note that the cline of the sign puts language in its place: it is not situated at the apex of a spiritual progression, as in Hegel's aesthetics, where poetry is the highest, because the most spiritual, form of art.

We are now in a better position to characterise what a *problem* is for Deleuze: it is not a question, it does not have solutions that put an end to it. It insists in the solutions offered and outlives them. It must therefore open up unexpected and creative vistas on its object, and yet it is not a case of 'anything goes': it must provide retrospective coherence for its object, it must be named by a single concept that must be constructed. In other words, a problem is the occasion for a strong reading. Or again, a Deleuzian problem is best described by the operation of the Lacanian stitching point (*point de capiton*). The chain of signifiers majestically goes from word to word. At one point, it is intersected by the backward loop of the chain of signifieds, which goes back from the stitching point of comprehension to the beginning of the chain, as the stitching point is the point where suddenly meaning emerges, but only retrospectively ('so *that*'s what it all meant'). My canonical example of this is 'Pride comes before a . . . vote of impeachment': so I was talking about Nixon all the time, not merely quoting the well-known proverb.

A strong reading, a reading for style, proceeds in similar fashion. We have a chain of signs of art, sentence after sentence, page after page, chapter after interminable chapter, that make up *La Recherche*. And we have a process of interpretation, of deciphering of those signs, which goes back from the stitching point of comprehension to the beginning of the chain. The intersected segment, from the stitching point backwards, is a reading of Proust: a reading that retrospectively, or against the grain of the text, extracts a problem. When the reading is achieved, it produces the concept that names it. For this is what reading for style is: reading towards style, in order to construct a concept of style. In Proust and, *en abyme*, in Deleuze, Deleuze's reading of Proust induces a counter-reading, where the historicity of his philosophy is put in perspective (as interpretation and metaphor play a major role and are not merely the butts of his philosophical satire) and where philosophy itself, rather than exploiting literature, using it for its own ends, for the elaboration of the concepts of which it is only dimly aware, becomes subservient to art, the only path towards essences.

Notes

1. D. Drouet, 'Index des références littéraires dans l'œuvre de Gilles Deleuze', in B. Gelas and H. Micolet (eds), *Deleuze et les écrivains*, Nantes: Cécile Defaut, 2007, pp. 551–81.
2. J.-J. Lecercle, *Deleuze and Language*, Basingstoke: Palgrave, 2002, ch. 6.
3. B. Baugh, 'How Deleuze Can Help Us Make Literature Work', in I. Buchanan and J. Marks (eds), *Deleuze and Literature*, Edinburgh: Edinburgh University Press, 2000, pp. 42–3.
4. G. Deleuze, *Cinema 2. The Time-Image*, London: Continuum, 2005, pp. 24–9 (38–45).
5. Ibid., p. 26 (41).
6. Cf. C. Panaccio, *Le Discours intérieur*, Paris: Seuil, 1999.
7. Deleuze, op. cit., p. 28 (45).
8. Ibid.
9. F. Guattari, *Molecular Revolution*, Harmondsworth: Penguin, 1984, pp. 189–90.
10. G. Deleuze, *Proust and Signs*, London: Continuum, 2008 (1960, 1970, 1977).
11. Ibid., p. 3 (9).
12. Ibid., pp. 3–4 (10).
13. For an analysis of these four types of signs, see A. P. Colombat, 'Deleuze and Signs', in Buchanan and Marks, op. cit., pp. 14–33.
14. Deleuze, *Proust and Signs*, op. cit., p. 4 (12).
15. H. P. Grice, 'Logic and Conversation', in *Studies in the Way of Words*, Cambridge, MA: Harvard University Press, 1989.
16. V. Woolf, 'The Mark on the Wall', in *A Haunted House*, Harmondsworth: Penguin, 1973, pp. 43–52.
17. G. Deleuze, *Empiricism and Subjectivity*, New York: Columbia University Press, 1991 (1953).
18. See Lecercle, op. cit.

4

Badiou Reads Mallarmé

Mallarmé is an important figure for Badiou. In the very first pages of *Logic of Worlds* he calls him 'his master' and claims that the first proposition he states: 'There are only bodies and languages, except that there are truths', is formulated in Mallarmean style.[1] And he has been a consistent reader of Mallarmé: in *Théorie du sujet*, we find a close commentary of two sonnets;[2] in *Being and Event*, the nineteenth 'meditation' is devoted to a reading of Mallarmé's famous spatial poem, 'Un coup de dés jamais n'abolira le hasard';[3] the early collection of essays, *Conditions*, contains an essay on Mallarmé's 'method'[4] in which the same two sonnets and another poem, *Prose (pour des Esseintes)*, are analysed; in *Handbook of Inaesthetics*, Mallarmé is evoked in two essays, in a discussion with the Polish poet Czeslaw Milosz and through a comparison with the Arab poet Labîd ben Rabi'a;[5] finally, at the end of *Logic of Worlds*, in a section entitled 'Commentaries and Digressions', Badiou, in reminiscent mode, evokes his intellectual debt to both Mallarmé and Beckett ('thinking under condition of Mallarmé', as he calls it) and even states that the whole of his philosophy has perhaps consisted of an attempt to understand the works of those two authors – this is no mean claim.[6]

So Badiou reads Mallarmé, compulsively and in detail, even if his is a restricted corpus (two sonnets and two longer poems): it is obvious he has a great book on Mallarmé in him. But it is equally true, as he himself insists, that Mallarmé reads Badiou: the shipwreck, the Mallarmean image which he privileges in his reading, is the poetic inscription of a Badiou event ('The "shipwreck" alone gives us the allusive debris from which (in the one of the site) the indecidable multiple of the event is composed'),[7] and the cast of dice as event is nothing but the event of the production of the very symbol of an event, a second degree event ('The event in question in *A Cast of Dice* . . . is therefore that of the production of an absolute symbol of the event. The stakes of casting dice "from the bottom of a shipwreck" are those of making an event out of the thought of the event').[8] This attitude to the poem is entirely consistent with Badiou's concepts of truth and event: procedures of truth only occur in the four fields of science, art, love and politics, the four conditions under which philosophy, which does not produce truths itself but only 'compossibilises' the truths produced in other fields, operates. And the poem is sometimes given an even more important role to play, as matheme and poem are the archetypal conditions under which philosophy develops (a situation consistent with Badiou's lifelong interest in mathematics, which he ascribes to the influence of his father, and his lifelong passion for poetry, which he ascribes to the influence of his mother) – it is either an event itself, the event of the inscription of the event, or part of an artistic configuration where the event occurs (the event, in that case, is a group of poems, or works of art): 'In the final analysis, the pertinent unit for the thinking of art as an immanent and singular truth is neither the work nor the author, but rather the artistic configuration initiated by an evental rupture').[9] The seriousness of the enterprise of reading Mallarmé therefore is not in doubt: the question that arises is not why Badiou reads Mallarmé (that he finds in his poetry an inscription of the very event of which he constructs the concept, that, in that sense, it is Mallarmé who reads Badiou, is abundantly clear), but *how* he reads him.

How Badiou reads Mallarmé

The most striking aspects of Badiou's reading technique are the closeness and explicit nature of the reading. What we have is an example of the French tradition of *explication de textes*, that glory of the French educational system which combines the most precise and detailed analysis of the text with the clarity that pedagogic exposition demands: an ex-plication in the etymological sense, not merely an interpretation of the text but an unfolding of its complexity. Badiou is not only a considerable philosopher, he is also a gifted teacher, and the closeness of his reading sharply differentiates him from Deleuze, who has a more distant and sometimes offhanded attitude to the text he reads.

The first reading occurs in *Théorie du sujet*, and the pedagogic aspect is partly explained by the fact that the book is the transcription (somewhat rewritten, I suspect) of an oral seminar: there are moments when Badiou is 'in front of the blackboard', drawing diagrams or clarifying things to a benighted audience.[10] Two sonnets, usually known by their first lines ('A la nue accablante tu' and 'Ses purs ongles très haut dédiant leur onyx'), are presented in two sessions of the seminar. Before reading the sonnets, at the end of a previous seminar, Badiou indicates the object of Mallarmé's poetic writing: precisely the vanishing of the object, the evocation of its lack, in necessarily allusive language, as the word is divided between its usual verbal value and the silence which the evocation of an absence calls, as in the poem even the lack, the trace of the absence of the vanished object, is lacking (this lack of the lack is, according to Lacan, the source of anguish, *angoisse*). The reference to Lacan at this point is not innocent, as the respective styles, identified by the complexity of syntax, of the psychoanalyst and the poet, are the first things Badiou mentions when he starts his reading. And the reason for this is that the very complexity of the syntax guarantees that there is a meaning in the text, and a single meaning.

Having thus evoked both the univocity of meaning in a Mallarmé sonnet and the role of syntax, Badiou proceeds to read the poem. He starts by quoting it in full: an *explication de texte* needs the physical presence of the text, so the reader can check the progress of the reading. We may imagine that, in the seminar, there was a handout or that the sonnet was written on the blackboard. The next move is more surprising: Badiou gives a prose translation of the sonnet ('What shipwreck has drowned even the masts and torn sails that were the last remnants of a ship? The foam that covers the sea, which bears the trace of the catastrophe, knows, but will not tell . . .'). Such a summary is coherent with the thesis that there is a unique meaning of the text: it becomes accessible to the puzzled reader, after syntactic parsing, in the form of the prose summary. The third move is precisely the syntactic parsing: thus the word *tu*, the last word of the first line, is the past participle of the verb *taire* and not the second person pronoun, even as the word *nue* is an archaic word for 'cloud' and not a feminine adjective, and so on and so forth. The combination of prose summary and syntactic parsing allows Badiou to develop the semantic structure as a series of metaphors and metonymic chains.

The metaphorical sequence is given in the following diagram:

$$\frac{\text{offsite}}{\text{splace}} \xrightarrow{M_0} \frac{\text{writing}}{\text{blank}} \xrightarrow{M_0} \frac{\text{foam}}{\text{cloud}}$$

M_0 is the mark of the metaphorical transfer from one couple of terms to the next. The interesting point is that the metaphorical chain begins with Badiou's two concepts for the description of a structure in *Théorie du sujet*, with their picturesque names (there is system of placement in the structure, named *esplace*, a space of places, as there is an element which rejects such placing, and finds itself *horlieu*, out of the space of the structure). And this accounts for the next couple of terms, as the splace of the blank page bears the traces of the offsite inscription of the words, even as the metaphorical offsite of the foam corresponds to the splace of the cloud. The object of Mallarmé's poem therefore is the evocation of the absence of the structural dialectic itself.

The next move is the identification of metonymic chains, associated with one word, *écume*, by way of two semantic hypotheses: the foam is the trace left by the shipwreck on the emptiness of the sea, and it is also the trace left by a diving, and drowning, siren. The apparition of the siren, in the form of its disappearance, redoubles the vanishing of the ship: it vanishes once in the shipwreck, and it vanishes a second time, and even more so, in a reinterpretation of the traces left on the surface of the sea, which suggest that the foam was not produced by a shipwreck but by a diving siren, so that there never was any ship. The shipwrecked boat and the drowning siren are evoked not directly as they are both absent from the scene of the poem, but by metonymic representatives: the mast of the vanished ship, the hair of the siren. The double semantic value of the word 'foam' presents the importance of the vanishing of the object, through a *terme évanouissant*, a vanishing term, but also the division (*clivage*, a term with strong Lacanian connotations) of the word between verbal meaning and silence.

The last move, which closes the reading in that session of the seminar, is a diagram of the semantic constitution of the poem, of Byzantine complexity, in which the metaphorical movements and the metonymic chains are faithfully charted. And the last paragraphs, curiously but also typically of *Théorie du sujet*, offer a transposition of the operation of Mallarmé's sonnet into the terms of revolutionary politics, where it appears that the spurious workers' state, the Soviet Union, with its belief in established and stable socialism, is not aware (this is 1976 and the Berlin Wall has not fallen) of the very instability of the structure of which the poet, with his vanishing siren, is fully aware.

In the next session of the seminar Badiou comes back to the sonnet by way of a discussion of Mallarmé's interest in the theatre, a discussion of the vanishing of the vanishing, exhibiting the causality of lack, in which the subject as literal exception emerges, and he criticises the closure of the sonnet on its fourteenth line. It is there that he makes his boldest move, by adding a new stanza, in his own writing, to the finished work of art. The objective is to reopen the sonnet, to reintroduce the vanished shipwreck that had been cancelled by the siren, in other words to reintroduce a form of infinity (the poem never ends) into the finitude of the sonnet (he adds, in his typical vein, that Stalin wanted to reach an end, but that Mao knew that the revolutionary process knew no end). This is of course anathema, as Badiou well knows (he is cocking a snook at the tradition of literary criticism): not only because Badiou is not Mallarmé and the added tercet is a paltry pastiche of the grand Mallarmean style, but because he goes against what is perhaps the main principle underlying the analysis of a work of art, which the work of Mallarmé consistently illustrates, the very closure of the work of art, the fact that it constitutes a self-contained totality, *tel qu'en lui-même enfin l'éternité le change*: every work of art is a Grecian Urn – a sonnet with seventeen lines is indeed a strange object. And it is significant that when Badiou reads the sonnet again in *Conditions*, the analysis takes only five pages of text, the prose summary is still there, as is the diagram of the metonymic chains, but the added tercet has vanished, in a shipwreck of theory.[11]

In the next session of the seminar, Badiou proceeds to the *mise à plat*, the 'flattening out', etymologically the explication of a second sonnet, 'Ses purs ongles très hauts dédiant leur onyx'. Again absence, the void, are prevalent in the sonnet: the dying day has not even left a trace, the sitting room is empty, and the sonnet contains a famous coinage, the word *ptyx* (the sonnet is a rhyming tour de force, rhymes in '-yx' not being frequent in the French language), which means nothing except the 'sonorous void of the signifier', in excess of the encyclopaedia of existing signifiers, but subtracted from the system of language in that no signified may be attached to it. The sonnet is in fact the staging of the three types of absence through subtraction, the vanishing (of the object), the cancellation (of the trace of the absence) and the forclusion (of the inexistent signifier). The method of analysis is the same as for the first sonnet: it begins with a prose summary of the sonnet, it goes on with the establishment of a univocal meaning of the sonnet (Badiou even discusses a letter by Mallarmé about an illustration for the sonnet: the univocal meaning can be made literally visible), followed by a translation of this meaning into concepts (void, forclusion, etc.) that belong to the philosopher's theoretical language and ending in a complex schema that again visualises the structure of the sonnet: a *mise à plat* indeed.

So if there is a method in Mallarmé (the essay in *Conditions* is entitled 'Mallarmé's method'), there is a method of reading Mallarmé in Badiou. This is usually called a poetics.

Badiou's poetics

A number of axioms, always made explicit at one moment or other of the text, guide Badiou's reading.

The first axiom is the axiom of the univocity of meaning. There is one and only one meaning in the text and it is the object of the reading to disclose it. Badiou here knows full well that he moves against the current of literary criticism (but he never hesitates to be *à contre courant*), the contemporary form of which is supported by the axiom of the infinite polysemy of the text. This is how he formulates the axiom in *Théorie du sujet*: 'In spite of its opaque appearance, the machinery of a Mallarmé poem, let us emphatically state it, admits of one meaning only.'[12]

The second axiom is that the univocity of meaning is guaranteed by syntax. Mallarmé's syntax is notoriously hermetic, but this hermeticism is not a cover for semantic chaos: syntax conforms to fixed rules and the most complex sentence can be parsed to yield only one syntactic interpretation. Syntax it is that sustains the architecture of the poem and guarantees the solidity of its structure. This is a point where Badiou's Mallarmean poetics can be generalised, as syntax is equally a guarantee for Pessoa's poems and it is obvious that the axiom of the guarantee of syntax involves far more than a poetics – an entire metaphysics (Badiou is fond of saying that he is not afraid of the term):

> I consider Pessoa's syntax to be the instrument of such a project [of building a modern metaphysics]. In this poet – beneath the images and the metaphors, as it were – there is a constant *syntactical machination* whose complexity prohibits the hold of sensation and natural emotion from remaining sovereign. On this point, in any case, Pessoa resembles Mallarmé: often, the sentence must be reconstructed and reread for the Idea to traverse and transcend the apparent image. Pessoa wants to endow language – as varied, surprising and suggestive as it may be – with a subterranean *exactitude* that I will not hesitate to declare algebraic. On this point, a comparison can be made to the alliance within Plato's dialogues between, on the one hand, a singular charm, a constant literary seduction, and, on the other, an implacable argumentative severity.[13]

As in Chomsky's picture of language, the deep structure of poetry is provided not by images and metaphors, but by syntax.

The third axiom is that of the precedence of prose. As we saw, Badiou systematically begins his analysis of the poems with a prose summary, something no self-respecting literary critic would dare to do, as it strongly suggests a conception of the poetic text where the poetic form is merely an ornament for a meaning if not better, at least more clearly expressed in prose. And Badiou is entirely explicit about it:

> In appropriating the Mallarméan poem at a philosophical level, which presupposes that the absence be restituted (i.e. the thinking, under the sign of Truth, of the operation of a thought), I shall always begin with a 'translation', a sort of 'review from scratch', or punctuation of the poem's syntactic unfolding.[14]

And such translation must be in prose: 'the first reconstructed state [of the poem], where any form of poetry is withdrawn from the poem, which is left to its latent prose, so that philosophy may start from prose *back* to the poetry, in order to reach its own ends.' [15] In the formulation of this third axiom, danger words abound: not only because philosophy 'appropriates' the poem, which sounds like a form of exploitation, but because the idea that there should be 'latent prose' in a poem is singular, and the practice is reminiscent of the commentary of a poem for beginners, in a pedagogic situation (but Badiou, as we have seen, is a born pedagogue). We must note, however, that the third axiom is coherent with the first two: if meaning is univocal and syntax is complex, a clarification inevitably takes the form of an unravelling of the syntactic complexity in order to make the one and only meaning entirely explicit. The prose summary is the equivalent of the grammarian's parsing of the sentence in the shape of syntagmatic trees.

The fourth axiom sums up the first three. It is most clearly formulated in the nineteenth meditation of *Being and Event*, when Badiou reads *A Cast of Dice* . . . Here, for once, Badiou does not provide a prose summary of the text: the poem is probably protected from such iconoclasm by its spatial nature, the layout of the words on the page being an essential part of the text. This, of course, raises interesting questions: 'ordinary' sonnets are treated as if the spatial layout had no importance, or as if the poetic 'layout' of the text could be safely neglected, as if the latent prose of the sonnets were closer to the surface. (This idea that prose is the deep contents of the poem and that the poetry lies on the surface is deeply worrying.) The fourth axiom, then, states that a poem is an enigma and that its meaning is concealed (under the poetic surface) and must be disclosed by the analysis. This is how the nineteenth meditation begins:

> A poem by Mallarmé always fixes the place of an aleatory event: an event to be interpreted on the basis of the traces it leaves behind. Poetry is no longer submitted to action, since the meaning (univocal) of the text depends on what is declared to have happened therein. There is a certain element of the detective novel in the Mallarmean enigma: an empty salon, a vase, a dark sea – what crime, what catastrophe, what enormous misadventure is indicated by these clues.[16]

Detective novel, crime, enigma, clues: the comparison is thorough. *Mallarmé, Agatha Christie, même combat!* It would appear that Badiou can only deal with poetry by getting rid of the poetry (he says: only provisionally), as if poetry were an outer garment, easily discarded when the weather gets too hot.

Annoying the literary critic

It appears that Badiou's poetics is in fact a counter-poetics, as the four axioms go counter to the axioms, whether explicit or not, that support the literary critic's critical practice. Thus the literary critic, duly annoyed, is inclined to speak roughly to Badiou, as the Duchess in *Alice in Wonderland* does in the famous ditty when she nurses what will turn out to be a pig:

> Speak roughly to your little boy,
> And beat him when he sneezes;
> He only does it to annoy,
> Because he knows it teases.[17]

Badiou's sneezes go against the four axioms of the literary critic. The first axiom is that a poem is infinitely polysemous, or rather, since this seems slightly exaggerated, that the function of the poem is to free the semantic potentialities of language, so that the poem cannot be pinned down to a single meaning but is rather a coalescence of various meanings. The second axiom is that the syntactic structure of the poem does not guarantee a single meaning since, if syntax does structure the text, it is not univocal itself, and the poem is the type of text that consistently plays with syntactic ambiguity or ambivalence. (The trope called 'double syntax' is a good instance of this constitutive slippage of syntax.) And if in a poem the syntax is not ambiguous, it may well be creative and subvert its own rules. This axiom follows from the first, as it simply transports it into the domain of syntax, even as Badiou's second axiom follows from the first. The third axiom is that there is no possible translation of poetry into prose: prose cannot in any way precede the poetic shaping of the text. A poem is a poem is a poem, and there cannot be any 'latent prose' in it, unless it deliberately plays with the prosaic idiom, as is often the case with the poetry of Rimbaud but certainly not of Mallarmé, at least of the texts Badiou reads. Any reduction of the poem to prose is inadmissible, as ludicrous as A. L. Rowse's transposition of Shakespeare's sonnets into modern English for the benefit of a philistine American public. The fourth axiom sums up the first three, even as Badiou's fourth axiom also sums up the three preceding ones: to treat the poem as an enigma to be deciphered, in the best style of Bletchley Park, is to adopt the rather simplistic theory of interpretation which I have called the 'tin-opener' theory of interpretation (if you peel down the thin layer of metal, you can tuck into the luscious sardines of meaning).[18]

But the literary critic soon gets even more annoyed. For he holds an essential fifth axiom, which Badiou's reading method implicitly denies. This fifth axiom states that in the matter of poetry, or indeed of any literary text, the signifier plays a central role: in literary texts, language can never be a mere instrument of communication, it can never be reduced to a transparent conveyor of signifiers (as it becomes when the poem is reduced to its latent prose). There is no analysis of a poem that does not ascribe a central function, in the construction of an interpretation, to rhyme, rhythm, assonance, alliteration and the material shape of the signifier, all of which Badiou, in spite of his Lacanian origins, blissfully ignores, as we saw with the second sonnet, which is written for an 'impossible' rhyme, the '-yx' rhyme. Badiou's metaphoric and metonymic chains, in which his close reading of the text mainly consists, operate at the level of the signified: that this cloud should be a *nue*, with the obvious lexical ambiguity with the feminine adjective meaning 'naked' (whereby the siren of the last line is already convoked) is of no importance. And it is significant that, although syntax is supposed to play an important part in Badiou's reading, no syntactic analysis, except the simplest translation into the 'normal' order of words, is suggested by Badiou. In order to understand this, all we have to do is to compare his reading to Jean-Claude Milner's reading of another Mallarmé sonnet: Milner, who is a Lacanian linguist, proceeds through a careful analysis of the syntax, in all its complexity (Mallarmé exploits all the resources that syntax gives, including all the possible ambiguities it involves), and one of his conclusions is that 'Mallarmé well knows the powers of homophony and all forms of playing with language'.[19]

In reading poems in this fashion, Badiou merely reproduces the practice of the most traditional form of literary criticism, which is erudite but literal and simplistic. In the Pléiade edition of the complete works of Mallarmé, which is the edition of reference, the sonnet has a note that tells us where it was originally published and mentions the existence of a manuscript version in a private collection. It goes on by providing a prose translation or summary of the poem, which reads exactly like Badiou's, and a syntactic re-transcription of the poem, with the following comment: 'This sonnet, which is considered to be one of the most difficult of Mallarmé's sonnets, loses any obscurity of meaning when, by cancelling the syntactic inversions, the order of the scattered words (suggestively so, like the debris of a shipwrecked boat) is recovered.' [20] That enlightened commentary was published in 1945: since then literary theory has somewhat progressed.

The five axioms that Badiou holds (the fifth, implicit axiom reads: in a Mallarmé poem, the signifier is negligible) are coherent in so far as they inscribe a philosophy of language of a traditional kind. That philosophy underpins the tin-opener theory of interpretation, which has the following four characteristics:[21] (1) the interpretation follows a path from the benighted first reading (the text has encrypted its meaning) to the enlightened reading that the interpretation produces, even as the interpretation of a dream is a passage from its manifest to its latent content; (2) this path is unique, the right path as opposed to the *impasse* of false understanding; (3) progress along the path of interpretation is achieved by *glossing* (translating the poetry into prose, syntactic reordering) and *guessing* (solving the enigma of the text); (4) progress along the path will be achieved by using critical tools, such as the construction of metaphoric or metonymic chains, and the result will be a matheme of the poem, inscribed in the diagram that gives its structure, or semantic skeleton (the flesh of the signifier being negligible).

This theory of interpretation in turn involves a philosophy of language which, because it remains implicit in Badiou, is nothing but the mainstream, or commonsense, philosophy of language. Badiou, as we have seen, resists the 'linguistic turn' in contemporary philosophy, and his system has no place for language, except in the shape of naming (the naming of the event is an integral part of it) – language itself, being the language of the situation and as such incapable of dealing with the radically new, that is the event, is of no consequence. But the repressed philosophy of language returns, here in the shape of a theory of meaning aptly captured by what is known as the 'conduit metaphor': ideas are objects, linguistic expressions are containers, communication is sending.[22] Or again, there is an intention of meaning in Mallarmé, which precedes the text (he knows exactly what he wants to say; he also wants to express his meaning obliquely, so that it will have to be deciphered by the clever interpreter). Such an intention of meaning is embedded in a form of linguistic expression that renders the meaning temporarily obscure. And successful communication is achieved when the poet encounters a reader subtle enough to understand what was meant and altruistic enough to make it clear to a mass of unenlightened readers. This conception of interpretation and of language is widely shared (it is apparently shared by Milner in the text I quoted: he also treats Mallarmé's sonnet as an enigma, even if his analysis is based on a careful study of the signifier, which is no longer negligible). It is nevertheless rather dubious.

Paradoxes

Am I being unjust to Badiou? His reading method is difficult to accept for a literary critic, but it is meant to yield results, and it does. So we have not only axioms, but a number of theorems on Mallarmé's poetry, of which the passage on Pessoa's syntactic machinations I quoted earlier gives an idea. A poem by Mallarmé fixes the place of an event. It stages the traces of the vanishing of the event, or rather their absence. It operates, by subtraction, on such absence. It can be treated as an enquiry into the appearance of the event, which results in its naming, in a procedure of truth from which a faithful subject emerges. The operation of syntax in the poem preserves it from the *pathos* of imaginary identification and the revelling in bodily affect: there is a *logos*, not a *pathos*, of poetry. And such interpretation of Mallarmé's poetry is compelling. Here, the literary critic may well argue that Badiou finds in Mallarmé exactly what he wanted to find in him, namely the concepts of his philosophical system, and that the result of the analysis precedes the analysis itself. But this argument is not sufficient, as the relationship may be inverted: Badiou thinks under the condition of Mallarmé, it is Mallarmé that reads Badiou. In a spirited defence of Badiou's reading of Mallarmé in *Théorie du sujet*, Oliver Feltham attempts to show that Badiou's reading method, far from being imposition and appropriation (of philosophical concepts on to the text, of the text by an invasive philosopher), actually treats Mallarmé's sonnet as a model for Badiou's theory, in the precise sense of the term which he developed in his first philosophical work, *Le concept de modèle*.[23] In Badiou's reading, 'semantic values, such as "foam" and "siren", are assigned to the syntax of the structural dialectic, and then the re-evaluated dialectic is tested for completion within the semantic field of the sonnet.' [24] So Badiou's interpretation does not stop at the tin-opener stage: there is not only parsing and the solution of an enigma (though there is also that), there is translation (of the text into the language of the theory) and modelling (of the theory by the text), which is a form of intervention (the text reads the theory that reads it). By a sort of *felix culpa*, dubious axioms deliver what is undoubtedly a strong reading. We find ourselves immersed in paradox. But paradox, the outside of *doxa*, is the very site of philosophy. Indeed, Badiou's poetics may be characterised by a number of paradoxes.

The *first paradox* is trivial enough. It concerns the philosopher who denies the centrality of language, has no place for language in his philosophical outlook and yet waxes eloquent in the denunciation of the despised medium. For philosophy, like poetry, is an exercise of/in language. This of course reminds us of Deleuze's essay, 'The Exhausted', which deals with Beckett's late television plays, where language there is none, but where Deleuze deals with the situation not only in terms of Beckett's language, but of three different types of language.[25]

Badiou does belong to that line of philosophers (rather rare these days) who resist the overwhelming importance of language for philosophy. He does this in two ways. He upholds the position of truth against the modern sophistry of the poststructuralists and postmodernists, and he rejects the linguistic turn taken by philosophy, both in the Wittgensteinian version (where all philosophical problems are grammatical problems) and in the Heidegerrian, hermeneutic, version, so that for him this first paradox is no paradox. Philosophy operates by subtraction, and what the subtraction mainly achieves is breaking the surface of language, where the Sophist has established himself.[26] This abandonment of language as a field of philosophical enquiry is a small price to pay for avoiding the position of the Sophist, for whom there are no truths but only techniques of utterance and sites for enunciation, and for whom there is nothing but a multiplicity of language-games, as being is inaccessible to thought.[27]

We have seen that there is a price to pay for this: the implicit reliance on a concept of language of the most traditional and doxic kind. But avoidance of the paradox is easy for Badiou: all he has to do is carefully separate natural language, a hindrance to philosophy, from the language of ontology, which is the language of mathematics.

Is this merely a restatement of Carnap's traditional position? It is not: Badiou does not use the contrast between natural and artificial languages, and, more important for us and a major difference with Carnap, he raises the question of the poem: perhaps there is a way, after all, of saving language for philosophy through a celebration of poetical practice.

This seems in fact to be Badiou's real answer: the operation of subtraction separates philosophical discourse from the poem. This is a Platonist gesture, the recognition of the constitutive diaphor (*diaphora*), or discord, between philosophy and poetry, between the poem and philosophical argument. We can express this through a correlation, with Greek names, for this philosophical battle was fought long ago on the Aegean, and we, on this distant northern sea, have merely inherited it: *poiesis* versus *dianoia*[28] (the vatic celebration of being is opposed to the slow and painful argumentative path that rises up to first principles), *pathos* versus *logos* (the poem is a site for the expression of affect, the philosophical text deals with argument and logic).

This solution to our first paradox, which separates a reasonable or purified use of language from its poetic uses, is essentially Plato's solution in his expulsion of poetry from the ideal *polis*. But it is still unsatisfactory, not least for Badiou: it tends to reduce the poem to an exercise in sophistry.[29] He duly notes that Plato, having explored the limits of *dianoia*, 'must himself resort to images, like that of the sun; to metaphors, like those of "prestige" and "power"; to myths, like the myth of Er the Pamphylian . . .'[30] It appears that there might be more to language than 'idealinguistery', the Lacanian term by which, in *Théorie du sujet*, he dismisses any attempt at a philosophy of language as mere sophistry.[31] Badiou's materialism implies the rejection of the idealism that any thinking of language inevitably carries with it. This is one of the things that, according to him, we learn from Celan:

> Contrary to the declarations of the modern sophists, there is indeed a fixed point. Not everything is caught in the slippage of language games or the immaterial variability of occurrences. Being and truth, even if now stripped of any grasp upon the Whole, have not vanished. One will find

that they are precariously rooted precisely at the point where the Whole offers its own nothingness.[32]

By the modern sophists he means practically every contemporary philosopher (Derrida, Lyotard, etc.), but not Deleuze, who shares his intense dislike for Witgenstein's philosophy.

But Badiou is, in this respect, singularly placed. Hence a second paradox.

The *second paradox* notes that Badiou, the arch anti-Sophist, he that almost single-handedly resists the linguistic turn, is, as a novelist and playwright, a technician if not of language in general (he is no linguist), at least of poetic language. As we know, he shares with contemporary Sophists a passion for literature. And like all those philosophers, he has constructed his own idiosyncratic canon, a number of poets whose names appear again and again in his work: Hölderlin, Mallarmé, Celan, Pessoa.

An elementary solution to the second paradox consists of producing a symmetrical position to that of the philosopher who becomes a surrogate poet: the position of the poet as surrogate philosopher. If, when the limits of argumentative thought, of *dianoia*, have been reached, philosophy waxes poetic, then we may call for a moment when, the vatic impulse of the poem being exhausted, the poem abandons *pathos* for *logos*. We may wish for a poetry of pure *logos*, the only object of which is the contemplation of ideas, the production of truths. Such a poem, as we saw, Badiou finds in the works of Mallarmé, a poem that presents itself as thought. And we may now rehearse the not unproblematic progression towards the poetic climax of the modern poem in Mallarmé.

It all begins, inevitably, with Parmenides: the first philosophical argument takes the form of a poem and the founding philosopher is also a poet. This is where the separation must operate: the first move in philosophy is the desacralisation of the poem, the interruption of the revelling in *pathos*, its substitution with rational argument, a violent form of intervention. Here is how Badiou describes the process: 'Philosophy requires [*exige*] that the authority of *profound* utterance [*profération*] be interrupted by argumentative secularization.'[33]

From this violent intervention, three types of relationship between philosophy and poetry emerge. First comes the Romantic tradition, from Parmenides to Heidegger, where poetic language is the natural site for authenticity and the disclosure of being and truth. This is clearly the wrong path, as it is the path that resists the separation between the two modes of language. Second comes the aesthetic tradition that begins with Aristotle, where the poem is no longer a source of knowledge but the object of the theoretical gaze of the philosopher, on a par with natural phenomena and no longer concerned with truth but only with verisimilitude. This path, too, is clearly wrong: it fails to do justice to the power of the poem. Third comes the Platonist gesture of exclusion, which rejects the poem because of its very power, of its charm in the etymological sense. Such a gesture recognises the extraordinary power of poetry and constantly re-enacts the movement of separation that constitutes philosophy, thereby also recognising, through a form of Freudian denial, that philosophy and poetry, at least at the beginning if not in principle, are inextricably mixed. The three positions are sometimes called by Badiou 'artistic schemata': Plato's schema is didactic in so far as it asserts that art is incapable of truth, although it exerts considerable charm and must therefore be kept under close surveillance. In an interesting, and faintly ironic twist, Badiou notes that the contemporary version of this schema is the Marxist position towards art, captured at its didactic best in Brecht – there lies his 'greatness'.[34]

Badiou's own poetics can be described as an effort to reach a fourth position, which would maintain the separation between the poem and philosophical discourse, but would accept that the poem is the site for the production of truths. (We remember that, for Badiou, truths always come in the plural: the concept of Truth is empty.) Such a position may be expressed through a *third paradox*, this time an entirely positive one.

On the one hand, the poem is a site for truth, and as such a *condition* for philosophy. If philosophy, as Badiou claims, is a procuress of truths (he uses the word *maquerelle*, with its fine eighteenth-century connotations), the poem creates any number of ravishing young persons, of either sex, for philosophy to thrive upon.

On the other hand, philosophy operates as a *deposition* of poetry: it demands of the poem that it should abandon its auratic search of or revelling in meaning, it demands the abandonment of all forms of *pathos*. Thus Deleuze must be criticised for taking his aesthetics seriously, that is literally, for constructing an aesthetics on the extraction of blocks of affects from affections, of percepts from perceptions, and thus sharply separating concepts from percepts and affects. The tables have been turned: it is Deleuze who accomplishes the Platonist gesture of separation between philosophy and the poem, whereas

Badiou's deposition relieves such separation in the Hegelian sense, which explains the proximity of philosophy to myth and metaphor, and also the distance between *logos* and *pathos*: deposition operates through the de-aesthetisation of the poem, the separation between the presence of the idea, which the poem captures, and the *pathos* of bodily affection, which it must discard.

In this type of poetics, a lot is demanded of literature: what the poem must renounce, what is deposed in it, is all that seems to concern the poem's relationship to language.

Here is Badiou in the essay tellingly entitled 'The philosophical recourse to the poem': 'Philosophy wants to and must be established in this subtractive point where language, divested of the prestige, or mimetic incitement, of images, of fiction and of narrative, is consigned [*s'ordonne*] to thought.'[35] Two pages later, he adds comparison and rhythm to this list. But of course Badiou is aware that not only the poem, but philosophy itself, has recourse to all those techniques of language. The difference between the poem and philosophy (deposition is merely the inscription of the necessity of this difference) lies in the fact that, in philosophy, such techniques are precisely *located*, at the place where a truth emerges that punctures meaning and defies interpretation. What is demanded of the poem, in order for it to condition philosophy, is that, in resisting the charm and incitement of fiction, image and narrative, it should choose truth, which does not make sense, against meaning, which all too readily makes conventional sense, and thereby fosters interpretation. For what fiction, narrative and metaphor, in their literary pervasiveness, produce is a plurality, or a surfeit, of interpretations.

Hence the poetry that Badiou calls for, and finds in Mallarmé. Such a poem has two singular characteristics: it is a poem of *logos*, a poem concerned with thought, and it is a poem capable of naming the event, of extracting from the advent of the event not affects and percepts but truths (where it appears that Badiou's poetics is the inverse of Deleuze's aesthetics).

It is easy to see why language is a problem in Badiou's poetics, why its importance for poetry, as indeed for philosophy, is obvious and crucial but deeply paradoxical. Language is always, at first at least, the language of the situation, in which the event cannot be named, in which the truths that follow from the event cannot be formulated. And yet the unnameable event *must* be named, and a new language, adapted to that naming, must be forged, a violent process. The language of the poem is paradoxical because it is the site of a violent birth: in order to attempt to name the unnameable, the poem must break and reconstruct language. There are revolutions in language, as there are in society. 'Mallarmé' is the name for this new operation of the poem. And indeed Badiou's poetics seems to be a reformulation of Mallarmé's poetic programme, as expressed by the famous sentence, *donner un sens plus pur aux mots de la tribu* ('give a purer meaning to the words of the tribe').

Having said this, we immediately encounter the *fourth paradox* with which I have already dealt at length, as it is at the heart of Badiou's technique of reading the poem: on the one hand, the poem, qua thought, has nothing to do with semantics and meaning and everything with 'negation' and with syntax; on the other hand, much to the surprise and the indignation of the literary critic, he begins with a prose translation of the poem. And since Badiou is too subtle a reader not to be aware of what he does (and of the literary critic's potential indignation), it is time to try and make positive sense of what he does.

I shall suggest a number of propositions.

The first thing to note is that this poetics is not an aesthetics. This is the note that defines his 'inaesthetics', at the very beginning of his *Handbook of Inaesthetics*:

> By 'inaesthetics', I understand a relation of philosophy to art, maintaining that art is in itself a producer of truths, makes no claim to turn art into an object for philosophy. Against aesthetic speculation, inaesthetics describes the strictly intraphilosophical effects produced by the independent existence of some works of art.[36]

This gives us a frame for a number of positive propositions about art *in its relation to philosophy*, that is art as it must be in order to condition philosophy (and conversely, philosophy as it must be in order to be conditioned by art: the relationship is not one-sided).

The first proposition is by now familiar to us: syntax is essential to the constitution of the poem. The contrast between semantics and syntax is a constant in Badiou's reflections on the poem: in this, he follows Mallarmé, whom he is fond of quoting on the subject ('We need a guarantee: syntax').[37] Hence the *syntactic machination* he finds in both Pessoa and Mallarmé: the poem disturbs the natural flow of reading and delays interpretation, a constant but mistaken urge; it does this in order to give time to the Idea to work through the immediate image. In his answer to the Polish poet Czeslaw Milosz, who deplores the hermeticism of modernist poetry, Badiou insists on the crucial function of such syntactic convolutions. This is of considerable interest for the literary critic, even if the claim is still largely formal (there is no real syntactic analysis in his readings, as we saw). It should be the task of the critic to develop such intuitions of the philosopher.

The second proposition is specific to Mallarmé's poems. In his reading, Badiou identifies three types of 'negation'. (This is one of the statements that I have called his 'theorems'.) The first is the *vanishing* that marks the absence of the event in the site of its emergence. Thus, in the first sonnet he reads, the absent word, 'shipwreck' (*le naufrage*), names the event and is represented in the text by a chain of metonyms of which it is the absent source. The second is the *cancellation*, which is a mark of the undecidability of the event. The traces left by the shipwreck on the surface of the sea may have been left by the vanishing siren: the vanishing of the ship is thus itself cancelled. The third is the *forclusion* that marks the absence of even the slightest trace, the paradoxical marking of the impossibility of the mark, the forceful absence of the radically unnameable. The foreclosed terms are that which no poetic truth can force into expression: the subject (the poet), the end (of the poem, of the subject: death), the material worked upon (language itself is foreclosed in the poem: you can poetically express any number of things, but not language). This, to the literary critic, is highly interesting in that it might be a characterisation of style: the forcing out (*forçage*) of language, when it is taken to its limits, towards its vanishing point into mere gibberish or silence. Except of course, there is no lyrical revelling in the ineffable in Badiou's poetics: such negations, such absences, are structural. A poetics of truth has the clarity and asceticism of rational structure, and the absence of the relevant term is part of the argument of the poem.

As a result of this, this is the third proposition, the poem is no lyrical celebration of affect or disclosure of meaning, but an *operation*: neither a description nor an expression.[38] Such an 'operation', when the reader has to accomplish it in her turn, is the inverse of interpretation: it does not claim to offer a key to the meaning of the poem that is being read, it provides an entry into the poet's syntactic machination. Let the poem itself operate: this is what the surface hermeticism of the text demands. The term 'operation' is chosen advisedly: it radically cuts off any reference to affect and the ineffable. A poetry of *logos* is a poetry of operations, not strictly mathematical ones, but certainly as rational as those of mathematics.

The fourth proposition is that this defines a poetics of purity and void. The 'purer sense' that the poem, in Mallarmé's phrase, gives 'the words of the tribe' is a reaching out for the purity of what he calls 'the Notion' and what the philosopher calls the Idea. Neither elegy, nor hymn, nor lyrical outburst, the poem is a reaching out for the purity of the Idea (this is the poetic version of the operation of subtraction). These are the four words in which Badiou sums up the operations of poetry qua thought, to be found in Mallarmé, Rimbaud, Hölderlin and Beckett: disobjectivation, disorientation, interruption and isolation. As we can see, such poetics relies on negation in the same sense as negative theology does, or in the sense that the Real in Lacan can only be grasped through negative description (it is senseless, indifferent, impossible, etc.): in the same vein, a truth for Badiou is undecidable, indiscernible, unnameable and generic. (The last term is as negative as the others: it means that no characteristic of such truth may be expressed in the prevailing encyclopaedia.)

I think that we now understand why such a poetics, obnoxious as it may appear to be to the literary critic, is so fascinating: it makes for what are undoubtedly strong readings, of Rimbaud, for instance (*Conditions* has an essay entitled 'Rimbaud's method'), and certainly of Mallarmé. In spite of the initial operation of translation, in spite of the precedence of prose, in spite of the dubious philosophy of language such method convokes, the readings of the Mallarmé poems are compelling. Suddenly the words of those hermetic poems come alive (I almost wrote 'make sense', which is exactly what, according to Badiou, they do not), and a coherence emerges around the concepts of event, naming and fidelity.[39] But can we go further? Can we find interest in this reading for the literary critic, independently of the philosopher?

The interest of such reading is that it ascribes its true power to poetry. Badiou is fond of the French phrase *à la hauteur de*. *Penser à la hauteur de Pessoa* (the English version, inevitably, loses the metaphor: '[thought] that is worthy of Pessoa'):[40] what is this 'height' which the philosopher must share with the poet? It is the singular power of language. We must beware of the traps of translation here, lest we fall back into the sophistic celebration of language which Badiou wishes to avoid at all costs. His phrase is *les puissances de la langue*, 'the powers of language'[41] – the lexicon is not entirely consistent, since a few lines later this *puissance* becomes *pouvoir* (translated as 'power'). But the general drift is clear: *potentia* is not merely power and *langue* is not language. In Mallarmé, such power is identified as the power eternally to state the disappearance of what presents itself, in other words to capture the emergence of the event. Such *hauteur* enables us to understand why the poem is indeed a condition of philosophy.

But other poetics, not least the Romantic tradition that gives all power to language, ascribe similar, if not greater, importance to the poem. So there is something else that, in Badiou's poetics, deeply satisfies the literary critic. It is a poetics of the anti-lyrical, of the impersonal, as opposed to the effusions of an affected subject (what Deleuze contemptuously calls his 'dirty little story' – and by which, unlike Badiou, he means what psychoanalysis is looking for). Badiou's poetics does not take as its elementary unit of poetic thought the single work or the personal author, but what he calls the artistic configuration, which is the true site for the emergence of the event and the production of truths. In this, Badiou shares the modernist poetics one can find in his contemporaries, Foucault or Deleuze.

Badiou's originality, however, lies in the articulation of the two seemingly independent words, 'poem' and 'thought'. This is of special interest to the literary critic, at least if he takes his task seriously and holds, as I do, that literature thinks. Badiou is the thinker of poetry as thought. In this he has truly found a fourth path, or site, for the relationship between poetry and philosophy, beyond the *aporia* of the contrast between *pathos* and *logos*, between auratic or lyrical vaticination and the exclusion of thought from poetry or poetry from thought. Badiou is one of the rare people, perhaps the only one, capable of making a decision, of solving the paradox the two terms form by firmly excluding one of them, the unexpected one, and turning the other, *logos*, into the very stuff that poetry is made of.

Yet, fascinated as the literary critic is, sometimes to the point of enthusiasm, he cannot conceal a feeling of unease. The strong reservations that Badiou's reading technique has suggested will not vanish. Let me propose three reasons for this.

The first reason may be entirely contingent. We can formulate in a *fifth paradox*. Badiou appears to be a novelist whose thinking about art well nigh ignores the novel. Apart from a few references to the artistic configuration of the novel, culminating in Joyce, and giving the impression that it is now exhausted, the Badiou canon seems to be entirely composed of poets (this is a major difference from Deleuze). Since what must be deposed from poetry in order for it to think is the mimetic, characterised as the combination of image, fiction and narrative, there seems to be no place for the novel in Badiou's poetics: where poetry is concerned with truth, the novel is concerned with fiction and make-believe. In other words, the novel is an Aristotelian genre. But I think such a view would be deeply mistaken. Truths in Badiou are generic in yet another sense: artistic truths are situated in a genre. So his poetics is not a general aesthetics, not even a poetics of literature, but a poetics of the poem as specific site for specific truths, which are different from the truths of the novel. After all, Badiou is singular among contemporary philosophers in that he is not only a philosopher but has a recognised artistic position, at least in the field of drama: a notable dramatist himself (in this, his only rival, and predecessor, is Jean-Paul Sartre), he is also a well-known theorist of the theatre, whose positions are at the centre of lively discussion. (A trace of this may be found in the *Handbook of Inaesthetics* in the shape of 'Theses for the theatre', the first of which, in a move that is by now familiar to us, states that 'the theatre thinks'.)[42] There remains a nagging suspicion, however, that for Badiou qua philosopher, the novel is not the literary genre where literature thinks par excellence, whereas for Badiou the artist, novel and drama are the two genres he practises. Perhaps we should remember that in the interview published at the end of Oliver Feltham's book, he describes himself as an optimistic thinker but a melancholy writer.[43] The poem presents the event which the novel can only represent: the optimism of capturing truth through artistic practice gives way to the melancholy of being able only to represent such truth in the language of the situation. We are not so far from Deleuze's definition of style as a-grammaticality and a reaching out to silence or images.

But the problem subsists, in the shape of a *sixth paradox*. As we have seen, Badiou's treatment of syntax is not yet *à la hauteur* of Mallarmé's dictum on syntax as guarantee. The limited examples he provides in his readings reduce syntactic analysis to mere parsing, which in turn opens the way for semantic glossing, the reality behind the 'prose preparation' of the poem. We have already formulated this paradox: syntax here is merely another name for semantics, it is merely the name for the imposition on the poem of a single, because true, interpretation of the text. But this need not be so. I have already alluded to the concept of *forçage*, 'a forcing of language enacted by the advent of an "other" language that is at once immanent and created',[44] as Badiou puts it: this opens up vistas of a truly syntactic analysis of the poem, in which, again, Badiou would be close to his philosophical other, Deleuze, who, as we just saw, defines style through a-grammaticality and who tries to define what he calls an 'intensive line of syntax'.⁴⁵

Nevertheless, the insistence on syntax as guarantee involves a *seventh paradox*, the paradox of the precedence of prose in a poem, or, which is the same, of an analysis of a poem that totally neglects the role of signifiers. If syntax offers a guarantee, we are entitled to ask what it is a guarantee of. And Badiou's answer is unequivocal: it guarantees the univocal meaning of the text, the solution of the enigma that the text encapsulates. It enables the reader to have a mental picture of the scene described, of the actors involved and of the events which the poem narrates. In other words, it allows the reader to gain access to the representation that the poem stages. This combination of stable syntactic rules and univocal meaning, however, provides an excellent description of the language of what Badiou calls the situation: the already established language that will be recognisable to any speaker or reader that belongs to the situation. So the reader of Badiou's reading will duly 'understand' the meaning of the poem when its syntax has been 'flattened out' (*mise à plat*). But this means that neither the poem nor the reading are *à la hauteur* of the event: they merely *represent* the event, they cannot *present* it, as such presentation, of the traces of the vanished event if not of the event itself, requires an entirely new language. In other words, the poem represents an event but cannot be an event itself. This paradox has a potentially unfortunate side: a preference for the arch canonical author that is Mallarmé, a defender of the aesthetics of *Parnasse* (a better version of Leconte de Lisle), over the rebellious or extra-canonical authors that are Rimbaud or Lautréamont, although Rimbaud too is part of the Badiou canon, as he devoted an essay to him in *Conditions*.⁴⁶ As the title of the essay states, Rimbaud, like Mallarmé, has a 'method'. He too is a thinker of the event, and therefore of subtraction: but his favourite form of subtraction is not absence or forclusion, but interruption. The specific 'machination' of the Rimbaud poem is the non-fulfilment of the poetic promise that it contains, inscribed within the work of prose within poetry. Prose is with us again, but this time not as the medium in which the meaning of the poem is made clear, but as what subverts the canonical language of poetry, the symbolist idiom of which Mallarmé is the archetypal representative. Here prose is what subverts the language of the canonical situation, as a result of which the evental nature of the poem is easier to grasp. We are not so far from Kristin Ross's reading of Rimbaud in terms of the emergence of social space, the right to laziness and the participation in that political event (in the strong sense) that the 1870 Paris Commune was.[47] Her reading of Mallarmé, however, is strikingly different from Badiou's as she interprets his poetry in terms of the fetishisation of the poetic text ('the thing which appears without a producer, which appears, according to Mallarmé's famous dictum, with "the elocutory disappearance of the poet" – in fact ends up promoting the reification it sought to resist').[48] She contrasts Rimbaud's strategy of resistance ending in flight with Mallarmé's denial of the social, and his insistence on the performative function of language, the violence of slogans and the operation of denotation as opposed to signification with Mallarmé's problematic of signifier and signified where poetic discourse replaces the referent, a typical strategy for the canonical avant-garde. As we read her reading of Rimbaud, we realise the paradoxical nature of Badiou's privileging of Mallarmé as the poet of the event.

A strong reading

Since paradox has a constitutive relation to philosophy, its is only natural that Badiou should consistently indulge in it. The result is undoubtedly a strong reading, so we can leave him the last word. In the essay 'Art and philosophy' in his *Handbook of Aesthetics*, he encapsulates the result of his reading of poetry in a number of propositions:

1. As a general rule, a work is not an event. A work is a fact of art. It is the fabric from which the artistic procedure is woven.
2. Nor is a work of art a truth. A truth is an artistic procedure initiated by an event. This procedure is *composed* of nothing but works. But it does not manifest itself (as infinity) in any of them. The work is thus the local instance or the differential point of a truth.
3. We will call this differential point of the artistic procedure its *subject*. A work is the subject of the artistic procedure in question, that is the procedure to which this work belongs. In other words, an artwork is a subject of an artistic truth.
4. The sole being of a truth is that of works. An artistic truth is a (infinite) generic multiple of works. But these works weave together the being of an artistic truth only by the chance of their successive occurrences.
5. We can also say this: a work is a situated *enquiry* about the truth that it locally actualises or of which it is a finite fragment.

6. The work is thus submitted to a principle of novelty. This is because an enquiry is retroactively validated as a real work of art only inasmuch as it is an enquiry *that had not taken place*, an unprecedented subject-point within the trajectory of truth.
7. Works compose a truth within the post-evental dimension that institutes *the constraint of an artistic configuration*. In the end, a truth is an artistic configuration initiated by an event (in general, an event is a group of works, a singular multiple of works) and unfolded through chance in the form of the works that serve as its subject points.[49]

We have noted the presence of the chain of concepts that make up *Being and Event*: event, truth, subject, enquiry, multiple. We also note the hesitation as to the nature of the work of art: is it an event or merely a fact of art, an element in the collective entity that is an artistic configuration? (In the next paragraph, Badiou states that the pertinent unit for thinking art is neither the individual work nor the individual author but the artistic configuration.) And Badiou's is undoubtedly a strong reading. The six characteristics of such a reading, as stated in the last chapter, are strikingly present in Badiou's reading of Mallarmé.

The first characteristic of a strong reading is that it goes against the grain of received *doxa*. It forces the reader into thinking. It insists on the violence of the practice of reading. And Badiou's reading of Mallarmé, which is traditional in its method, certainly goes against the grain of current interpretations, not least in its neglect of the role of the signifier. Thus we learn that the poet's hermeticism is only superficial and that the *préciosité*, the euphuistic complexity, of his style is merely transitory, an unavoidable passage to the univocal meaning of the text which is what really counts.

The second characteristic inscribes this forcing of thought in the shape of the extraction of a problem. Even as Deleuze extracted the problem of the learning of signs from his reading of Proust, Badiou extracts the problem of the paradoxical presence of the absence of the vanished event.

The third characteristic moves from the extraction of a problem to the construction of the concept that grasps it. In the case of Deleuze's reading of Proust, the concept was a non-Saussurian concept of sign. In the case of Badiou, his reading of Mallarmé, or Mallarmé's reading of him, engages the construction of the system of concepts (event, truth, subject, fidelity, etc.) which *Being and Event* expounds.

The fourth characteristic of a strong reading is its sheer persistence. The right problem, and the correct concept that grasps it, do not vanish once they have been respectively extracted and constructed: they persist. And even as Deleuze compulsively returns to his reading of Proust, Badiou keeps going back to his reading of Mallarmé and to the same few texts. Thus to say that Mallarmé consistently conditions Badiou's thinking is no exaggeration.

The fifth characteristic is that the consequence of such extraction, construction, persistence and insistence is an intervention rather than an interpretation. In the case of Deleuze, the best test of such an intervention was its capacity to shock the critical tradition of readings of Proust. That Badiou's reading of Mallarmé is meant to annoy the literary critic who believes in his *doxa* is, I think, clear. Badiou's reading is as outrageous as it is compelling.

The sixth characteristic of a strong reading is that its very strength is a provocation for readers. In other words a strong reading is an instance of what Harold Bloom calls a creative misprision, a blatant misunderstanding that produces positive artistic or critical effects. As such, it calls for a *counter-reading*. Such, for instance, is the effect produced upon readers of Deleuze by Badiou's reading of Deleuze in his eponymous book. Such, as we saw, is the effect on the literary critic of his reading of Mallarmé. However, the literary critic, being an unredeemable sophist, rejoices at this characteristic, as it ensures the unending continuation of the chain of interpretations: a strong reading calls for a strong counter-reading.

Notes

1. A. Badiou, *Logic of Worlds*, London: Continuum, 2009, p. 4 (12).
2. A. Badiou, *Théorie du sujet*, Paris: Seuil, 1982, pp. 92–109 and 118–27.
3. A. Badiou, *Being and Event*, London: Continuum, 2006 (1988), pp. 191–8 (213–20).
4. A. Badiou, 'Mallarmé's Method: Subtraction and Isolation', in *Conditions*, London: Continuum, 2008, pp. 49–67 (108–29).
5. A. Badiou, 'A French Philosopher Responds to a Polish Poet' and 'A Poetic Dialectic: Labîd ben Rabi'a and Mallarmé', in *Handbook of Inaesthetics*, Stanford, CA: Stanford University Press, 2005.
6. Badiou, *Logic of Worlds*, op. cit., p. 548 (573).
7. Badiou, *Being and Event*, op. cit., pp. 192–3 (214–15).
8. Ibid., p. 193.
9. Badiou, *Handbook of Inaesthetics*, op. cit., p. 12 (25).

10. Badiou, *Théorie du sujet*, op. cit., pp. 92–128.
11. Badiou, *Conditions*, op. cit., pp. 49–53 (108–13).
12. Badiou, *Théorie du sujet*, op. cit., p. 92.
13. Badiou, *Handbook of Inaesthetics*, op. cit., p. 42 (70).
14. Badiou, *Conditions*, op. cit., p. 49 (109). This 'review from scratch' in French is a *mise à plat*, a flattening out or etymological ex-plication.
15. Ibid., p. 110.
16. Badiou, *Being and Event*, op. cit., p. 191 (213).
17. L. Carroll, *Alice's Adventures in Wonderland*, Harmondsworth: Penguin, 1994, p. 72.
18. J.-J. Lecercle, *Interpretation as Pragmatics*, Basingstoke: Macmillan, 1999.
19. J.-C. Milner, *Constats*, Paris: Gallimard, 1999, p. 149.
20. S. Mallarmé, *Œuvres Complètes*, Paris: Gallimard (Bibliothèque de la Pléiade), 1945, p. 1503.
21. See Lecercle, *Interpretation as Pragmatics*, op. cit., pp. 4–5.
22. M. J. Reddy, 'The Conduit Metaphor – A Case of Frame Conflict in Language about Language', in A. Ortony (ed.), *Metaphor and Thought*, Cambridge: Cambridge University Press, 1979, pp. 284–324.
23. A. Badiou, *Le concept de modèle*, Paris: Maspéro, 1969; new edition: Paris: Fayard, 2007.
24. O. Feltham, *Alain Badiou. Live Theory*. London: Continuum, 2008, pp. 129–31.
25. G. Deleuze, 'The Exhausted', in *Essays Critical and Clinical*, London: Verso, 1998, pp. 152–74.
26. Badiou, *Conditions*, op. cit., p. 24 (81).
27. Ibid., pp. 18–19 (74).
28. Badiou, *Handbook of Inaesthetics*, op. cit., pp. 17–18 (33).
29. Ibid., p. 18 (33).
30. Ibid., p. 19 (36).
31. Badiou, *Théorie du sujet*, op. cit., p. 204.
32. Badiou, *Handbook of Inaesthetics*, op. cit., p. 33 (56).
33. Badiou, *Conditions*, op. cit., p. 36 (94).
34. Badiou, *Handbook of Inaesthetics*, op. cit., p. 6 (16).
35. Badiou, *Conditions*, op. cit., p. 43 (101).
36. Badiou, *Handbook of Inaesthetics*, op. cit., p. xiv (7).
37. Badiou, *Conditions*, op. cit., p. 49 (109).
38. Badiou, *Handbook of Inaesthetics*, op. cit., p. 29 (50).
39. Ibid., pp. 139–40 (213–14).
40. Ibid., p. 36 (62).
41. Ibid., p. 24 (43).
42. Ibid., pp. 72–7 (113–20).
43. Feltham, *Alain Badiou*, op. cit., p. 137.
44. Badiou, *Handbook of Inaesthetics*, op. cit., p. 23 (41).

45. See J.-J. Lecercle, *Deleuze and Language*, London: Palgrave, 2002, ch. 6.
46. A. Badiou, 'La méthode de Rimbaud', in *Conditions*, op. cit., pp. 130–54.
47. K. Ross, *The Emergence of Social Space*, London: Verso, 2008.
48. Ibid., p. 65.
49. Badiou, *Handbook of Inaesthetics*, op. cit., p. 12 (24–5).

5

A Modernist Canon? Badiou and Deleuze Read Beckett

A modernist canon

Badiou and Deleuze both indulge in a canon, which means two things: they defend a number of writers about whom they write extensively; and this personal choice they project onto a theory of literature based on a discrimination of great art and a rejection of false or doxic art, what Badiou calls the art of communication and commerce. There is no cultural relativism in either Badiou or Deleuze: there are great texts, faithful either to the event or to life, and the task of the philosopher-critic is to find them and extol their greatness.

Being the result of personal taste and biographical chance (as is the case with Deleuze's admiration of Anglo-American literature), their canons somewhat differ. But, which is much more relevant, they also intersect to a considerable extent: in a word, both their canons are modernist canons. Thus Deleuze's canon will include Proust, Kafka, Artaud, Beckett and Woolf, with extensions to Carroll, Sacher Masoch and Melville, whereas Badiou's canon will include Beckett, Pessoa, Celan and Mandelstam, with extension to Mallarmé and Rimbaud. In his 'Third Sketch for a Manifesto of Affirmationist Art', Badiou takes mischievous delight in the adolescent game of making a list of great twentieth-century artists: Pessoa, Picasso, Schönberg, Brecht, Zadkine, Chaplin, Faulkner, Merle Cunningham; but also Wallace Stevens, Mandelstam, Celan, Berg, Bartok, Pirandello, Claudel and Brancusi; and again, Woolf, Mansfield, Beckett and Malraux.[1] I have not quoted the list in full, but we note that, if we except the absence of Proust (for whom, unlike Deleuze, Badiou has little taste) and D. H. Lawrence, this is essentially a modernist canon, vigorously defended in these our postmodern times (the French version of Badiou's text appeared in 2004).[2] We also note that for Badiou there is no unified art of literature (unlike painting – represented in the list by Picasso, music – Schönberg, or sculpture

– Zadkine), as 'literary' texts are distributed across the poem (Pessoa), the theatre (Brecht) and the novel (Faulkner).

And of course, we note that the core of the intersection of Deleuze's and Badiou's canons is Beckett, to whom they both devoted a separate, if brief, text and to whose work they come back repeatedly in the course of their *oeuvre*.[3] The English version of Badiou's collected texts on Beckett has three essays on top of the text of the short book,[4] and the index of literary references in Deleuze's works has a whole page and no less than fifty-two entries.[5]

The adoption of a modernist literary canon is not original to Badiou and Deleuze: they share it with the so-called 'poststructuralist' philosophers, a category that includes Derrida, Lyotard and Foucault, that sometimes includes Deleuze (a somewhat doubtful ascription) and emphatically fails to include Badiou (for whom they are the modern Sophists). The question, therefore, is raised of this rather strange consensus.

There is a general answer to this question in Jameson's critique of what he calls 'the ideology of modernism' in *A Singular Modernity*: for him, the very idea of a canon is a modernist stance, and consequently a canon is always a modernist canon.[6] My question, therefore, is naive: it is always-already answered. But Jameson's assertion is highly questionable, not least in that it talks of *a* canon: we have learnt to come to terms with the fact that there is more than one canon, that our academic canon, even if it is the best, is no longer the most influential, etc. Even if we forget about the vulgar middle-brow canons that dominate the current field (the canons of publishers, school boards and reading groups), the canon is still declined in the plural: Lukács's realist canon is not a modernist canon. And one might expect that 'poststructuralist' philosophers would adopt a postmodernist literary canon. But they don't.

Deleuze and Badiou, however, do believe in a canon of 'great' literature. And this apparently essentialist view of literature needs to be explained. Jameson himself provides another answer: Deleuze, Foucault and Lyotard are 'quintessentially' modernist philosophers. Thus, 'like Deleuze, Lyotard was himself in many ways a quintessential modernist, passionately committed to the eruption of the genuinely, the radically and, dare one say, the authentically new: a commitment which ultimately marks the politics of both men [. . .] as aesthetic.'[7] We note the innuendo in the last words of the quote, which remind us of Benjamin's characterisation of the politics of

A Modernist Canon? Badiou and Deleuze Read Beckett

national-socialism as aesthetic, although the commitment to the radically new does concern both Badiou and Deleuze.

Nevertheless, Jameson is aware of our question, as the following passage shows (he is speaking of the aesthetics of de Man and Adorno):

> [E]ach is certainly to be counted as a modernist in his own fashion (as are, philosophically and aesthetically, yet in their various unique ways, Deleuze, Lyotard and Foucault, whose 'poststructuralism' – to raise a flag of passionate discord and heated debate – might rather have seemed consistent with some larger narrative of the postmodern).[8]

A few pages later he even contends that one cannot even call Deleuze a 'closet' modernist because of his explicit commitment to art and to the New.[9]

We need not necessarily adopt Jameson's definition of modernism as the cult of the New, which may sound more than a little reductive. But I shall briefly explore the intuition that Deleuze, but not Badiou, is a 'quintessentially' modernist philosopher.

Modernism in Foucault and Jameson

An elementary characteristic of literary modernism, which it is supposed to share with poststructuralist philosophers, is its critique of representation. The modernist break with realism and its attempt at representation finds its equivalent, for instance, either in the contrast between presentation and representation that sustains the argument in Lyotard's *Discours, figure*,[10] or in the theory of literature sketched by Foucault in two famous passages of *The Order of Things*. The first passage occurs at the end of the second chapter, a chapter entitled 'La Prose du monde'.[11] Foucault is trying to characterise the passage from Renaissance *episteme* to the two *epistemai* that can be called 'modern', the classical *episteme* of the seventeenth and eighteenth centuries, and the truly modern *episteme* of the nineteenth and twentieth centuries. He is analysing 'the moments when things and words parted for good', 'an immense reorganisation of culture', as he calls it. This involves a characterisation of the function of literature, of its essence, and an account of its appearance, a periodisation. For literature, it seems, as symptom and heuristic device, plays a considerable part in our attempts at periodisation (this is strikingly the case in Rancière's theory of literature).[12]

The second passage occurs at the end of Chapter 4, entitled

'Parler'.[13] The chapter deals with the place of language in the classical *episteme*, and the text provides an account of both language and literature around the practice of naming: it stresses the crucial importance of the work of Sade (a typical hero of this canon, from Lacan to Adorno, even if his 'modernism' is questionable).

A general theory of literature is thus offered (the boldness of the gesture, in these our anti-essentialist times, hardly needs to be emphasised). But it has a function: it serves to bolster up the periodisation of Foucault's archaeology, which is divided into four periods. Jameson's account provides a convenient summary.[14] There are four historical moments. The first is the pre-modern moment 'in which elements of the medieval are combined with the more superstitious features of the Renaissance'. The second is the classical moment of representation. The third is characterised by Jameson as 'the very moment of the invention of modern history as such, the moment of historicism, vitalism and humanism.' We could call this the moment of literature. But there is a fourth period, one that is hardly with us yet, 'a shadowy and prophetic realm, the realm of language and death, which lives in the interstices of modernity as its negation and denial.' That literature is also concerned with this moment, that it is in fact the privileged inscription of this moment (a privilege that is embodied in the choice of a canon), is clear: and that moment may rightly be called the moment of modernism.

We understand why Badiou cannot be called a modernist: he certainly does not belong to that 'fourth moment', the moment of language and death, as he rejects any centrality of language to philosophy and his thought is one of infinity as opposed to finitude, and the immortality to which the human subject must aspire rather than the obsession with death that characterises the melancholy side of contemporary philosophy. We also understand why Deleuze might be called a modernist philosopher. We note the appearance, in Jameson's account, of a concept to which Deleuze is not indifferent, the concept of vitalism. We also note, which is more to the point, that the 'dogmatic image of thought' which Deleuze wishes to overturn has representation for its central characteristic. Deleuze's 'modernism', if there is such a thing, will be closely associated with his critique of representation.

A critique of representation

We may start with a puzzle well known to students of Deleuze and which we have already encountered: the contradiction between his notorious hostility to metaphor (there are numerous passages in his work that insist on this) and his equally notoriously metaphorical style.[15] It is all very well to claim that metaphor is one of the reasons why one must despair of literature or to coin the slogan 'not metaphor but metamorphosis', but there is a problem if one, in the same breath, describes a face as a combination of a black hole and a blank wall. The black hole is a metaphor borrowed from one of the hard sciences and the whole construction of the concept of 'face' (and the co-occurrent concept of 'faciality', 'visagéité') is itself metaphorical (which does not mean that the concept has no interest – witness the use Garin Dowd makes of it in his study of Beckett after Deleuze and Guattari).[16]

There is, however, good reason for Deleuze's hostility to metaphor: it is part and parcel of a thoroughgoing critique of representation. We may start from a well known passage in the second chapter of *Anti-Oedipus*, in a section entitled, in the English translation 'The Imperialism of Oedipus':

> The whole of desiring *production* is crushed, subjected to the requirements of *representation*, and to the dreary games of what is representative and represented in representation. And there is the essential thing: the reproduction of representation, in the process as well as theory of the cure. The productive unconscious makes way for an unconscious that knows only how to express itself – express itself in myth, in tragedy, in dream.[17]

We find here, in a nutshell, the essence of Deleuze and Guattari's critique of psychoanalysis, in the contrasts between production and representation, which is linked to reproduction, and between the productive and the representative unconscious (on what psychoanalysts are fond of calling *l'autre scène*). Let us try to decline the moments of this critique of representation.

The critique, naturally, will start from the double ambiguity of the term: like all deverbal nouns ending in '-tion' (interpretation for instance), it is ambiguous between process and result (the process of representing yields, as its end-result, a representation), and the prefix 're-' is ambiguous between the 're-' of repetition (representation is second degree presentation) and the 're-' of regress (representation is a moving away, and backwards, from presentation). Familiar philosophical contrasts are thus evoked: similitude versus resemblance, presence versus separation, difference and repetition, etc. The last of these contrasts, of course, is closest to Deleuze's philosophical concerns.

To put it briefly, from the linguistic analysis of the ambiguities of the term, a concept of representation may be constructed around the five following characteristics:

1. Representation is characterised by a *difference* between representative and represented: they do not belong to the same order of being.
2. Representation is characterised by the *separation* between representative and represented: there is no contiguity or continuity between them.
3. The third characteristic is *replacement*: the representative is present in the absence of the represented, for that is the essence of his (or its) representativeness.
4. The fourth is *hierarchy*. The representative and the represented are not only separated, but differently valued. The direction of the hierarchic relation may vary: often the representative dominates the represented, but the opposite may be true as well.
5. The fifth and last characteristic is the *generalisation*, or *abstraction*, of the representative from the represented.

It would be easy to decline the five characteristics of representations here suggested in all the fields where the concept operates, from image and word to politics. Thus the word is different from its referent; it is separated from it, except in the case of labels or Swift's island of Laputa; it replaces it in its absence (that is the essential characteristic of a sign); it is deemed to be less important than its referent, being a tool for reference that satisfies the needs of communication (although sometimes the relation, or the direction of fit, as Searle calls it, is reversed, as in the case of performative utterances); and it generalises and abstracts, as the word is the carrier of a linguistic notion, which in the best of cases becomes a philosophical concept.

We could play the same game with political representation. The King, or the MP for that matter, in spite of proclamations to the contrary, is different from his subjects, or constituents, in terms of money, power, lifestyle and Spitting Image puppet (remember that the King has two bodies: one more than the average subject). The system of democratic representation is, as we know, a system in which everybody is eligible but only the elect are elected. Not anybody can be a candidate with a chance of succeeding and the metamorphosis is a long process. The King, but also the MP, is separated from his subjects or constituents, not being answerable till the next election, if there is one, and not being obliged to keep his promises: thus Tony

A Modernist Canon? Badiou and Deleuze Read Beckett

Blair goes to war and Nicolas Sarkozy is elected on the basis of electoral promises he has no means of keeping. The King, or the MP, replaces his subjects or constituents, he acts in their place. This is not a Swiss canton or the *agora* in Athens, and not everybody can have a seat in parliament. The King, naturally, is in a hierarchic position vis à vis his subjects. So is, in spite of proclamations to the contrary, the MP. Lastly, the King, or the MP, is abstracted from the generality of subjects or constituents: this is embodied in the fiction that the MP represents not only the constituents that have voted for him, but the totality of his (the word is significant) constituents.

But the five characteristics of representation can also account for the contrast between the metaphoric and the metamorphic, using the characteristic Deleuzean device of the correlation. Metaphor first (as the climax of the logic of representation and the point where it gives rise to another logic). First, metaphor is based on difference: there must be sufficient distance between tenor and vehicle for the metaphor to work: you do not choose your metaphors if the objects of the implicit simile are too closely related. Second, this difference involves separation: if the literal relation is by definition true (a rose is a rose is a rose), the metaphorical relation is blatantly false (Sally is *not* an English rose). The metaphorical sign is a false sign, separated from the literal sign that picks out the referent. Thirdly, metaphor involves replacement. The evoked tenor of the metaphor (the literal lion that Richard is not) is doubly absent: replaced by the true sign, displaced in the metaphorical sign. In Plato's gradient of representation via signs, metaphor is the idol to the literal icon: it completely cancels the point of departure of the signifying process, which normally starts with the referent. Fourthly, metaphor involves hierarchy. That relation has always been central to the theory of metaphor. The usual posture is that literal meaning, in so far as it is 'true', is more valuable than metaphorical meaning, which it precedes. But this is not always the case: the tradition of hostility to metaphor (from Locke and Hobbes onwards) is now opposed by another tradition, of the centrality of metaphor, from Rousseau and Vico to de Man. Lastly, metaphor involves abstraction. Whether ontological, orientational or structural (I am using Lakoff and Johnson's classification here),[18] metaphor abstracts and generalises.

This position of metaphor as the climax of representation can be systematically contrasted with metamorphosis. With metamorphosis, in spite of the obvious ontological difference between mice and horses, a pumpkin and a carriage, there is no parallelism in the links between words (taken literally or metaphorically) and their referents, because words and things are taken as being on the same ontological level, and a direct word–object linking which shortcuts the sign process becomes possible: words no longer represent objects because they are themselves objects (they have material shape, they exert force, they mix with objects). Secondly, there is no separation through obvious falsity: a metamorphic Richard *is* a lion. From this point of view, metaphor is seen as an attempt to deflate the violent potential of words, their ability to intervene, as objects, among objects: suddenly, like the werewolf in our favourite horror film, Richard roars in his rage and claws his opponent into shreds. Thirdly, there is no replacement of tenor by vehicle. In metamorphosis, as in a dream, the chessboard actually turns into a railway and the train, not its image, is in the mind (you have recognised the world of Lewis Carroll's *Through the Looking-Glass*). Neither element in the transformation is allowed to stand for the other. Metamorphosis connects what metaphor, in spite of its revolutionary aura, carefully keeps apart, at a safe distance. Fourthly, since there is neither difference nor possible replacement, there is no hierarchy between the two terms involved in metamorphosis. What we have is not a hierarchic tree, whatever its direction, but an anarchic rhizome. Deleuze's ontology is sometimes said to be 'flat'[19] because all entities exist on the same plane of immanence. Lastly, metamorphosis fails to abstract and generalise for reasons that are by now entirely clear: the world of metamorphosis is a world of singularities, not abstractions. It appears, therefore, that Deleuze's preference for metamorphosis over metaphor is a modernist stance.

Deleuze as modernist

In Foucault's periodisation, we might be inclined to interpret modernism as the literary expression of the second modern period, the period of literature, which would make postmodernism the incarnation of the shadowy fourth period, in the interstices of modernity. The immediate historical problem is that, for Foucault, that period goes from the nineteenth century to structuralism, with the relevant break occurring roughly with Romanticism, a traditional candidate for the break with classicism. Hence the question of the historical place of modernism is still unanswered.

There is an answer in Jameson, where modernism is the literary name for modernity as a whole, conceived as an internal critique of

A Modernist Canon? Badiou and Deleuze Read Beckett

both *epistemai*: a critique of the classical *episteme* of representation, and a critique of the nineteenth-century *episteme* characterised by humanism and historicism. Hence the rightful place of modernism is the fourth period, where this double critique is enacted. Modernism is the literary incarnation of a double cultural shift.

The consequences of this are interesting. We have already seen some of them. First, modernism is synonymous with literature, and the canon of literature can only be the canon of modernism. Second, modernism not only precedes, but is always already beyond, or in advance of, postmodernism. Third, we may even go further and state that postmodernism, in the field of literature, cannot exist, as its positions are always already pre-empted by modernism. So, if, for the needs of critical contrast, we wish to find the natural opponent of modernism, there is no point in looking for it in postmodernism.

But there is a place where such contrast can be usefully found, thus allowing us to produce non-trivial characteristics of modernism (beyond the Jamesonian 'obsession with the New', which is too pat): in the debate with Marxism, its arch-enemy. One only has to think of the direct polemics between Lukács, Brecht and Bloch in the 1920s, or of the indirect polemics, later on, between Lukács and Adorno. Lukács still remains the critic who preferred Thomas Mann and Romain Rolland to Joyce and Beckett.

In Eugene Lunn's book on modernism and Marxism we find a characterisation of modernism. I shall take that necessarily simplistic account with the necessary pinch of salt, but it will provide a starting point. Lunn ascribes the four following characteristics to modernism:[20] (1) aesthetic self-consciousness or self-reflexiveness; (2) simultaneity, juxtaposition or *montage*; (3) paradox, ambiguity and uncertainty; (4) the demise of the integrated individual subject. When contrasted with the four equivalent characteristics he ascribes to realism (typicality, individuality, organic plot construction and the presentation of humans as subjects as well as objects of history), they make a fairly clear, if slightly gross or exaggerated, picture: the picture of the opposition between realist representation and modernist presentation (even if the first characteristic ascribed to modernism, reflexivity, is shared, at least in Foucault's interpretation, with classical representation). So the general name of the game is the presentation of chaotic experience in its state of near chaos, rather than the ordering of representation. And there is a link between this feature, which is the central one, and the demise of the integrated subject: the integrated individual subject it is that orders chaos into a representation.

If we take this as a very rough picture of modernism, we are in a position to account for Deleuze as a modernist: we may consider that his philosophy exemplifies the four characteristics ascribed by Lunn to modernism, without forcing the text of either Deleuze or Lunn.

Thus the aesthetic self-reflexiveness of literary modernism is reflected in the conscious writerly stance of the work of Deleuze and Guattari: philosophy as a kind of writing, with a vengeance. Witness the all too famous opening of *Anti-Oedipus*, with its provocative linguistic playfulness: 'It is at work everywhere, functioning smoothly at times, at other times in fits and starts. It breathes, it heats, it eats. It shits and fucks. What a mistake to have ever said *the* id. Everywhere it is machines – real ones, not figurative ones . . .'[21] We note of course the usual paradox: the text expresses Deleuze's hostility to metaphor, here in the guise of the 'figurative', and yet it engages in a series of rhetorical tropes, the object of which is the third person pronoun, 'it', on which the text opens (for instance, the narrative trope of topicalisation, of the *quis* who will be revealed as the hero of the tale).

The second characteristic, the fragmentation of literary modernism (juxtaposition or *montage*), finds consonance not only in Deleuze's keen interest in the cinema (*montage* is no longer a mere technical device, it becomes a philosophical concept), but in his conception of the text as rhizome (rather than a tree, with univocal branching causality and hierarchy, as in Chomsky's conception of syntax), with concomitant effects of juxtaposition (Deleuze, being a philosopher of surfaces, is the philosopher of cartography and *calque*), of intensities and regimes of signs.

The third characteristic of literary modernism, paradox, is familiar to readers of Deleuze, being the central concept of *Logique du sens*, which is divided not into chapters, but into 'series of paradoxes', some of them originating in Lewis Carroll. Such paradoxes provide the characterisation of sense (as opposed to the fixed meaning of *doxa* which in Deleuze goes under the names of good sense and common sense).[22] The very concept of sense as opposed to meaning is based on systematic ambiguity: it is that which (chrono)logically precedes meaning, and therefore has neither the shared consensual fixity of common sense, nor the right directionality of good sense (here of course Deleuze is punning on the two meanings of the French word *sens*). In the words of the medieval philosopher Nicolas d'Hautrecourt, the formula of sense is *contradictoria ad invicem idem significant* ('contradictories have the same sense'). From this theory of meaning and sense Deleuze derives nothing less than a fully fledged theory of language.[23]

The fourth characteristic of literary modernism, the demise of the integrated individual subject, is perhaps the one that is most spectacularly exemplified in Deleuze's philosophy. It is perhaps in his philosophy more than in anyone else's that the all-pervading concept of subject (from philosophies of consciousness to psychoanalysis) is most explicitly superseded – this is a striking difference from Badiou, who clings to a concept of a subject, albeit not the subject traditionally conceived as a unitary centre of consciousness or action. And it is superseded in two ways or two directions: in the multiplicity and ontological mixture or rather 'flatness' of the collective assemblage of enunciation; and in the individuation of an a-personal, a-subjective, pre-individual haecceity.

So the choice of a canon of modernist writers is coherent with crucial aspects of Deleuze's philosophy: his adoption of those texts is not merely due to a blind following of the current avant-garde: he can in fact be called a modernist philosopher, perhaps even a modernist linguist. For this is the interesting paradox of this characterisation which sharply distinguishes Deleuze from Badiou: in many ways, in the tradition of Bergson, Deleuze resists the linguistic turn taken by contemporary philosophy. But his 'modernism' means that he has a concept of language (remember that Jameson defines Foucault's 'fourth period' as 'the realm of language' and such a reflexive concept of language is characteristic of literary modernism, in advance of postmodernism). I have tried elsewhere to show that language is a point of entry, in the shape of a problem, to Deleuze's philosophy.[24] We understand the consonance of Deleuze's philosophy with literature, the art of language (Deleuze, unlike Badiou, has a concept of *écriture* and style), which explains the sheer range of his literary corpus and the privileging of modernist writers as the centre of his literary canon. But there remains a question: where is Badiou situated in all this?

Badiou reads Beckett

Badiou is emphatically not a modernist philosopher (and Jameson is careful not to include him in his list). His rejection of the linguistic turn is *sans appel*, he refuses to let concepts of language and style play a role in his philosophy and the four characteristics of Lunn's simplified theory of modernism do not in the least fit him: although he is a writer himself, there is no aesthetic self-relexiveness in his writing of philosophy, rather the asceticism of formalisation; the total coherence of his chain of concepts (Badiou is the archetype of systematic philosophers) has nothing to do with juxtaposition and montage; he has no time for the ambiguity and uncertainty in which modernism and postmodernism revel: his is a philosophy of strong affirmation and Badiou is not much troubled by ambiguity or doubt; and, as we saw, he retains a concept of subject, even if his subject is not the 'integrated and individual subject' whose demise modernism celebrates. For Badiou the subject is collective, as in the couple who construct a procedure of fidelity to the event of a *coup de foudre*; and the subject of art is neither the author nor the reader, but the work itself. Rancière, however, has argued that Badiou cannot be called an unqualified modernist because of his rejection of the role of language in art (of the languages of art) in favour of the Platonist Idea, but that he is nevertheless a 'twisted modernist' in his insistence on subtraction, an anti-mimetic position that absolves art of any obligation to imitate external reality, and in his assertion that the truths of art are proper to it: for Rancière these are two characteristics of modernism, which makes Badiou an 'undoubted', if twisted, modernist.[25]

It is no wonder, therefore, that Badiou is an obsessive reader of modernist literature, with two qualifications: his corpus is almost exclusively poetic (in spite of the presence of Faulkner, Woolf and Mansfield in the list quoted above, he does not really engage with the modernist novel – as we saw, a paradox for an author who is a novelist himself) and not exclusively modernist as Mallarmé and Rimbaud figure prominently in it. But he does read Beckett obsessively.

Badiou's reading of Beckett is now well documented. His texts have been collected in an English translation, complete with a long introduction by Nina Power and Alberto Toscano and a postface by Andrew Gibson, and Andrew Gibson has devoted a massive volume to Beckett and Badiou.[26] And this reading has a number of striking characteristics.

1. Badiou's reading goes against the grain (a familiar tactic with him) of traditional and doxic readings of Beckett as an existentialist writer, 'a writer of the absurd, of despair, of empty skies, of incommunicability and eternal solitude'.[27] It is true that Beckett criticism has moved away from this, as Gibson demonstrates in his postface, but Badiou blissfully ignores such criticism: he is in fact nostalgically evoking his own youth and himself as a Sartrian 'young cretin'[28] (he

ascribes that interesting quality not only to himself but to youth in general), whose task, as he then thought, was 'to complete Sartre's theory of freedom by means of a careful investigation into the opacities of the signifier.'[29] Perhaps this is the source of his later refusal to treat language as an object worthy of philosophical analysis, as the inconsistent alliance between nihilism and the imperative of language was typical of the young cretin that he claims to have been. Against this critical *doxa*, the older Badiou constructs a reading of Beckett as the writer of tireless desire (or desire unstoppable), of exactitude and courage, but also of joy, the joy that provokes not the grin of irony but the frank laughter of comedy. That such a reading goes against the *sensus communis* of traditional readings of Beckett is obvious.

2. This reading is also a strange reading, in that a concept of beauty lies at the centre of it. 'Beauty' has come to be a danger word for literary critics, and you would be hard put to find a contemporary analysis of Keats's poems that would be conducted in terms of their beauty. But Badiou, as always, is indifferent to such *doxa*, especially as the term, which might be taken to make trivial sense in the case of Keats, appears to be singularly ill-chosen in the case of Beckett: you would hardly describe the two lovers on their bench in the opening pages of *Watt*, or the reaction of Mr Hackett who is annoyed by their presence on his bench, as 'beautiful'. But 'beauty', the title of the second section of Badiou's *Beckett*, is given a technical meaning in three ways. First, beauty is the specific characteristic of literature as the art of language, in so far as it works on and subverts ordinary or natural language. In a move that is reminiscent of Deleuze's analysis of Beckett as that Irishman who writes in French and thus turns every language, including his own, into a foreign tongue, Badiou links beauty with Beckett's specific practice of language:

> Beckett truly was a constant and attentive servant of beauty, which is why, at a distance from himself (at a distance from nature, from a 'natural' language, and at a distance from the mother, from the mother-tongue) he called upon the services of a secondary and learnt idiom, a 'foreign' language: French.[30]

So beauty is in that distance from nature, from the natural tongue and of the writer from himself. Secondly, beauty is captured by a number of stylistic operations:

> Rectification, or the work on the isolation of terms. Expansion, or the poetic incision of memory. Declaration, or the function of emergence of

prose. Declension, or the tender cadence of disaster. Interruption, or the maxims of comedy. Elongation, or the phrased embodiment of variants.³¹

The names of these operations all make stylistic sense, in that they seem to describe what might be called the 'Beckett sentence'. Yet some of the glosses of these names seem to forget language: I can understand that 'elongation' (of the Beckett sentence) should be 'the phrased embodiment of variants', as this corresponds to the reader's experience of a Beckett text as the exhaustion of possibilities (a stylistic device that is prevalent in *Watt*), but I cannot make stylistic sense of 'declension' (a technical word in grammatical discourse) as 'the tender cadence of disaster'. This is because the third characteristic of beauty takes us way beyond language: '[T]he destiny of beauty, and in particular of the beauty that Beckett aims at, is to separate. To separate appearance, which it both restores and obliterates, from the universal core of experience.' ³²

3. Badiou's reading of Beckett, being, as may be expected, a strong reading, is based on an intervention in the Beckett corpus. In a move reminiscent of Althusser's separation, through epistemological break, between the young, humanist Marx and the later, scientific Marx, he holds that there is a break in Beckett's *oeuvre* in the 1960s with *How It Is*, when the three 'functions' of movement (how to move, how to rest), being (what there is, questions of identity) and language (the imperative of language, the centrality of silence) are supplemented with a fourth, the encounter with the other. In such supplementation, Badiou sees the abandonment of Beckett's Cartesianism and a conversion to a form of Platonism, an opening up to the thought of the event. Naturally, such intervention provokes counter-readings. Even Andrew Gibson, the Beckett critic most sympathetic to Badiou, casts doubts on the brutality of this *coupure*: it is doubtful that such a clear-cut separation can be discerned. Nevertheless, in this matter, Badiou is not alone; he follows one of the critical traditions among Beckett scholars, and we may note that in 'The Exhausted', Deleuze also holds that *How It Is* is a landmark in Beckett's *oeuvre*.³³

4. The main word has been uttered: what Badiou reads in Beckett is an ascesis towards thought, the thought of the event. Beckett's is a Platonism of the event:

> We can see that the ascesis – metaphorically enacted as loss, destitution, poverty, a relentlessness based on almost nothing – leads to a conceptual

economy of an ancient or Platonic type. If we disregard (and Beckett's prose is the movement of this disregard, of this abandon) what is inessential, what distracts us (in Pascal's sense), we see that generic humanity can be reduced to the complex of movement, of rest (of dying), of language (as imperative without respite) and of the paradoxes of the Same and the Other. We are very close to what Plato, in *The Sophist*, names as the five supreme genera: Being, Sameness, Movement, Rest, and Other. If Plato the philosopher uses these to determine the general conditions for all thinking, then Beckett the writer intends, through the ascetic movement of prose, to present in fiction the atemporal determinants of humanity.[34]

Reading for the event means that there is a consonance between Beckett's literary thought and the thought of the philosopher who reads him. Indeed, Badiou's reading often sounds like a roll call of the main concepts of his system. This is how Andrew Gibson, whose reading of Beckett is closest to Badiou's (even if it is often critical of him), sums up this consonance:

> I have argued for the relevance to Beckett's work of many of the key terms in Badiou's philosophy: subtraction, restricted action, actual infinity, the event, subjectification, the logic of appearance, naming, fidelity, apagogic reason, the waiting subject, investigations, inexistents, patience, vigilance, objectivity, undecidables, indiscernibles and unnameables, *événementialité* and the event of the event.[35]

Even if we note an inflexion which is Gibson's own (apagogic reason, *événementialité*, the event of the event are his terms as much as Badiou's), even if he immediately adds that although they offer an understanding of Beckett's 'extreme brilliance of purpose', Badiou's use of them to read Beckett is somewhat 'unsatisfying', we note the presence in that list of the chain of concepts that make up Badiou's theory of the event (subtraction, subjectification, naming, fidelity, etc.), with a hint of the later work (logic of appearance).

5. There is one last aspect of Badiou's strong reading of Beckett which is relevant to my analysis. A strong reading, as we have seen, is not afraid of paradox. One of the paradoxes of Badiou's reading of Mallarmé is that he reads the poems for their latent prose (which justifies the prose summary of the sonnets with which he begins his reading). Now that he is reading Beckett's prose, he celebrates the 'latent poem' that governs it:

> The effect of this oscillation and this caesura is that no single literary genre can command the comprehension of Beckett's enterprise. The

novel form is still perceptible in *Molloy*, but in *The Unnameable* it is exhausted, though it is not possible to say that the poem prevails – even if the cadence, the disposition of the paragraphs and the intrinsic value of the visions indicate that the text is governed by what could be defined as a 'latent poem'.[36]

The passage has two interesting aspects. The first is the appearance of stylistic terms like 'cadence', which suggest that reading the literary text for its language might be relevant after all, even if the remark about 'the disposition of the paragraphs' is immediately followed by 'the intrinsic value of the vision', where we have abandoned the materiality of the language of the text. The second is the recurrence of the word 'latent' (the latent prose, the latent poem), which inscribes the paradox I mentioned: the Freudian connotation of the term confirms the idea that Badiou's concept of literary reading is predicated on what I have called the 'tin-opener' theory of interpretation. But Badiou's theory of reading is in fact more complex. Reading for the latent poem applies to a moment in Beckett's work, the moment of transition, the moment of *The Unnameable*, neither fowl nor fish, neither novel nor poem. It must be abandoned when we come to the break. Thus *Worstward Ho* (which is sometimes called a novel but hardly reads like one) 'is not governed by a sort of latent poem' and must be read otherwise. How? As a philosophical treatise: 'It is entirely possible to read *Worstward Ho* as a short philosophical treatise, as a treatment in shorthand of the question of being.'[37] The paradox rebounds: we no longer read the prose text for its latent poem, we read the work of literature for its latent (or not so latent) philosophy: a shorthand kind of philosophy, which presumably needs the gaze of the philosopher to articulate its condensed philosophical contents in full. As we shall see, this paradoxical method of reading raises serious problems: Beckett risks being taken for a proto-Badiou, a literary John the Baptist announcing the advent of his philosophical Christ, and the status of the event whose truth procedure the literary text constructs becomes highly problematic.[38]

Because all this is rather abstract, let us look at how Badiou reads a single text, *Ill Seen Ill Said*. In the course of a chapter in the Beckett book entitled 'The event and its name', Badiou reads the following paragraph:

> Alone the face remains. Of the rest beneath its covering no trace. During the inspection a sudden sound. Starting without consequence for the gaze the mind awakes. How explain it? And without going so far how say it?

> Far behind the eye the quest begins. What time the event recedes. When suddenly to the rescue it comes again. Forthwith the uncommon common noun collapsion. Reinforced a little later if not enfeebled by the infrequent slumberous. A slumberous collapsion. Two. Then far from the still agonizing eye a gleam of hope. By the grace of these modest beginnings. With a second sight the shack in ruins. To scrute together with the inscrutable face. All curiosity spent.[39]

Badiou gives a brilliant account of the movement of what Gibson, in his reading of Badiou's reading of the passage, calls 'a phenomenology of the event' (and he stresses the importance of the passage for Badiou's understanding of Beckett as a whole).[40] This movement goes through the following stages: (1) the 'inspection' of the situation that serves as a starting point, through the normal activity of seeing; (2) in this situation an event occurs, whose presence is marked by a 'sudden sound'; (3) 'the mind awakes', as 'thought is vigilant under the effect of an event'; (4) the reaction of the mind to the event is not one of understanding (the question of interpretation) but of naming: 'how say it'; (5) the name, inscribed in two rare words, an 'uncommon common noun', 'collapsion', and the adjective 'slumberous', bores a hole in ordinary language – and Badiou notes that the putting together of adjective and noun in a single phrase is paradoxical, as the adjective both 'reinforces' and 'enfeebles' the noun; (6) lastly, the naming of the event produces a 'gleam of hope'. Badiou concludes: 'And though it is certainly nothing more than a commencement, a modest beginning, it is a commencement that comes to the thought that it awakens like an act of grace.'[41] And he adds that such gleam of hope marks the hope of the advent of a truth:

> A truth begins with the organisation of an agreement between, on the one hand, a separable event 'shining with formal clarity' and, on the other, the invention in language of a name that from now on retains this event, even if – inevitably – the event 'recedes' and finally disappears. The name will guarantee within language that the event is sheltered.[42]

Beckett is the poet of the event, as the chain of concepts, event, naming, truth, etc. can be extracted from his text, even if the nature of the event in question is not clear, and the name that Beckett has chosen for it, 'slumberous collapsion', is neither helpful nor hopeful: the name is both uncommon and common, and the common meaning it conveys, that of a collapse, seems to contradict that 'gleam of hope' and 'effect of grace' Badiou reads in the text. Indeed, Gibson, who is too skilful a reader of Beckett not to be slightly worried by the reading he admires, notes that Badiou's reading is based on a single passage of the text: in spite of the title, he notes, what Badiou calls the 'poetics of nomination' is hardly central to the text as a whole; the term 'event' has only one occurrence in the whole text, in this passage (he accounts for this by the rarity of the event); and the larger part of the text 'is representational, if hardly in a Balzacian manner'.[43] And it is true that an old woman waiting for death is an unpromising witness to the radical novelty of the event. But there is worse. Beckett's text is written in paragraphs, and I have quoted the whole paragraph. Badiou, however, does not. He omits the first two and the last two sentences, and it is easy to understand why: they hardly confirm his affirmative interpretation of the text, which is centred on that gleam of hope. The absent sentences provide a negative framework to the advent of the event: 'alone', 'no trace', 'the shack in ruins'. And the *chute* of the paragraph, 'all curiosity spent', introduces a note of resignation if not despair, hardly conducive to the construction of a procedure of truth, with its eager enquiries and fidelity to the radically new. Badiou's reading proceeds through a double extraction: of the passage from the text as a whole; of the core of the passage from the paragraph that frames it. As if the sole presence of the word he was looking for, 'event', was sufficient to colour the whole paragraph and the whole text in the exact shade required. What disappears from Beckett's text is its resolute ambivalence (what Badiou finds is indeed in the text, only to be immediately denied), what Gibson, in his own, even if Badiou inspired, reading of Beckett, calls 'the pathos of intermittency'.

Badiou's reading of this short passage raises a question that can be generalised. If the object of the work of art worthy of that name is the naming of the event, the specificity of the single text is compromised: there is a risk that the event in question is always the same event, the event in general, what Gibson calls the event of the event. This is how Rancière, reading Badiou reading Mallarmé, puts it:

> The inscription of the name and the declaration of the maxim are posited as effects of the poem-form – which is to say, of an apparatus of naming – and following good Althusserian logic, philosophy is then summoned in order to discern the truths encrypted in the poem, even if this means miraculously rediscovering its own, which it claims to have been divested of [. . .] At a stroke, the Mallarmean poem, which is already an allegory of the poem [. . .] becomes in Badiou an allegory of the form of the event in general and of the courage of the thought that withstands its ordeal in particular. Which also means that in this regard it is comparable with

every other poem that allows itself to be bent to the same demonstration, to be assigned the same task of speaking twice, to say the same event of the Idea twice: the first time as a maxim, the second time as an enigma.[44]

What Rancière is suggesting is that Badiou's reading method always yields the same result, whatever the poem or literary text he reads: that it finds what it wanted to find, namely the event and its naming, at the cost of 'bending' the text to its 'demonstration'. It also suggests that, contrary to Badiou's doctrine, the poem cannot really think the truth it encrypts, and needs philosophy to decrypt it, which re-establishes the superiority of philosophy to the text of art, in spite of Badiou's declarations of modesty (philosophy does not produce truths, it only 'compossibilises' the truths that emerge in other fields). In fact, the term 'compossibilise' is the site of a problem: why should the truths of art, politics, science and love need to be 'grasped together', if not in order to produce a general concept of truth (a possibility which Badiou denies, even if his philosophy's main task is to construct it)? It seems to me we are back with the conception of philosophy defended by Third International Marxism under the name of dialectical materialism: one claims to respect the capacity of each science to produce its type of knowledge independently, and the task of philosophy is to produce the general laws (the laws of the dialectic) that apply to every science and compossibilise all sciences. By this means philosophy, which claims to be the servant of science, 'miraculously' recovers its position of superiority, as the science of generalities.

Rancière's critique raises two other problems related to the first. First, if the task of the poem is to speak 'the event of the Idea', we are back to the transparency of language which we already noted when we read Badiou reading Mallarmé: such a decrypting of an encrypted truth ignores the materiality of the language of the text, or, in other words, there is no concept of *écriture* in Badiou (since the task of the reader is to solve the enigma of the text, the role of the language of the text is simply to conceal the truth that it contains). When Badiou, in *Logic of Worlds*, analyses a painting by Hubert Robert, it is in terms of the world it presents and 'the transcendental construction of phenomena'. He pays lip service to the painter's technique and to the materiality of the work, but his analysis is conducted almost exclusively in terms of what the painting represents, so that in a painting, as he says, the figurative or abstract character of the work is not relevant.[45] It would be instructive to compare this attitude to painting to that of Deleuze in his Bacon book, where the materiality of the pictorial gesture is at the centre of the analysis. Secondly, the specific nature of the event in a literary text is not clear. A text, as Badiou says, is not itself an event, but an element in an artistic configuration which seeks to construct the truth of an event: the text, then, is rather a subject in this truth-seeking process of enquiry and fidelity. But an artistic event in that sense cannot be other than a change in artistic paradigm, a literary revolution (even as the event in politics is a revolution, in science a change in paradigm). However, Badiou appears to read the single text for the event to which it bears witness, which is encrypted in it and only recoverable in the traces it has left. And it is obvious that there is more to a Mallarmé sonnet than the trace of the Parnassian poetic 'revolution', if there is such a thing. Three solutions have been offered to this paradox. Badiou sometimes suggests that Mallarmé is to be understood in terms of the traces that a political event, the Paris Commune, with its glorious failure, has left in the situation: in which case, literature seeks to capture an event which has not occurred in its own field, it has a representative rather than a presentative function. Andrew Gibson introduces the concept of 'the event of the event' ('Mallarmé makes an event of the thought of the event'),[46] which again places literature, among the evental fields, in a singular position: its event is a second-degree event, and literature is both less important than other evental fields (there is no direct event in literature) and more so (it has a reflexive function, a function traditionally attributed to philosophy). Nina Power and Alberto Toscano, in their introduction to Badiou's collected texts on Beckett, describe a typology of literary events in the texts Badiou reads: Mallarmé deals with the consequences of the event, his text is situated after the event; Rimbaud deals with the event at the time it occurs, and immediately interrupts the process of fidelity his recognition of the event implies; Beckett tries to think the possibility of the event that is to come, he anticipates it.[47] These three attitudes towards the event are embodied in three qualities of the texts: Mallarmé's patience, Rimbaud's impatience, Beckett's courage.

It would appear that, in spite of such defences, Badiou's reading of literary texts is deeply flawed. It appears to exploit the text, treat it as a pretext for philosophy. Badiou seems to find something in the text only because he sought it, and what he finds is always philosophical propositions, and always the propositions of his own philosophy. The strength of such reading is the strength of the bulldozer. Yet, after this firm condemnation of an exaggeratedly strong reading practice, we are left with a problem, and you will have noted the tentative modal verbs in the first sentences of this paragraph: in spite of the flaws of the reading, Badiou's accounts of single literary texts, of Mallarmé and of Beckett, are compelling and often brilliant. The bulldozing of the text uncovers archaeological treasures. Perhaps those defences are not as off the mark as it seems. Perhaps, when Badiou reads Beckett and finds in his work the rudiments of his philosophy, it is also Beckett that reads Badiou.

Beckett reads Badiou

This is the position of Power and Toscano in their introduction: Beckett is not merely a site for the miraculous rediscovery of Badiou's system. His work raises questions for the system and induces revisions of it: Badiou reading Beckett is also read by him, and the system is not left untouched by the reading. And the point where the system is modified is of extreme interest to us, as it concerns language, which the system so far deliberately neglected. This is how they make their point:

> Beckett does demand from Badiou the recognition, otherwise foreign to his doctrine, of an irreducibility proper to language or speech as a 'region of existence'. Moreover, though language is not itself an object of speculation (whether structural or hermeneutic) or adulation (it is the very stuff of our earthly ordeals), it is nevertheless identified as an ineluctable and ineliminable 'function' of the human, an essential compound of that capacity for thought that determines the existence of humanity. It is this role of language that Badiou is obliged to assume and, in a qualified manner, affirm. What his reconstruction of Beckett does not involve, however, is any specific attention to the 'texture' of language itself – to the operations undergone in Beckett by grammar, to the usage of certain tropes, etc. While the linguistic dimension is indeed ineliminable, what captivates Badiou when it comes to Beckett as a thinker is precisely what emerges from a subtraction *of* and, of course, *through* language.[48]

You will have noted the convoluted and defensive tone of that account. We must rejoice at the thought that Badiou has finally recognised that language was 'an ineluctable function of the human'. Even if such recognition is 'qualified' and reluctant, we should be grateful to Beckett for having provoked it. And you will have noted that such recognition remains abstract, as language cannot be an object of speculation, and the texture of the text is not worthy of the philosopher's attention. Yet, Power and Toscano have a point, and we must look more closely at the treatment of language in Badiou's texts on Beckett.

At first sight, however, we shall be disappointed. The treatment of language in Badiou's texts on Beckett is limited (there is a section entitled 'Being and Language' in the Beckett book, and the order of the terms is relevant), and limited to a small number of ever recurrent propositions or themes:

1. The first is the insistence on reading the latent poem that underlies Beckett's late prose:

    I would say that the prose – segmented into paragraphs – will come to be governed by a *latent poem*. This poem holds together what is given in the texts, but it is not itself given. The thematic recurrences appear on the surface of the text, characterised by their slow motion. Beneath the surface, however, this movement is regulated or unified by an inapparent poetic matrix.[49]

    I am afraid this 'poetic matrix' of the poem is reduced to thematic recurrence, and the ghost of the tin-opener theory of interpretation has not been laid to rest.

2. The second is the statement of the imperative of language. Not only is language an inescapable human function, but saying, in the works of Beckett, has become an imperative: the subject and her language strive towards silence, but language never entirely disappears. 'On. Say on. Be said on.' is the famous opening of *Worstward Ho*.

3. The third is the centrality of naming. This is the main characteristic of Beckett's late prose as regards language: he has renounced his hermeneutic quest for the operation of naming – naming, not meaning (or the absence thereof) is the order of the day.

4. The fourth is that there is a form of violence involved in the operation of naming, a violence done through language and to language: naming subverts the established significations. This is an integral part of the doctrine of the event: naming is itself part of the event and it bores a hole in the language of the situation. A Beckettian way of formulating this is: saying is always ill-saying, well-saying being defined by the adequacy of the saying to the said, which implies that we remain within the language of the situation.[50]

5. In the Beckett book, there is an opening towards the role of fiction and an attempt to think, among the 'pretty three in one', the triple subject in Beckett's texts, the subject of enunciation (the other two are the subject of passivity and the subject of the question).[51]

A Modernist Canon? Badiou and Deleuze Read Beckett

It would be easy to dismiss this by saying that Badiou has a concept of language that is both vague and skeletal. It appears that he has no concept of the material workings of language in the play of signifiers (nor does he want to have one), that he has only the most superficial concept of syntax and that the poetic character of the poem is reduced to the work of the lexicon, to the subversion of established language by naming, whether it takes the form of coinage or of the emptying and resignification of the common noun into a name. What he calls the 'cadence' of Beckett's language in his late prose, surely one of the most striking characteristics of the text, is reduced to the division in paragraphs and a form of repetition in slow motion: Badiou's limited poetics do not equip him to capture this, which is so neatly captured by Deleuze's concept of 'stuttering'.

But that would be to miss the very centre of Badiou's reading of Beckett, or rather of Beckett's reading of Badiou: reading the text for the event means being aware of the ever renewed stylistic work whereby the text worries a common noun, as a dog worries a bone, to abstract or extract from it a thought, the thought of the anticipated event. And we may go even further: what Beckett brings to Badiou by reading him is a development of the concept of event, which is no longer as univocal as the doctrine suggests. After reading Beckett, and Badiou on Beckett, we must realise that there are four levels, or types of events, in Badiou's use of the term.

The first type is what the doctrine describes: there is an ontological deduction of the emergence of events in the four evental fields. We may call this type of event a revolution. In the field of art, the single work of art is not an event, but an element in a chain of works, an artistic configuration, which constructs the procedure of truth initiated by the event of an artistic revolution (for instance the break between the baroque and the classical styles of music).

There is one of the four evental fields in which the event is not only an occurrence, the source of a procedure of truth, but where it is represented or staged. This field is of course the field of art. Let us call this second event the staged event: the work of art stages an event that occurs in one of the three other fields. Thus with Rimbaud, Mallarmé and the Paris Commune. Note that this is not a return to the old Marxist theory of literature as reflection: what is staged is not the event itself, which is indiscernible, but the traces it leaves, its vanishing, absence or irremediable pastness (Mallarmé), the interruption of the procedure of truth and fidelity that its occurrence initiates (Rimbaud), the anticipation of its coming, or failure to come (Beckett). And here lies the first contribution that Beckett makes to the theory of the event in his reading of Badiou: he helps Badiou to think the temporality of the event as in the *future anterior*. When the procedure of truth is initiated, the prospective subject of such truth must make a decision, the decision that what she is being faithful to will turn out to have been an event (you will have noted the appearance of the grammatical markers of a past in the future, or future anterior).

But the work of art, being capable of staging or representing events in other fields, is also capable of reflexively staging the event in its own field. The artistic event represented in the artistic work is *the event of the event*, or the *événementialité* of the event, as Andrew Gibson develops it.[52] What the text of art represents here is the general characteristics of what it takes to be an event. We are moving from representation and staging towards abstraction. And this is the second specific contribution that Beckett's reading of Badiou makes to the doctrine: he stages the abstraction of *événementialité* as both the object of the work of art and a mode of access to the event. The importance, in Beckett's text, of the operations of abstraction, subtraction and extraction, operations that are mimicked in Badiou's reading of him, is clear.

But there is a fourth level of eventhood, when we reach the level of philosophy. There is, as we know, no procedure of truth in philosophy, which is not an evental field. But the generalised event that the work of art abstracts through the operation of naming (whose centrality in Badiou's treatment of Beckett's language is now clear) remains precisely what it is: an abstraction. The thought of the event in the work of art can never be successfully achieved: it requires the light that a *concept* of event, which only philosophy can offer, will provide. And it requires precisely the concept of event that Badiou extracts from it and transforms into a doctrine, through the philosophical operation of compossibilisation, which, as we saw, is not as modest as it seems.

Event (revolution), representation of the event (staged event), *événementialité* (event of the event), concept of event: my four types of event are rather four levels of a hierarchy. It would seem that transcendence is hard to kill. That is exactly the criticism Deleuze and Guattari in *What Is Philosophy?* level at Badiou.

Deleuze reads Beckett

Deleuze is not as copious or consistent a reader of Beckett as Badiou is. He never wrote a book about him, only one long piece and a very brief essay.⁵³ The longer piece, however, was originally published as an afterword to the French translation of Beckett's late television plays, which suggests a kind of proximity, if not with the writer himself (the French text was published after Beckett's death), at least with his literary executors.⁵⁴ And Beckett does occupy a central position in Deleuze's modernist canon: there are myriads of references to him in his works throughout his publishing career.

There are four types of presence of Beckett in Deleuze's works. First, Deleuze is fond of quoting, repeatedly so, a number of 'formulas' of Beckett, extracted out of their context and imported into Deleuze's current concerns. Secondly, Deleuze comes back repeatedly to certain scenes in Beckett, which are inserted in his own philosophical argument as stepping stones rather than illustrations. The most consistently mentioned of such scenes concerns Molloy's four pockets and sixteen stones. Thirdly, there is the close reading of the television plays, from which Deleuze unexpectedly extracts the problematic of language: the unexpectedness concerns both Beckett (as language, in those plays, has vanished) and Deleuze (whose resistance to the linguistic turn of philosophy, if it is not as definitive and radical as Badiou's, is nevertheless notorious). Lastly, Beckett plays a central part in the literary canon that enables Deleuze to construct a concept of style as stuttering. In the last two instances, it can be said that Beckett reads Deleuze as he reads Badiou, as he contributes to the development of Deleuze's thinking in an area that turns out to be of crucial importance.⁵⁵

'Formula' is a Deleuzian word. His essay on Melville is entitled 'Bartleby; or, the formula', and his deliberately provocative treatment of Kant, his old philosophical opponent, takes the form of a 'summary' of Kantian philosophy by way of four 'poetic formulas' extracted from Shakespeare, Rimbaud and Kafka.⁵⁶ The essay on 'Bartleby', as its very title indicates, offers a theory of the Deleuzian formula. Bartleby's famous rejoinder, 'I would prefer not to', is analysed in terms of its agrammaticality. The formula is profoundly agrammatical, even if it respects the rules of morphology and syntax. It pushes language to its limits, it creates an event in language ('it hollows out a zone of indetermination that renders words indistinguishable, that creates a vacuum within language').⁵⁷ It is contagious, it disturbs the usual contrast between affirmation and negation, it turns the maternal or national language into a foreign tongue: 'by means of driftings, deviations, de-taxes or sur-taxes (as opposed to the standard syntax)', Bartleby's formula makes the English language 'slip' (*fait filer la langue*).⁵⁸ Therein lies the 'eccentricity' of Bartleby (*un original*).

But the ex-centricity of the formula goes further than this: for Deleuze the formula is a way of ex-centring thought. The formula has a provocative value: like a live metaphor, or like a conceit, there is something blatantly false or exaggerated, as in the famous opening sentence of Beckett's *Murphy*, 'The sun shone, having no alternative, upon the nothing new'.⁵⁹ Because it is agrammatical in this extended sense, the formula jogs language into thought, it deterritorialises it. We recognise the familiar Deleuzian theme of the violence necessary for thinking: we are forced into thought by the formula. What is interesting here is that – herein lies a difference to Badiou – such violent entry into thought is managed by and with language, which obtrudes, which is no transparent medium for thought nor (this is closer to Badiou) a mere hindrance to thought, an inevitable torture. This is where the formula, in the terms of Garin Dowd, provides sites for the unexpected encounter between philosophy and literature: Deleuze himself is a philosophical Bartleby.

Here are a few examples of Beckettian formulas in the work of Deleuze. Beckett is being provocative about the uselessness of travel, in the manner of Roussel, who is supposed to have gone through Peking in a closed car, all windows obscured: 'We don't travel for the fun of it, as far as I know; we're foolish, but not that foolish' – the French word is rather stronger, as a result of which the English version of the formula loses much of its strength.⁶⁰ This obviously delights Deleuze, who despised conferences and rarely travelled himself. In another passage, Beckett provides a dismissive *chute* to a convoluted Deleuzian argument against theories of the cinema inspired by linguistics, where the thought of the image is modelled on language: to the verticality that governs both the hierarchical conception of language (to be found, for instance, in Chomsky's contrast of deep and surface structure) and our visual world, he opposes the thought of the plane, of horizontal surfaces, on which the inscription is not that of hierarchical language but of diagram. And this is where Beckett's formula, which on the face of it has little to do with the current problem, clinches his argument: 'As Beckett says, it's better to be sitting than standing, and better to be lying down than sitting.'⁶¹ No wonder another gem of Beckett's comes to comfort the vision of Kant's philosophy through Hamlet's dictum, 'The time is out of joint': Hamlet is a deeply Kantian character 'whenever he appears as a passive existence', and this in turn evokes Murphy's 'metabulia'.⁶²

A Modernist Canon? Badiou and Deleuze Read Beckett

Beckett's formulas are crystals of thought: they open up a world of thought, they jog us into thought, they force a conclusion upon us, which their offhandedness immediately questions – they are Deleuzian philosophemes, temporary accretions on the plane of immanence that relay or relaunch the lines of flight of thought. We understand why they are the sites of the encounter between philosophy and literature: their workings are those of wit, and Deleuze is not merely a philosophical Bartleby, an ex-centric of thought, he is also a philosophical Oscar Wilde. No wonder again he, like Badiou, stresses the importance of laughter in Beckett, far from any sinister or absurdist interpretation of his work.

The episode of Molloy, his pockets and his sucking pebbles or stones is well-known, and Deleuze is not the first to read it. It is presented as a kind of algorithm ('Taking a stone from the right pocket of my greatcoat, and putting it into my mouth, I replaced it in the right pocket of my greatcoat by a stone from the right pocket of my trousers . . .' – and so on and so forth till all the combinations are exhausted),[63] and Deleuze compulsively returns to it. As a result of this, there is a history of the scene in his works. The first occurrence is to be found in the second chapter of *Difference and Repetition*, as Deleuze is making ready to deal with the syntheses of time:

> In all his novels, Samuel Beckett has traced the inventory of peculiarities pursued with fatigue and passion by larval subjects: Molloy's series of stones, Murphy's biscuits, Malone's possessions – it is always a question of drawing a small difference, a weak generality, from the repetition of elements or the organisation of cases. It is undoubtedly one of the more profound intentions of the 'new novel' to rediscover, below the level of active syntheses, the domain of passive syntheses which constitute us, the domain of modifications, tropisms and little peculiarities.[64]

Although the context is highly specific and concerns the analysis of 'repetition for itself', as the title of the chapter indicates, the main elements of the recurring analysis of that scene are already present: the larval subject, no longer a centre of action; the series of elements and its exhaustion; the link between the waning of the subject, the exhaustion of the series and the concept of synthesis; and lastly, but not least, a characterisation of the scene as typical of the current state of the novel (this 'new novel' is of course the French *nouveau roman*, to which *Molloy* is, perhaps a little too easily, associated).

When the scene reappears, in *Anti-Oedipus*, it embodies the Guattarian concept of machine, or rather of machinic assemblage, thus justifying Garin Dowd's reading of Beckett 'after Deleuze and Guattari' in terms of abstract machines.[65] The importance of the concept for the *Capitalism and Schizophrenia* project, its origin in the early work of Guattari,[66] the systematic contrast between the machinic and the mechanical (the body is a machine and a machine of machines, it is not mechanical – the machine is defined as a 'neighbourhood' of heterogeneous independent elements),[67] all this is well-known, as is the transformation of the concept of machine into the concept of assemblage (the machine is the original form of what became a machinic assemblage of desire). Beckett's Molloy scene can in fact be considered, if not as the source, at least as the archetypal inscription of the machinic assemblage: as early as the second page of *Anti-Oedipus*, the Beckett desiring machines are duly mentioned – not only Molloy's stones, but Watt's strange way of walking. (In fact, the metaphors of rolling and pitching, by which Deleuze characterises style as the stuttering of language, are not, as we might think, nautical metaphors but accurate descriptions of Watt's idiosyncratic manner of walking). A few pages later, a link is made between machines, series (the distinct Deleuzian contribution to the construction of the concept of assemblage which comes from *The Logic of Sense*) and synthesis – where we shall recognise our old friend the disjunctive synthesis. This time, it is not Molloy and his stones but Malone and his possessions that occupy the centre of the stage, but, as we have seen, they are linked by a relation of metonymy:

> Thus the schizophrenic, the possessor of the most touchingly meagre capital – Malone's belongings, for instance – inscribes on his own body the litany of disjunctions, and creates for himself a world of parries where the most minute of permutations is supposed to be a response to the new situation or a reply to the indiscreet questioner. The disjunctive synthesis of recording therefore comes to overlap the connective synthesis of production. The process as process of production extends into the method as method of inscription.[68]

Beckett's characters are constructed through disjunctions, by the schizophrenic affirmative use of the disjunctive synthesis, whereby 'everything divides, but into itself'.[69] This induces a concept of subject which is, if not 'larval', at least marginalised: the subject is a residual product of the machinic assemblage. Thus the typical Beckett character, the unnameable, Murphy, Watt or Mercier, is 'with no fixed identity, forever decentered, *defined* [*conclu*] by the states through which it passes'.[70] In the end, Molloy sucking his stones becomes the

A Modernist Canon? Badiou and Deleuze Read Beckett

figure of the schizo-analyst, who is neither a theatre director nor an interpreter, but 'a mechanic, a micromechanic'[71] and Beckett is the literary master of syntheses.

But the machinic assemblage of desire does not stand on its own: it is associated with a collective assemblage of enunciation. And here also Beckett is an inspiration. Deleuze never tires of referring to his bilingualism: an Irishman writing in both English and French is the best example (with a Czech Jew writing in German), of the minorisation of the standard dialect and of the creation of style by carving a foreign language in one's own tongue. This is *Mille Plateaux*, but similar passages may be found in *Dialogues*, in *Kafka*, in *Superpositions*:

> What is called a style can be the most natural thing in the world; it is nothing other than the procedure of a continuous variation. Of the dualisms established by linguistics, there are few with a more shaky foundation than the separation between linguistics and stylistics: Because style is not an individual psychological creation but an assemblage of enunciation, it inevitably produces a language within a language. Take an arbitrary list of authors we are fond of: Kafka once again, Beckett, Gherasim Luca, Jean-Luc Godard.[72]

'Stylistics' here must be understood in its French acceptation: not as a form of grammatical analysis of texts, but as an equivalent for literary theory. And it appears that Deleuze's specific canon, undoubtedly a modernist one, is not merely the reflection of his literary taste: it is the canon he needs to construct his concept of style. We shall not wonder, therefore, at the references to Beckett as a typical novelist, as the allusion to the *nouveau roman* above already suggested. Deleuze is fond of bracketing together Beckett and Chrétien de Troyes, the author of a medieval proto-novel, as archetypal novelists, a *rapprochement* that will leave the historian of literature gasping. But such linking is not as provocative and arbitrary as it seems: as we saw, one of the things Deleuze has found confirmed in Beckett is the centrality of disjunctive syntheses.

What emerges from this journey through the historical layers of the Deleuze corpus is the growing importance of the question of language. Deleuze, we have seen, is wary of language, in the tradition of Bergson, and in this he resists the linguistic turn: he shares with Badiou the idea that there is something in thought that language alone cannot capture. But, unlike Badiou, or to a much greater extent than Badiou, his philosophical reading of literary texts, of Beckett in particular, has convinced him that language was for philosophy an object of thought. So when he indulges in the close reading of a text by Beckett, in the afterword to *Quad*, he reads it from the point of view of language.

In Beckett's late television plays, *Ghost Trio*, ... *but the clouds* ..., *Quad* and *Nacht und Traüme*,[73] what Badiou calls 'the imperative of language' seems not to be imperative any longer, as language is hardly present in the first two plays and has completely disappeared in the last two, with the usual paradox that they are now published in the collected dramatic works and therefore consist of strings of words, even if those words are reduced to stage directions and the legends of diagrams. This paradox is central to Deleuze's essay, which naturally deals with the exhaustion of language in late Beckett.[74] Towards the end of his trajectory, the famous playwright moves away from language, the stuff that drama is made off, altogether. He does so in all possible ways, by moving on to other media, like music and the visual arts, by striving for complete silence as the climax, but also the substitute, of language, or, when language persists, by exiling it to the margins of the play, the voice off of commentary or the stage directions. Deleuze, however, in his reading carefully avoids taking such an obvious path for his commentary and offering us a disquisition on the dereliction of language in late Beckett. On the contrary, he constructs his reading around a theory of Beckett's language, even a theory of three types of language in Beckett.

He begins by extracting a problem from the text, the problem of *exhaustion*, in all the senses of the term: physical exhaustion (the characters in the plays obviously suffer from terminal fatigue); logical exhaustion of all possible combinations (the primitive scene in *Molloy* is with us again), but also the exhaustion of language, which is the exhaustion of the characters, who no longer speak, but also of the writer, who no longer writes, having no language at his disposal. But he goes on by describing not one but three types of language in Beckett.

Language no. 1 is a language of *names*. It is already far from language as we know it. We no longer find the syntactic constructions that yield meaning, the references that propositions convey: names qua words are disjunct atoms, their sequence forms enumerations or lists, not propositions, and their combination is algebraic rather than syntactic. Outlandish as it sounds, however, such language is still closer to our language than the next.

Language no. 2 is the language of *voices*. In the first language,

A Modernist Canon? Badiou and Deleuze Read Beckett

there is still a subject, the speaker, who is in charge of naming: he offers the guarantee of a form of reference, albeit disjointed and non-propositional, to the world. But in the second language, which it is difficult still to call a 'language', this is no longer possible, as words have disappeared, with two striking consequences. First, such language is no longer *our* language, a language that we can share with Beckett and his characters, since we fail not only to make sense out of it, but to grasp it as an expression of meaning. Second, meaning has of course absconded: such language, if a tongue at all, can only be a foreign tongue, a tongue of which I am ignorant, uttered by the utterly Other. Deleuze takes advantage of this situation to sketch a theory of the Other as a possible world, whose only point of contact with the world of our reality is the Voice that no longer makes sense. Yet, foreign as it is, this second language is still closer to language as we know it than the third.

Language no. 3 is the language of *images* and *spaces*. Its name of 'language' is highly dubious, as it seems to have abandoned all the characteristics we ascribe to language and to have moved towards other media, the auditory and the visual. We no longer have series, as in language no. 1, or a voice, as in language no. 2: language no. 3 consists merely of impersonal images, both in sound and picture. We no longer have a message, with its syntax, however rudimentary; we no longer have a sender, with her voice; all we seem to have is a heap of broken images. Why call it a language still? Because there is still an addressee, the audience, and there is still something going on, the process of emergence of those images, which, reflexively, is the process of emergence of language itself, when art takes it to its limits, closer and closer to silence, to which it aspires, and which it achieves with this 'language'.

Deleuze describes the progression from the first to the third language in terms of the development of Beckett's *oeuvre*: like Badiou, he orders the texts into a historical narrative. Language no. 1 corresponds to the first novels, above all *Watt*; language no. 2 is to be found in novels and plays; language no. 3 appears with a prose text, *How It Is* (like Badiou, he ascribes a function of epistemological break to this text), and flourishes with the television plays. But the progression is also a logical one: there is a form of progress in the development of Beckett's *oeuvre*, as language becomes purified of what is 'annoying' about it. For language as we practise it, the language Beckett tries to get rid of, is not only deceitful in the ambiguity of its words, it is laden with all the paraphernalia of communication and interlocution: intentions, significations, memories and clichés – all of which freeze and poison our words and stifle us, their speakers. The speaker is always foiled by her language: a wet blanket of signification damps down any attempt at expression. Hence the necessity, as Deleuze formulates it, of 'boring holes' in language to find out 'what is hidden behind'. Only a change in medium, the combination of image and music in *Nacht und Traüme*, can achieve this.

The Exhausted concludes, in a manner reminiscent of Badiou, on poetic language as ill seen ill said:

> Is there then no salvation for words, like a new style in which words would at last open up by themselves, where language would become poetry, in such a way as to actually produce the visions and sounds that remain imperceptible behind the old language ('the old style')? Visions or sounds: how can they be distinguished? So pure and so simple, so strong, they are said to be *ill seen ill said* whenever words pierce themselves and turn against themselves so as to reveal their outside. A music proper to a poetry read aloud without music.[75]

As in Badiou, the 'ill said' of poetic language (whether latent or explicit) subverts the language of communication. Unlike Badiou, however, this process of boring holes in language to take it to its limit in silence or other media is described in terms of style. This is indeed the climax of Deleuze's reading of Beckett: his works play a central part in Deleuze's construction of a concept of style.

The essay, 'He Stuttered' is the site of the most comprehensive and explicit construction of such a concept in Deleuze. The beginning is innocuous enough: 'It is sometimes said that bad novelists feel the need to vary their dialogic markers by substituting for "he said" expressions like "he murmured", "he stammered", "he sobbed" ...'.[76] But bad novelists soon give way to the canon of practitioners of style, and to the systematic construction of the concept, around the paradox of 'style = non-style'. The gist of the theory appears in the following passage:

> *When a language is so strained* that it starts to stutter, or to murmur or stammer ... *then language in its entirety reaches the limit* that marks its outside and makes it confront silence. When a language is strained in this way, language in its entirety is submitted to a pressure that makes it fall silent. Style – the foreign language within language – is made up of these two operations, or should we speak with Proust of a nonstyle.[77]

This definition of style as a straining of language is based on a concept of syntax as the most important aspect of language: the writer creates a syntax that makes language stammer. I have developed elsewhere this Deleuzian concept of the centrality of syntax (a Chomskyan theme, but one to which Deleuze gives a totally different content) under the name of 'the intensive line of syntax'.[78] But Deleuze's definition has two further characteristics. The first is his insistence on the *impersonality* of style: the subject of style, which is both individual (Cézanne's style) and collective (the style of a school of painting, or of Mods and Rockers) is in no way reducible to a person, and the old tag, 'the style is the man', cannot be further removed from his conception of style. Secondly, the possibility of style is conditioned by the fact that the workings of language cannot be captured, as 'scientific' linguistics tries to do, by a system of rules and functions, but must be described as an array of continuous variations (in other words, Deleuze prefers the linguistics of Labov and Hjelmslev to the linguistics of Saussure and Chomsky).

The determinations of the concept are of course much more precise than that, and the essay charts the progress of language from meaning to silence through style. The language of everyday communication produces meaning, which is a function of common sense and good sense and corresponds to Beckett's 'well saying'. The work of style, the torsion that the writer imposes on language, makes it forego meaning and strive after silence: silence is the limit towards which language strives, and the means and medium of such striving is style. That Beckett should be central to the canon of practitioners of style in this sense will come as no surprise: indeed the concept in its determinations seems to be made especially for Beckett's style.

The meaning to silence progression goes through no fewer than eleven stations, all spelt out in the essay. Here is the glorious list: disequilibrium, continuous variation, trembling (zone of vibration), line, minorisation, stuttering (rolling and pitching), repetition, digression, line of syntax, rhythm, limit (in silence or in other media).

It all starts with the instability of language. Language stutters and style encourages it to do so: it is not a stable or fixed system, but a system of variations, in a constant state of *disequilibrium*. This does not mean that language is entirely chaotic. This is why I have kept the word 'system', understood as a system of *variations*: no element is fixed in its place; each element occupies a zone of variation. This zone of variation is a zone of *vibration*. Style makes language tremble: it vibrates like a musical instrument or hums like a machine. Such vibration occurs along a *line*: language is no longer conceived as a system of hierarchic trees or modules, as in Chomsky, but as a vibrating line, it is 'stretched along an abstract and infinitely varied line'. This line, which is a line of flight, or what Deleuze calls a 'witch's line', is what enables style to *minorise* the standard dialect of communication, to counteract its attempts at stabilisation through good sense and common sense and lets it move towards its limits. With *stuttering*, which marks the very middle of the progression of style (a position Deleuze is fond of: one must always start from the middle), we reach the essential characteristics of style: it makes language stutter, or, in two Beckettian metaphors, it makes it pitch and roll, through inclusive disjunctions and reflexive connections. Since those are the two main concepts through which Deleuze constructs his concept, I must quote the relevant text:

> Language is subject to a double process, that of the choices to be made and that of the sequence to be established: disjunction or the selection of similars, connection or the consecution of combinables. As long as language is considered as a system in equilibrium, the disjunctions are necessarily exclusive (we do not say 'passion,' 'ration,' 'nation,' at the same time but we must choose between them) and the connections progressive (we do not combine a word with its own elements, in a kind of stop-start or forward-backward jerk). But far from equilibrium, *the disjunctions become included or inclusive, and the connections reflexive,* following a rolling gait that concerns the process of language and no longer the flow of speech. Every word is divided, but into itself (*pas – rats, passions – rations*) and every word is combined with itself (*pas – passé – passion*). It is as if the entire language started to roll from right to left, and to pitch backward and forward: *the two stutterings*.[79]

The two types of stuttering describe the subversion, *which is inscribed in the very constitution of language*, of the two types of structuring that linguistics (aptly called 'structural') ascribes to language: paradigm and syntagm, the two axes of selection and combination. Their philosophical constitution is expressed according to the Deleuzian analysis of syntheses, that is in terms of disjunctions and connections: but here both types of synthesis become paradoxical, as disjunctions include instead of excluding (we recognise a version of the disjunctive synthesis) and connections reflexively connect their own elements (instead of connecting elements that are at first separate).

The last five characteristics may be considered as developments of those two types of stuttering. Thus *repetition* is a form of literal stuttering. *Digression* works against the determination and fixity, the teleology of meaning; it enforces an open-endedness of sense. The *intensive line of syntax*, 'a ramified variation of language', an iconic rather than arbitrary sequence of linguistic signs, marks the creative aspect of language intended not as a fixed system but as a system of variation, that is as a process of becoming. Such syntax is endowed with *rhythm*, as in Artaud's *mots-souffles* and *mots-cris*, or in Beckett's haunting repetitive style in *Worstward Ho*. Lastly, and this is what style makes language strive for, a *limit* is reached, what is *the* outside of language and yet not outside language (you will have recognised the usual paradox of the concept of limit): there are still words, but hardly so, as in Beckett's second language, and language is moving towards silence, sounds or images, as in Beckett's third language. Beckett's three languages chart this progression from meaning to silence, which style organises.

The Deleuze canon is constituted around these eleven characteristics of style. Gherasim Luca, the Romanian poet who writes in French, practises compulsive reflexive connection (the *pas, passé, passion* sequence comes from one of his poems, which runs to twenty pages); Charles Péguy is as well-known for his repetitive style as Raymond Roussel is for his structural use of systematic digression; the agrammaticality (in a wide sense) of Bartleby's formula shows that Melville is aware that syntax develops along an intensive line, as is e. e. cummings in his poetry; Artaud, as we just saw, incarnates the moment when language becomes unintelligible because rhythm has taken over; and Céline illustrates the moment when style has been pushed to the limit and language has become not a system of arbitrary signs but an iconic reflection of being and becoming.

In this canonical list, Beckett is everywhere, but especially in the middle, where the two stutterings occur, and a whole page is devoted to him. The following two quotations give us the gist of Deleuze's account:

> Beckett took his art of inclusive disjunctions to its highest point, an art that no longer selects but affirms the disjointed terms through their distance, without limiting one by the other or excluding one from the other, laying out and passing through the entire set of possibilities. Hence, in *Watt*, the ways in which Knott puts on his shoes, moves about his room, or changes his furniture. It is true that, in Beckett, these affirmative disjunctions usually concern the bearing or gait of the characters: an ineffable manner of walking, while rolling and pitching.[80]
>
> Beckett's procedure, which is different from Luca's, is as follows: he places himself in the middle of the sentence and makes the sentence grow out from the middle, adding particle upon particle [. . .] so as to pilot the block of a single expiring breath [. . .]. Creative stuttering is what makes

language a rhizome instead of a tree, what puts language in perpetual disequilibrium: *Ill Seen Ill Said* (content and expression). Being well spoken has never been either the distinctive feature or the concern of great writers.[81]

Style is a function of stuttering, a term which must be understood in the active as in the passive sense: language stutters because the great writer stutters language (this trope is of course itself an example of stuttering in Deleuze's sense). In Beckett, such stuttering is intimately linked with the practice of disjunctive synthesis, with starting in the middle, that is with producing an image of language as a rhizome, not as a tree. And the quotations aptly finish on a reference to the title *Ill Seen Ill Said*, a phrase that has obviously struck Deleuze as much as it has struck Badiou. And the two analyses have strong similarities, in the contrast between the ill said of the great writer (as we have seen, neither of our philosophers is shy of making value judgements, that is of constructing a canon) and the well said of the language of ordinary communication. But they are also considerable differences: in Deleuze, the workings of language in Beckett are not merely thematised, they are analysed in the detail of their stylistic operations. This is why Deleuze has a concept of style and a non-trivial concept of language where Badiou has neither, with the two consequences that Deleuze's account of Beckett is closer to the critical mainstream than Badiou's (Deleuze's Beckett is a modernist writer where Badiou's is not) and therefore less original and in a way less compelling. But it is much more detailed, as Deleuze engages with the materiality of Beckett's language, with the literariness of the literary work of art, which makes his account, in another way, much more compelling than Badiou's. Perhaps the close proximity, in the French edition, of Deleuze's essay, 'The Exhausted', to Beckett's own text, is indeed more than a fortunate coincidence: perhaps it is a symptom.

Notes

1. A. Badiou, 'Third Sketch for a Manifesto of Affirmationist Art', in *Polemics*, London: Verso, 2006, pp. 141–2.
2. A. Badiou, *Circonstances 2: Irak, foulard, Allemagne/France*, Paris: Lignes, 2004.
3. A. Badiou, *Beckett*, Paris: Hachette, 1995; S. Beckett, *Quad, suivi de L'Epuisé, par Gilles Deleuze*, Paris: Minuit, 1992.
4. A. Badiou, *On Beckett*, Manchester: Clinamen Press, 2003.

5. D. Drouet, 'Index des références littéraires dans l'œuvre de Gilles Deleuze', in B. Gelas and H. Micolet (eds), *Deleuze et les écrivains*, Nantes: Cécile Defaut, 2007, p. 553.
6. F. Jameson, *A SingularModernity*, London: Verso, 2002, pp. 179, 210.
7. Ibid., p. 4.
8. Ibid., p. 181.
9. Ibid., p. 203.
10. J.-F. Lyotard, *Discours, Figure*, Paris: Klincksieck, 1971.
11. M. Foucault, *Les Mots et les choses*, Paris: Gallimard, 1966, pp. 58–9.
12. J. Rancière, *Politique de la littérature*, Paris: Galilée, 2007.
13. Ibid., pp. 134–5.
14. Jameson, op. cit., pp. 61 ff.
15. G. Deleuze and F. Guattari, *Kafka*, Paris: Minuit, 1975, p. 40; G. Deleuze and C. Parnet, *Dialogues*, Paris: Flammarion, 1977, p. 25; G. Deleuze, *Pourparlers*, Paris: Minuit, 1990, p. 44.
16. G. Dowd, *Abstract Machines*, Amsterdam: Rodopi, 2007, ch. 2.
17. G. Deleuze and F. Guattari, *Anti-Oedipus*, London: Athlone Press, 1984, p. 54 (63).
18. G. Lakoff and M. Johnson, *Metaphors We Live By*, Chicago: Chicago University Press, 1980.
19. S. Žižek, *Organs Without Bodies. On Deleuze and Consequences*, London: Routledge, 2004, p. 53.
20. E. Lunn, *Marxism and Modernism*, London: Verso, 1985, pp. 34–7.
21. Deleuze and Guattari, *Anti-Oedipus*, op. cit., p. 1 (7).
22. It is even possible to read the whole of Deleuze's *oeuvre* from the vantage point of a number of paradoxes, as P. Montebello does in his *Deleuze*, Paris: Vrin, 2008.
23. J.-J. Lecercle, *Deleuze and Language*, Basingstoke: Palgrave, 2002, ch. 3.
24. Ibid.
25. J. Rancière, 'Aesthetics, Inaesthetics, Anti-aesthetics', in P. Hallward (ed.), *Think Again*, London: Continuum, 2004, p. 222.
26. A. Badiou, *On Beckett*, eds N. Power and A. Toscano, Manchester: Clinamen Press, 2003; A. Gibson, *Beckett and Badiou*, Oxford: Oxford University Press, 2006.
27. Badiou, *On Beckett*, op. cit., p. 38 (6).
28. Ibid.
29. Ibid., p.39 (7).
30. Ibid., p. 42 (14).
31. Ibid., p. 44 (16).
32. Ibid.
33. See Gibson, op. cit., pp. 131–2; Dowd, op. cit., p. 163.
34. Badiou, *On Beckett*, op. cit., p. 47 (24).

35. Gibson, op. cit., p. 285.
36. Badiou, *On Beckett*, op. cit., p. 41 (12).
37. Ibid., p. 40.
38. On Badiou's reading of *Worstward Ho*, see Dodd, op. cit., pp. 219–21.
39. S. Beckett, *Ill Seen Ill Said*, London: John Calder, 1981, p. 55.
40. Gibson, op. cit., p. 217.
41. Badiou, *On Beckett*, op. cit., pp. 58–9 (44–6). See Gibson's analysis of this passage, op. cit., pp. 127–8.
42. Ibid., p. 59 (46).
43. Gibson, op. cit., p. 217.
44. Rancière, 'Aesthetics, Inaesthetics, Anti-aesthetics', op. cit., p. 227.
45. A. Badiou, *Logic of Worlds*, London: Continuum, 2009, pp. 204 ff. (216 ff.).
46. Gibson, op. cit., p. 185.
47. N. Power and A. Toscano, 'Introduction', in A. Badiou, *On Beckett*, op. cit., pp. xx–xxi.
48. Ibid., p. xxv.
49. Badiou, *On Beckett*, op. cit., p. 17.
50. Ibid., p. 90.
51. Ibid., p. 53 (36).
52. Gibson, op. cit., pp. 138–42 and *passim*.
53. G. Deleuze, 'The Exhausted' and 'The Greatest Irish Film (Beckett's « Film »)', in *Esssays Critical and Clinical*, London: Verso, 1998, pp. 152–74 and 23–6.
54. Beckett, *Quad, suivi de L'Epuisé, par Gilles Deleuze*, op. cit.
55. On this, see Lecercle, op. cit.
56. G. Deleuze, 'Bartleby, or: The Formula' and 'On Four Poetic Formulas that Might Summarize the Kantian Philosophy', in *Essays Critical and Clinical*, op. cit., pp. 68–90 (40–9) and 27–35 (89–114).
57. Deleuze, 'Bartleby, or: The Formula', op. cit., p. 73 (95).
58. Ibid., p. 72 (93).
59. S. Beckett, *Murphy*, London: John Calder, 1963 (1938), p. 5.
60. G. Deleuze and F. Guattari, *A Thousand Plateaus*, London: Athlone, 1988, p. 199 (244). The French says: *nous sommes cons, mais pas à ce point*.
61. G. Deleuze, *Negotiations*, New York: Columbia University Press, 1995, p. 53 (77).
62. Deleuze, *Essays Critical and Clinical*, op. cit., p. 30 (43).
63. S. Beckett, *The Beckett Trilogy*, London: Picador, 1979, p. 64.
64. G. Deleuze, *Difference and Repetition*, London: Continuum, 2004, p. 100 (107–8).
65. Dowd, op. cit.
66. F. Guattari, 'Machine et structure', in *Psychanalyse et transversalité*, Paris: Maspéro, 1972.

67. Lecercle, op. cit., pp. 180–4.
68. Deleuze and Guattari, *Anti-Oedipus*, op. cit., pp. 12–13 (19).
69. Ibid., p. 76 (91).
70. Ibid., p. 20 (27).
71. Ibid., p. 338 (404).
72. Deleuze and Guattari, *A Thousand Plateaus*, op. cit., p. 97 (123).
73. S. Beckett, *The Complete Dramatic Works*, London: Faber, 1986.
74. See Lecercle, op. cit., pp. 1–7; Dowd, op. cit., pp. 58–61.
75. Deleuze, *Essays Critical and Clinical*, op. cit., p. 173 (*Quad*, op. cit., pp. 104–5).
76. Ibid., p. 107 (135).
77. Ibid., p. 113 (142).
78. Lecercle, op. cit., ch. 6.
79. Deleuze, *Essays Critical and Clinical*, op. cit., p. 110 (138–9).
80. Ibid., pp. 110–11 (139).
81. Ibid., p. 111 (139–40).

6
Reading the Fantastic after Badiou and Deleuze

So far, in their reading of literature, Badiou and Deleuze have dictated the agenda. Reading Mallarmé with Badiou and a host of writers, modernist and otherwise, with Deleuze has confined us to the narrow, or not so narrow, ambit of their respective canons. The time has come to try to put their strong readings to work on texts which they themselves blissfully ignore. There is no mention of either *Frankenstein* or *Dracula* in Badiou, because when he is not reading *poems* for their latent prose, he is reading avant-garde prose for its latent *poem*: something which cannot easily be done with prose narratives, with novels and tales. And if Deleuze is not shy of dealing with prose narratives, as his belief in the superiority of Anglo-American literature inclines him to do, from the short stories of Melville and Fitzgerald to Stephen Crane's *The Red Badge of Courage* and the tales of Lewis Carroll, his interest does not extend to the gothic: there is no allusion to Dracula in his complete works, and only one to Frankenstein, taken, as we shall see, as a counter-example.

The gothic, however, or rather the literary genre the French have called *le fantastique*, may well lend itself to the type of strong reading our philosophers practise. A gothic novel, even the most illustrious one, may not be the site of a literary event in the sense of Badiou. But if my surmise is right that there is a slippage in the concept which allows a literary text not only to be the site of an event but to stage it, the gothic text may well be an excellent candidate for the staging or capture of a Badiou type event. And a gothic text may also be the site of processes of becoming, of deterritorialisation, of minorisation that will be aptly accounted for in Deleuzian terms. So I shall try to read the gothic, or rather the fantastic, with Badiou and Deleuze. But first, I must clarify exactly what I mean by 'the fantastic'.

The narwhal and the unicorn

In the Christmas issue of the French daily, *Le Monde*, in 1972, the sociologist and poet Roger Caillois published a short piece, entitled

'The Narwhal and the Unicorn', based on the following proportion: the fantastic is to the marvellous what the narwhal is to the unicorn.[1] The object was a definition of *le fantastique*, that French invention which seeks to capture a subpart of what the English call fantasy: tales of horror and the uncanny, rather than fairy tales or tales of the supernatural, dismissed under the name of *le merveilleux*, the marvellous. The question of the fantastic was once very much in fashion among French literary theorists, the standard text being Tzvetan Todorov's *Théorie du fantastique* (*The Fantastic: A Structural Approach to a Literary Genre*), where the genre was defined by its recourse to ambiguity (the reader is never sure whether the ghost is real within the fiction, or merely a figment of the narrator's overheated brains) and the canonical text was *The Turn of the Screw*.[2]

Caillois has a different view of the fantastic, which for him is defined by its subversion of the normal order of the world, which the marvellous, in spite of its frequent recourse to the supernatural, comforts. The gist of his argument was that the two beasts, the narwhal and the unicorn, have inverse and symmetrical characteristics: one really exists, the other is a mythical creature; the one that exists subverts the order of the world, the non-existent one comforts it. Here, a word of explanation is in order. The narwhal does exist (less and less so): it is a small whale found in the Arctic, characterised by a two-yard long horn protruding from its jaw, the function of which is obscure. But it subverts the natural order: the horn is in fact its upper left eye-tooth, grown immoderately long, which makes the beast an exception to a law governing the external appearance of animals, the law of sagittal symmetry, which states that if you cut an animal into two lengthways, you will get two symmetrical halves, as far as the external organs are concerned. If you cut an elephant into two along the sagittal axis, each half will have one tusk, half a trunk, two legs and half a tail. A spider treated in the same way will have four legs for each half. And the viscount in Calvino's famous tale, who was cut into two in a battle, yielded two perfectly symmetrical selves.[3] Not so the narwhal, as its horn will be on the left half, an asymmetry that only one another animal possesses, a crab with one pincer considerably larger than the other. Note that the unicorn, although it does not exist, conforms to sagittal symmetry, as its horn stands right in the middle of its forehead. And the unicorn comforts the natural but also the moral order of the world. In medieval times, its horn was deemed to have medical properties and one could purchase vials of water in which a unicorn's horn had been dipped as one buys paracetamol today. And if a father had doubts about the virtue of his daughter he could take her into the forest and leave her to the unicorn, which was gentle with the virtuous but stabbed the errant ones with its phallic horn.

No doubt you will have asked yourself a question: how can the horn of a non-existent beast be dipped into water and sold as medicine? The answer is that the medieval reality of the non-existent unicorn's horn was the existent narwhal's horn, a precious possession, which led to the animal being over-fished and today almost extinct. That is the rationale behind Caillois' proportion, which develops into a correlation in the following way: like the narwhal the fantastic uses the *realia* of our ordinary world (it has no need of the supernatural), which it seriously subverts by introducing an impossible element (there is a link, therefore, between the fantastic and paradox); like the unicorn, the marvellous indulges in the supernatural, but it comforts the moral order of the world, as in the end villains are duly chastised and the hero and heroine are happy and have many children. Kafka's *Metamorphosis*, where the cockroach makes an unwelcome appearance in the comfortable petty-bourgeois world of the Samsa family, is an archetypal fantastic text, and *Cinderella*, with its mice turned into horses and its pumpkin turned into a carriage, not to mention a glass slipper, is an archetypal marvellous text.

The correlation is coherent with the definition of the fantastic Caillois gives in another text, his introduction to an anthology of fantastic paintings:

> The fantastic operates a break with established order, it captures the irruption of the inadmissible within our inalterable daily legality; it does not involve the substitution of an exclusively supernatural world for the real world.[4]

The fantastic has no need of invasions from outer space, or of a double world as in *Harry Potter*: all it requires is the world of our daily life, and an element that cannot belong to it and subverts it. The archetypal fantastic story would go like this. You are walking in your home town and you come across a small street that you had never noticed before. You enter the street in a spirit of exploration. Through an open window, you hear the best violinist you have ever heard. When he stops, you vow to come back the next day and listen again. And the next day, the street is no longer there: the two buildings at the corner of the street are joined up and there is no opening. This is why, unlike a marvellous tale, which requires a certain length to construct that alternative world, a fantastic story may be very brief, the narrative equivalent of a *haiku*. This is the shortest story I know, which Calvino maintained was also the best. Its author is the Guatemalan writer Augusto Monterroso:

And when he woke up, the dinosaur was still looking at him.[5]

According to this type of theory, a fantastic story needs the presence of four elements: (1) a world which is our world, which we recognise, and in which the 'inalterable daily legality' reigns; (2) a narrator, the hero of the tale, who is an ordinary inhabitant of the world; (3) a phenomenon, that is an alien element, whose presence threatens the disintegration of the normal world (the word is to be understood in its strong sense, as when we talk of a success that is 'phenomenal'); (4) an encounter between the hero and the phenomenon, which transforms the life of the hero, who becomes a witness to the phenomenon, sometimes with dire consequences to himself, as nobody else believes in the phenomenon and he passes for mad.

It is easy to see that Mary Shelley's *Frankenstein*, for instance, is a fantastic tale in this sense: the city of Geneva and the university of Ingolstadt provide recognisable elements of a normal world; the monster is a good example of a phenomenon, in that he appears in the normal world but is entirely out of it (he does not even have a name); the encounter between the phenomenon and the character, Victor, comes through an act of creation, but it has all the qualities of an encounter: hardly has the monster opened one eye when his creator experiences an overwhelming feeling of revulsion and tries to deny his existence by taking flight; and the character's life is irrevocably changed by the encounter: his younger brother, his friend and his fiancée are murdered, he passes for mad, nobody will believe in the existence of the monster, etc.

We can sum up this theory of the fantastic by using a deliberately down-to-earth formula: the problem with the phenomenon is that it cannot fill in a passport application form, in other words it is deprived of identity in our world in which it appears, a monster in all the senses of the term. The table below provides a typology of fantastic phenomena; it also explains why Frankenstein's monster is a fantastic phenomenon, whereas count Dracula is not.

Passport application form	Contribution to identity	Type of fantastic phenomenon	Frankenstein	Dracula
1. Photograph	Recognition	Vampires	+	–
2. Name	Insertion within the tribe	Frankenstein's monster; *Them*	–	+
3. Christian name	Insertion within a lineage	Frankenstein's monster; Rosemary's baby	–	+
4. Date of birth	Insertion within history, a generation, an individual destiny	*She*, Dracula, Lovecraft's Charles Dexter Ward	–	--
5. Place of birth	Insertion within a neighbourhood	Alien	+	+
6. Nationality	Insertion within a nation state	Conrad's *Secret Sharer*	–	+
7. Address	Electoral register; supports a football team	Melmoth the Wanderer and the wandering Jew	–	+
8. Signature	Capacity to be a party to legal transactions	Madman, Lovecaft's archaic monsters	–	+
9. Official stamps	Official guarantee	Outlaws and various criminals	–	---

A few words of explanation are in order. The left-hand column lists the items of information the applicant must provide on a passport application form. Failure to do so will prevent you from getting papers establishing your identity.

The next column spells out the contribution of those items to the construction of the social identity of the applicant: it is all a question of recognition (I recognise myself, I am recognised by others) and integration (I am who I am because I am a member – of a nation, a neighbourhood, a profession, etc.).

The next column again suggests that a fantastic character, the embodiment of the phenomenon, is simply a creature that, not for a temporary or accidental reason, is unable to fill in one or several rubrics in a passport application form. Thus, if we think of someone whose photograph cannot be taken because he or she has no mirror image, we are thinking of a vampire. A creature which cannot be named will be in the same situation as Frankenstein's monster, or the mutant ants in the American horror film *Them*, which are so monstrous they cannot be named and can only be described by the vague pronoun that gives its title to the film. In the same vein, Polanski's Rosemary's baby, whose father is the devil, has no Christian name, nor for that matter has Frankenstein's monster, who has no ancestors. Count Dracula, the heroine of Rider Haggard's *She* or the eponymous hero of H. P. Lovecraft's *Adventures of Charles Dexter Ward* dare not confess their date of birth since, as they are unnaturally old, no official would believe them, even as the monster in the series of *Alien* films would not be able to mention a credible place of birth. Conrad's 'secret sharer' owes his aura of mystery to the fact that he comes from nowhere and goes nobody knows where – he is an alien in the legal sense of the term, as are the contemporary French *sans papiers*, those real-life embodiments of a fantastic character. The wandering Jew has no fixed address, the madman cannot sign a legally binding document (nor can Lovecraft's archaic monsters, for lack of a hand to hold the pen) and outlaws of all description cannot obtain the official stamps which guarantee that, legally and socially speaking, all is as it should be. In the end, what emerges from this column is a typology of fantastic characters: going down the rubrics of the passport application form is like visiting a museum of horrors.

The last two columns are attempts by Frankenstein's monster and count Dracula to fill in their passport application form. Where it appears that although the count cannot provide a photograph or mention his real date of birth, which will deprive him of the official stamps, he can fill in all the other rubrics: he has a name, a lineage, an address, a nationality, etc., whereas the poor monster, who can provide a photograph (of extraordinary ugliness) can only give a place of birth (provided he does not mention that his birth took place in a laboratory, by unnatural means). We can safely conclude that he is much more of a fantastic phenomenon than the count: if we go back to Caillois' correlation, and treat the contrast as a gradient, Frankenstein's monster will occupy the fantastic pole, whereas Dracula will be closer to the marvellous pole.

A few conclusions may be derived from this table:

1. The object of the fantastic text is the destruction of social identity and the subversion of the world that such identity constructs, the world of our reality, as opposed to the Lacanian Real. The object

of the marvellous text is to resist such dissolution or subversion by comforting our social identity.
2. The fantastic crisis is caused by a void in the world of our everyday reality. The absence of only one element in the construction of identity, symbolised by the inability to fill in only one of the rubrics of a passport application form (provided that such inability is not merely contingent) is sufficient to precipitate the crisis.
3. The contrast between the fantastic and the marvellous is better thought of as a gradient (the degree of fantastic is marked by the number of rubrics the fantastic phenomenon would be unable to fill in). In this theory of the fantastic, *Frankenstein* is in the position of the archetypal fantastic text (the role played by *The Turn of the Screw* in Todorov's theory), whereas *Dracula* is a mixture of fantastic and marvellous elements.

The question naturally is: in what way does the theory of the fantastic that I have just sketched concern Badiou and Deleuze?

Reading the fantastic after Badiou

The account of the four elements necessary for a fantastic text can easily be retranslated into the terms of Badiou's theory of the event. A fantastic text needs a world, in other words a situation: a multiple of multiples – settings, characters, customs and habits, the world as we experience it, or the *realia* on which the fantastic text thrives. Something emerges in that situation that makes manifest the void on which it is based, something impossible, an embodied paradox, an unnameable element, the phenomenon which is at the heart of the fantastic text. A monster is created, a nose acquires its independence, as in Gogol, a clerk is metamorphosed into a cockroach, as in Kafka. This phenomenon is the incarnation and the trace of an event, *the* event, whether it be creation, metamorphosis or quasi miraculous emergence, that gave birth to it. Being indiscernible, the event has escaped the notice of ordinary members of the situation, as it cannot be named in their language. There occurs, however, an encounter, between the phenomenon, the trace of the event, and a character, the narrator of the tale, who starts the process of enquiry, bears witness to the retroactive existence of the event and engages the procedure of truth. This encounter produces the subject of the procedure of truth: monster and creator, vampire and vampire hunter, the subject is always dual, as in a procedure of love. A world or situation, a narrator-hero as part of a subject, a phenomenon as trace of an event, and an encounter as the beginning of a procedure of subjectivation and of truth: the theory of the fantastic I have sketched is indeed translatable in the terms of Badiou's philosophy. We may reformulate it in the following manner: the object of a fantastic text is the inscription and capture of an event in the sense of Badiou and the staging of its consequences.

However, 'inscription', 'capture', 'staging' are danger words, in so far as we are moving from the enactment or presentation of an event, which Badiou's philosophy describes, to its representation in literature. But we saw in the last chapter that the concept of event was understood in more than one sense: the event proper, or revolution; the staged event, originating in another evental field, and re-presented, in its anticipation, its traces and its consequences, in the field of art; and the 'eventuality', or *événementialité* of the event, art having the capacity to stage not only a specific event (the Paris Commune in Rimbaud or Mallarmé) but the general conditions of all events, what Gibson calls the event of the event. The last two senses may be deviations from the straight and narrow path of Badiou's theory of the event, but they are what literature is about, or, if you prefer, they are the specific contribution of literature to the construction of a theory of the event, when literature reads the philosophy of Alain Badiou. In a sense, this is where Badiou the writer reads Badiou the philosopher as, in his latest novel, *Calme bloc ici-bas*, what we have is a staging of events in the four fields where they may occur: the field of politics (the traces left by a vanquished regime of political commissars, the new historical sequence determined by the movement of the masses – there is a sense in which Badiou's novel is a modern version of Jack London's *The Iron Heel*, that classic of the revolutionary socialist novel), the field of science (the toucan, or very large, cardinal number which one of the characters constructs), the field of love (a devastating passion is described) and literature (one of the characters is composing a long and particularly abstruse poem, out-Mallarmeing Mallarmé, and we are given extracts). All these events are caught in a narrative framework, in other words they are represented, even if the representation is no mere attempt at reflection, being expressed, for instance, in the three different styles in which the novel is written.

We may therefore treat the fantastic as the inscription of Badiou events in their three senses. We might, for instance, make a case for the constitution of an artistic configuration to which the 'fantastic' would give a name: a name originating in nineteenth-century France and making unified sense of a series of texts, all the way through the tradition of world literature, and bringing together apparently unconnected or little connected texts like *Frankenstein*, the works of Kafka or the tales of Borges. Caillois' correlation of the marvellous and the fantastic might be understood in this way, the fantastic text marking a break, an evental break, with the tradition of fantasy. But that is the subject of another book.

For the time being I shall concentrate on a more modest task: I shall try to put to work Badiou's theory of the event to produce an interpretation of *Frankenstein*. I shall try to ascertain whether Mary Shelley's tale inscribes an event in another field, the field of politics; and I shall try to see whether it is the narrative enactment of the eventuality of an event, whether it deals with the occurrence of an event, with the traces it leaves and their consequences for the situation and for the characters immersed in it, and with the construction of a procedure of truth, with the co-occurring process of fidelity and subjectivation. Badiou's philosophy of the event will have been fruitfully 'put to work' if it casts a non-trivial light and 'compossibilises' elements of the narrative, on which interpretation stumbles, into a coherent account. For instance, it may be wondered why Victor Frankenstein, having sacrificed everything to the fabrication of his creature and having finally succeeded in doing what nobody before him except God had done, is immediately seized with a feeling of revulsion and horror rather than calmly waiting for the attribution of the Nobel prize for biology.

Let us take these two enquiries in order. At first glance, there is little history in *Frankenstein*. A gothic novel is not a historical novel: the castle of Otranto has nothing to do with the eponymous Italian town and its history, and the castle of Udolpho is erected in a historical and geographical no man's land. However, there is a reference to time, at the very beginning of *Frankenstein*: captain Walton's first letter to his sister is dated 'St Petersburgh, *Dec 11th, 17–*'. The action, therefore, takes place in the eighteenth century. And in the second chapter of volume III, we do find a historical allusion, when Victor, on his way to Scotland (where he intends to give the monster a bride) stops at Oxford:

> From thence we proceeded to Oxford. As we entered the city, our minds were filled with the remembrance of the events that had been transacted there more than a century and a half before. It was there that Charles I had collected his forces.[6]

Reading the Fantastic after Badiou and Deleuze

This passage gives us a date, 1642, the year when Charles I fled London to prepare for the civil war. 'More than a century and a half after' means that the narrative cannot take place before 1792, and Walton's letter tells us it cannot take place after 1800: the action takes place between those two dates, in other words *at the time of the French Revolution*. We shall not, of course, interpret these indirect references as an attempt at historical realism, but we must take them as a symptom. The Europe which provides the backcloth to the tale is torn by war and revolution, yet there is not the slightest mention of those historical events in the text, and the characters are able to travel freely all over the continent. But there is a trace of the political event of the French revolution in the character of the monster, who wreaks havoc not in society at large but among Victor's family and friends. Contemporary readers did perceive this symptom, as the monster was soon taken as the metaphor for all sorts of revolutionary or rebellious mobs, the archetype of which were the Parisian sans-culottes, and the historical incarnation of it was Napoleon, that child of the French Revolution who was also Bony, the scarecrow with whom unruly British children who refused to go to bed were threatened. We understand why the revolutionary monster, but also the irresponsible intellectual who had created him, must die at the end of the novel: to allow the bourgeoisie to breathe a sigh of relief at the closure of that historical sequence. And we also understand that, the event having produced a truth that is eternal and survives the end of the historical sequence of its birth (the spirit of the French Revolution still lives), the dead monster remained eternally very much alive, in the form of the myth: very few people nowadays know who Mary Shelley was, but everybody knows Frankenstein, and believes that it is the name of the monster.[7]

But it is not enough to decide that the tale bears witness to a political event in the sense of Badiou. We must look at the staging of the traces in more detail, especially since, as I suggested, such traces are the traces of the *événementialité* of an event. We must be able to tell the tale of Victor and his monster in the language of Badiou.

It all starts with the initial situation, a multiple of multiples: Victor's family circle and their history (the story of Victor's mother and of her untimely death), the town of Geneva as it was at the end of the eighteenth century, the state of knowledge prevailing at the university of Ingolstadt, in other words an encyclopaedia of knowledge and belief and the language necessary to phrase it. And, within that language, we remember the contradiction between an archaic conception of science as alchemy and the more modern version defended in the university: Victor's scientific breakthrough takes the paradoxical form of a return to the archaic concept of science.

In a situation, as described by Badiou, when an event occurs, since it is indiscernible, evanescent and unnameable, it can only be grasped in the future anterior, it *will have* occurred, and it will be grasped retrospectively through a process of enquiry. But it is the privilege of narrative to stage what is not immediately perceivable, and to represent it as a miracle, as an epiphany. Here is how Victor Frankenstein conceived his wondrous idea – the scientific event that might have changed the world and certainly changed his life:

> I paused, examining and analysing all the minutiae of causation, as exemplified in the change from life to death, and death to life, until from the midst of this darkness a sudden light broke upon me – a light so brilliant and wondrous, yet so simple, that while I became dizzy with the immensity of the prospect which it illustrated, I was surprised, that among so many men of genius who had directed their inquiries towards the same science, that I alone should be reserved to discover so astonishing a secret.
>
> Remember, I am not recording the visions of a madman. The sun does not more certainly shine in the heaven, than that which I now affirm is true. Some miracle might have produced it, yet the stages of the discovery were distinct and probable. After days and nights of incredible labour and fatigue, I succeeded in discovering the cause of generation and life; nay, more, I became myself capable of bestowing animation upon lifeless matter.[8]

What is striking in this passage is the intertwining of two discourses, the discourse of epiphany and miracle, and the discourse of science, of causation, enquiry and experiment. The event itself, the spark of light of the idea that disperses the cloud of unknowing and shatters established knowledge, is ineffable, and can be captured only in the metaphorical language of light inserted in the discourse of theology – this is indeed Victor Frankenstein's encounter on the road to Damascus. But the event, being evanescent, always already past, can only be confirmed by a process of enquiry and a procedure of truth that in turn will produce a faithful subject.

So a subject is constituted, but it is not an individual subject (the mad scientist pursuing his solitary task in his 'workshop of filthy creation'),[9] but a couple, as in the event of love: what Victor creates when he assembles the monster from bits of corpses is the subject of the event. We understand why the technicalities of such fabrication are of no importance and are passed over by Mary Shelley in a few vague sentences, and we also understand why the creator and his creature are inseparable, why, when the former dies, the latter must commit suicide. Here is the famous scene, the most remarkable aspect of which is its brevity:

> It was on a dreary night of November that I beheld the accomplishment of my toils. With an anxiety that almost amounted to agony, I collected the instruments of life around me, that I might infuse a spark of life into the lifeless thing that lay at my feet. It was already one in the morning; the rain pattered dismally against the panes, and my candle was nearly burnt out, when, by the glimmer of the half-extinguished light, I saw the dull yellow eye of the creature open; it breathed hard, and a convulsive motion agitated its limbs.[10]

'A spark of life': that is all we shall ever know of the actual making of the monster – a vague reference to the marvellous powers of newly discovered electricity.

The constitution of a subject is the outcome of a series of enquiries and the initiation of a procedure of truth requiring fidelity. And Victor does undergo such a process. When he sees the light, he abandons his old life in order to devote himself to his enquiries: he forgets his family and friends, neglects his fiancée, no longer attends the lectures at the university, shuts himself up in his laboratory. He has become a monomaniac, the militant of a single idea, which is a truth, and to which he must be faithful whatever the cost. He is engaged in a process of *fuite en avant*, he is carried away by his research, at the expense of his social identity: unlike the monster, he would have no difficulty filling in a passport application form, except that he has become, if not an outlaw, at least a hermit.

But here we encounter the strangest turn in the story of Victor. The continued engagement in this procedure of truth should have induced him to accept the possibility of a race of *Übermenschen*, by him created, no longer monsters but creatures stronger, more intelligent, and very likely morally better than common-or-garden humanity. In other words, he should have nurtured the innocent monster, educated him and enthusiastically given him not only a bride but brothers and sisters. But he does not. The scene of creation is immediately, in the next paragraph, followed by a scene of violent and irrational repulsion:

> How can I describe my emotions at this catastrophe, or how delineate the wretch whom with such infinite pains and care I had endeavoured to form? His limbs were in proportion, and I had selected his features as

beautiful. Beautiful! – Great God! His yellow skin scarcely covered the work of muscles and arteries beneath; his hair was of a lustrous black, and flowing; his teeth of a pearly whiteness; but these luxuriances only formed a more horrid contrast with his watery eyes, that seemed almost of the same colour as the dun white sockets in which they were set, his shrivelled complexion and straight black lips.

The different accidents of life are not so changeable as the feelings of human nature. I had worked hard for nearly two years, for the sole purpose of infusing life into an inanimate body. For this I had deprived myself of health and rest. I had desired it with an ardour that far exceeded moderation; but now that I had finished, the beauty of the dream vanished, and breathless horror and disgust filled my heart.[11]

Overwhelmed by such strong feelings, Victor leaves the room and goes to bed, where, in correct gothic fashion, he dreams he embraces the corpse of his dead mother, only to wake up and see the monster looking at him, upon which he flees the house and abandons his creature. And you will have noted the tensions that animate the language of our passage, the inversion of feelings that the birth of the monster provokes, when love turns to hatred, as well as the contradictory description of the monster's physical appearance, a mixture of the *blason* of courtly love, when each part of the loved object's body is celebrated in turn ('his hair was of a lustrous black, and flowing, his teeth of a pearly whiteness' – this is the lover praising the beauty of his beloved) and of the teratological description of an unnatural creature, with those 'dun white' eye sockets and those black lips (this is no longer the loved object, this is the Devil himself).

So the procedure of truth is brutally interrupted, the subject dissolved, with dire consequences. But such interruption is described in Badiou's system: not all subjects remain faithful to the event, not all procedures of truth endure. The account of such failure occurs twice in his works, in the theory of evil, to be found in his *Ethics*, and in the renewed 'metaphysics' of the subject in *Logic of Worlds*, where the older theory of the subject developed in *Théorie du sujet* is revisited in the light of the theory of the event.

In *Ethics*, evil is not primary, it is not an unfortunate but inevitable part of human nature, but what occurs when a procedure of truth goes wrong.[12] Accordingly, there are three varieties of evil. *Terror* is produced by a commitment not to a truth but to its simulacrum, when the procedure is initiated not from the void of the situation, from an indiscernible and unnameable element that does not belong to the situation, but from one particular section of the situation, which is therefore already given, the object of a form of knowledge or belief, and only too easily named in the language of the situation. The example Badiou gives is the spurious Nazi 'revolution', which does not revolutionise the situation, only projects a part of it, the German *Volk*, on to the whole. *Betrayal* occurs when a genuine procedure of truth is initiated, but its subject is unable to pursue it and ends up denying the event of which he had made himself a militant. The canonical example is provided by the French *nouveaux philosophes*, who begun as militants of the political event of May '68 and ended up as supporters of the capitalist status quo, not to mention a few imperialist wars. *Disaster* occurs when a procedure of truth has been conducted but the fragility and inbuilt incompleteness of the process is forgotten and the truth is imposed on the new situation it has engendered: that truth is no longer predicated on the void, it becomes a form of absolute knowledge. The canonical version of this is the Stalinist transformation of the political truth of the October revolution into a dogma, the consequence of which is not only a freezing of revolutionary Marxism into the dogma of historical and dialectical materialism, but the Gulag.

In *Frankenstein*, Victor has initiated a genuine procedure of truth: the creation of the monster is the embodiment of such a procedure; it marks Victor's fidelity to the scientific event which occurred in a flash, in the sudden discovery of the secret of creation. The creation acknowledges the fact that the event is always situated in the future anterior, as the scientific event will have occurred when the monster, who is the living proof of it, is created. And the creation of the monster also creates the dual subject of the event. So, when Victor falls into evil, it is not through terror and simulacrum as the procedure was genuine. It is not through disaster either, as he does not attempt to impose the truth of his discovery on the world he and the monster inhabit, but rather renounces the truth and tries to deny the existence of the monster, first by taking refuge in sleep, then by sheer flight. This is a characteristic example of betrayal, of not having the courage to go on with the truth of which one has had a glimpse. Truth is difficult, the path is uneven, and the subject of truth finds himself in the situation of the character of Beckett's *The Unnameable*, whose situation is summed up in the famous last words of the text: 'You must go on, I can't go on, I'll go on.' [13] Not so Victor Frankenstein, who goes away instead of going on, and seeks to destroy what he has created. In so doing, he actively betrays the event of which he was a subject not so much by denying it (as reality will insist, and the monster will soon remind his creator of his existence) as by reversing the procedure of truth into a procedure of untruth, or of evil, which ends up in his and the monster's annihilation.

The second *locus* for the account of the failure of the procedure of truth occurs in the first book of *Logic of Worlds*, which is entitled 'Formal Theory of the Subject (Meta-Physics)'.[14] In the wake of *Being and Event*, the subject is conceived as the outcome of a procedure of subjectivation, in other words a procedure of truth: it is a consequence of the event. In *Being and Event*, only one subject was envisaged, the subject faithful to the truth she follows. But in *Logic of Worlds*, account is taken of the possibility that the procedure of truth should abort and the procedure of subjectivation should continue, producing the wrong subjects. There are two of those, the reactive subject and the obscure, or obscurantist, subject. The first book is devoted to a demonstration of the structure, or matheme, of each of these three subjects, a structure that involves three elements: the traces of the vanished event, the body produced by the advent of the event (Badiou is a materialist, the traces of the event are inscribed on bodies, and the subject emerges from the body, or from its repression) and the present, defined as the consequences in the world of the presence of the traces of the event. Each subject combines those three elements (and their denial or repression) in a different way.

The faithful subject, whose figure is Spartacus, the leader of the revolt of the slaves, affirms the event in its traces, incarnates such affirmation in a cleft body (there are always parts of the body that evade capture by the traces of the event) and faces the consequences of this decision in the evental present. In the case of Spartacus, the faithful subject is that part of the body of revolting slaves that is willing to form a united army in order to do battle with the Roman legions.

The reactive subject, whose figure is the conservative slave who is terrified at the thought of revolt, or the *nouveau philosophe* (Badiou singles out André Glucksmann, the former militant Maoist turned supporter of imperialism), denies the actuality of the traces of the event and represses the structure of the faithful subject which he once was or tried to be, thus 'switching off' the present (*il éteint les lumières de l'événement*: the French language has the same word for 'light' and 'enlightenment').[15] The obscure subject, whose figure is the religious fundamentalist, is bent not on affirming the present as a consequence of the event, but on obscuring it, which means a return to the past of tradition (there is nothing new under the sun, there never was an event) and the affirmation of an eternal transcendence which underpins the radical lack of novelty: the function of the priest is to substitute a fetish for the traces of the event.

If we go back to *Frankenstein*, we understand what happens to Victor, who fits the description of the reactive subject: an event has indeed occurred, which has left traces in the world and produced a dual subject. But his subject immediately divides into two. There is a faithful part, embodied by the monster, who wants to 'hold the point' of the event, as Badiou calls it, in other words make the series of decisions called for by the fidelity to the event, and who also wants to affirm the consequences of the event in the present, in the form of the creation of a race of *Übermenschen* who will replace our puny humanity. But there is also a reactive part, embodied by Victor, who denies the traces of the event, refuses the present that is their consequence, and represses his erstwhile fidelity to the event. This is why he feels an overwhelming repulsion at the sight of the incarnation of the event in the living monster, why he makes his escape in sleep and sheer flight, why later he actively tries to destroy the traces of the event of which he was the subject by pursuing the monster to the end of the world. Only the strength of such denial, where the reactive subject reacts against what he once was and hates the result of his work, can explain the suddenness and violence of Victor's change of heart.

Frankenstein is the fictional account of the advent of an event, of the traces that it leaves, of the procedure of truth that it initiates, and of the process of subjectivation that ensues, a process that produces a reactive subject in the person of Victor. And the eventual field in which the event occurs is the field of science: Victor Frankenstein is a genius at chemistry and biology, and Mary Shelley has firmly placed her tale under the auspices of Dr Darwin, Charles's grandfather. But it is, as we saw, a characteristic of the event as narrated by literature that it can also stage events in an indirect fashion, as well as present the general characteristics of any event, its *événementialité*. This *Frankenstein* does in two ways. First, as we saw, there are traces of the event of the French revolution in the tale, where the presence of the political event can be paradoxically inferred from the absence of any mention of it. And we could go a little further by interpreting Victor's relation with his creature, the labour of love that finds its outcome in the creation, followed by the immediate and violent inversion of affect, as a description of another event and another process of subjectivation, the event of love, here denied by the hatred at first sight that both creates and destroys the inseparable couple of creator and creature. Secondly, the tale is the site of an event which occurs in its specific field, the field of literature. The novel is not merely a product of the gothic tradition: it initiates what Badiou calls an artistic configuration, a series of works that constitute the procedure of truth typical of the field of art. Whether we call this artistic configuration the fantastic or science fiction (it has been asserted that Mary Shelley invented science-fiction with *The Last Man*, but the same may be more plausibly said of *Frankenstein*) is irrelevant. The literary consequences of this invention are still with us.

So *Frankenstein* stages an event and its consequences not merely in its own, artistic field, but in the three other fields where events occur. And I think we understand why *Frankenstein* is more of a fantastic text than *Dracula*. There is no trace of an event in *Dracula*, and no process of subjectivation. The vampire, an archaic form of evil, almost as old as the Devil himself, is always already part of the situation: his tale is narrated in ancient tomes, his feeding habits are known to the enlightened few, as are known the traditional methods, from consecrated wafers to cloves of garlic, of combating him. Van Helsing, no modern scientist in spite of his love of telegrams, is the recipient of this traditional knowledge. As a result of this, the vampire never lacks a name, unlike Frankenstein's monster, who is unnameable: not only has Count Dracula an immemorial social identity, but what he is called, a vampire, is sufficiently known to strike terror in the heart of human multiples of the situation. An occurrence which has always already happened, whose origin is lost in a long forgotten past, cannot be an event, its traces cannot constitute a present and initiate a procedure of truth. *Dracula* is a tale of ascendance turned towards the past, towards a long lineage of vampires of which the count is the last representative: it is a reactionary tale, the tale of the ritual expulsion of an evil that is too well known, whereas *Frankenstein* is a tale of descendance, turned towards the future, towards the utopian development of a race of better humans: the monster is not only more agile and more intelligent than the rest of us, he is also morally superior, more virtuous, at least when he is born, before unjust rejection has embittered him and converted him to evil because he is miserable. In other words, *Frankenstein* is a progressive tale, a tale of the epoch of revolutions, not a medieval resurgence. That is why it initiates a new artistic configuration, which is still alive (Badiou has written a short essay on the philosophical import of *The Matrix*, a worthy member of the artistic configuration of science-fiction),[16] whereas

Dracula is, at the very end of the nineteenth century, a late survivor of the long exhausted genre of the gothic.

Reading Dracula *after Deleuze*

There is no more mention of fantastic texts in Deleuze than in Badiou, unless we decide that the works of Kafka and Borges are an integral part of the genre: a few allusions to Poe, none to Hoffmann and only one mention of *Frankenstein*. In plateau no. 7 of *A Thousand Plateaus*, 'Year Zero: Faciality', Deleuze and Guattari are contrasting their concept of faciality with the concept of gaze, whether in phenomenological garb, as in Sartre, or in psychoanalytic parlance, as in Lacan. And they are particularly hostile to the psychoanalytic concept of part object:

> An approach based on part objects is even worse: it is the approach of a demented experimenter who flays, slices, and anatomizes everything in sight, and then proceeds to sew things randomly back together again. You can make any list of part-objects you want: hand, breast mouth, eyes ... It's still Frankenstein. What we need to consider is not fundamentally organs without bodies, or the fragmented body; it is the body without organs, animated by various intensive movements that determine the nature and emplacement of the organs in question and make that body an organism, or even a system of strata of which the organism is only a part.[17]

So poor Victor is no longer a scientist who deserves a Nobel prize, but a demented experimenter. His dabbling with part objects in order to construct an organism (the result of his celebrated visits to various graveyards) goes against the germinal unity of the body without organs, which precedes and eventually produces the organism.

There is, however, a deeper reason why the fantastic is not mentioned in Deleuze, whose reading of narrative is extensive. If, with the help of Caillois, but also of Badiou, we define the fantastic as the genre whose object is the capture of/by the event and the staging of the consequences of such capture, the concept of event referred to will always be close to Badiou's concept: a radical novelty, a subversion of the order of the world, a hole in the situation. But such a concept of event is alien to Deleuze, whose conception of what an event is is entirely different. Thus the two concepts of event in Badiou and Deleuze may be systematically contrasted. (For a systematic study of the similarities and differences in the concepts of event in Deleuze and Badiou, see James Williams's remarkable essay.[18]) The Badiou event is a flash of lightning; the Deleuze event is a mist. The Badiou event is extremely rare, as rare as a political revolution or a change of scientific paradigm; the Deleuze event is everywhere, it is occurring all the time – every accident finds its virtual counterpart in the event it actualises. (Williams stresses the ubiquity of the Deleuze event: 'There is an event whenever there is a change in intensity accompanying novel effects along actual and ideal series.' [19]) The Badiou event is impossible, but only too real, according to Lacan's definition of the real as the impossible (it is impossible in the situation, being indiscernible and having no name, but it is real in its traces and in the procedures of truth and subjectivation it initiates); the Deleuze event is virtual, and actualised in the accident, with its mixture of bodies in the approved Stoic fashion. The Badiou event is not the object of a hermeneutic quest, it does not provide meaning, but destroys the established meanings of the language and encyclopaedia of the situation; the Deleuze event makes sense, in the precise meaning that term takes in Deleuze's philosophy. In Deleuze, the event is an in-between element, attributed to a state of affairs (this is captured by the Deleuzian concept of phantasy) and expressed in a proposition (this expression is captured by the concept of sense). The Deleuze event is a ghost, a phantasm, hovering over the mixtures of bodies; in so far as it is what is expressed in propositions, it becomes inseparable from the words that express it, from the thoughts the proposition is made of, and its name under that aspect is sense. Finally, the temporality of the Badiou event is the future anterior, whereas the temporality of the Deleuze event is not the time of the accident, *chronos*, the time of present past and future, but the a-temporal time of the infinitive, *aion*, the time of a present outside time's arrow, inscrutable and neutral.

In Deleuze, the concept of event is developed in *Logic of Sense*, but, unlike other concepts, it survives in later works. In the earlier work, it is developed through a reading of a literary text, Stephen Crane's *The Red Badge of Courage*. The archetype of the event is the battle, as experienced by the hero of the tale, who is very much part of it as this is a tale of fear and bravery, but who can never perceive it as a determinate object of experience as the battle is both everywhere and nowhere: it does not reside in the actions and passions of the participants, yet it envelops them like a vapour, always present and always elusive. The event is that mist that trails over the battlefield. This is how Deleuze, in a late text, accounts for it:

> Now, if we go back up in the opposite direction, from states of affairs to the virtual, the line is not the same because it is not the same virtual [...]. The virtual is no longer the chaotic virtual but rather virtuality that has become consistent, that has become an entity formed on a plane of immanence that sections the chaos. This is what we call the Event, or the part that eludes its own actualization in everything that happens. The event is not the state of affairs. It is actualized in a state of affairs, in a body, in an experience, but it has a shadowy and secret part that is continually subtracted from or added to its actualization: in contrast with the state of affairs, it neither begins nor ends but has gained or kept the infinite movement to which it gives consistency. It is the virtual that is distinct from the actual, but a virtual that is no longer chaotic, that has become consistent or real on the plane of immanence that wrests it from chaos – it is a virtual that is real without being actual, ideal without being abstract.[20]

We understand the difference between the Deleuze event and what common sense calls an event. Deleuze's 'pure' event belongs to the realm of the virtual, it is ideal but not abstract, real but not corporeal. It is also unique, must be spelt with a capital E, the Event, in and through which all individual events communicate: the one dice-throw, another name for the one Being. Badiou, in his critique of Deleuze, takes advantage of such formulations to describe Deleuze's philosophy as a metaphysics of the One. This is what he has to say of Deleuze's 'true throw of the dice':

> It is *unique*. For were there (really, ontologically) several throws, the statistical revenge of the Same would be ineluctable. This is, no doubt, the point at which Deleuze's philosophy as philosophy of the One is at its most concentrated. For, if there is only one throw of the dice, if the 'throws are formally distinct, but with regard to an ontologically unique throw, while the outcomes implicate, displace and recover their combinations in one another throughout the unique and open space of the univocal', then one has to uphold that the plurality of events is purely formal, and that there is only one event, which is, as it were, the event of the One. And we have seen that Deleuze does not, in fact, draw back from this consequence. Being is indeed the unique event.[21]

We understand why Deleuze and Badiou cannot mean the same thing under the term 'event'. The Badiou event is conceived in the emphatic plural, and it is both real and actual: or rather, Badiou utterly rejects the virtual that Deleuze inherited from Bergson.

We understand why there is no marked interest in the fantastic in Deleuze: the creation of Frankenstein's monster cannot be usefully described as a Deleuze event. Or rather it is an event in so far as, in every occurrence, the event is the part that resists actualisation. But in this, the rather extraordinary creation of a totally new being is in no way different from any other occurrence. Deleuze is trying to make philosophical sense of ordinary occurrences, and indeed the theory of the event in *The Logic of Sense* is linked to the theory of sense on which it rests. If the battle is the best image of the pure event, the only access we have to it is through the proposition that expresses it and that allows it to be attributed to the state of affairs. And that proposition is best exemplified by a literary proposition, by a literary text: it takes a Tolstoy, a Stendhal or a Stephen Crane to express the event of the battle, to make us perceive it. Only in the eternal and motionless surface of the text can the event, in its virtuality, be captured. So the fantastic text is not the best text for a Deleuzian reading of literature, for two related reasons: the fantastic event can no longer be taken as extraordinary, as phenomenal in the intensive sense of the term, as a result of which the capture of the event in a fantastic text loses any specificity; and the fantastic text, if we wish to concentrate on its specificity, is not the best text to capture the essence of the event, because it focuses on the radically new rather than on the vaporous virtual nature of the event that accompanies every accident.

However, there is another type of fantasy that may strike a chord in the Deleuzian philosopher, the type of texts Caillois contrasts with fantastic texts, which he calls marvellous texts because of their recourse to the supernatural. *Dracula*, in which there is no trace of a Badiou event, might be treated as such a text: as we saw, it was far less of a fantastic text than *Frankenstein*. And there may be elements in it which the reader of Deleuze will readily recognise.

The problem with Caillois' contrast, strongly supported as it is by Badiou's theory of the event, is that it creates a hierarchy with implicit value judgement. The narwhal is a more interesting creature than the unicorn, which is supernatural but trivially moral. As we saw, Caillois mentions the medieval legend which suggested that if a father had doubts about the virtue of his daughter, all he had to do was to expose her to the unicorn in the nearby woods: the beast, a conservative and highly moral creature, a servant of the *doxa*, fawned on the virtuous ones and stabbed the fallen ones with its horn. As a consequence, the fantastic text, a para-doxical text, is greater than the marvellous text, which is tendentially confined to old wives' tales, superstitions and what is usually known as paraliterature. And when I sought to demonstrate that from the point of view of the passport application form, that is from the point of view of the situation, *Frankenstein* was a more fantastic text than *Dracula*, I implicitly endorsed the hierarchy and the value judgement.

There is, of course, every reason to decide that *Frankenstein* is a better text than *Dracula*. The so-called monster in *Frankenstein* is a round character, capable of putting forward his point of view with considerable eloquence, of obtaining the reader's sympathy, in spite of his nefarious deeds – he is a complex and contradictory character, indissolubly both good and evil, and he provokes the passions of pity and fear in the reader like the tragic figure that he is. The count, on the other hand, hardly ever talks, and never in the first person (a few of his conversations are reported by Jonathan Harker), and therefore he cannot hope for the reader's sympathy; he is a flat character, a walking embodiment of evil, an object of abhorrence and little else. The two novels also differ in so far as *Frankenstein* is progressive in the political sense whereas *Dracula* is reactionary. *Frankenstein* basks in the philosophical and ideological light of the Enlightenment, it is a European tale (Victor wanders throughout Europe in the course of the narrative: from Geneva to Germany, then to England and Scotland, before the monster attracts him to the end of the world), and there is not the slightest trace of nationalism and masculinism in the tale (the fact that it was written by a woman is no assurance). On the other hand, *Dracula* is a woman-hating tale, but also a tale of rejection of all aliens: the vampire is, in the immortal words of Tony Blair, a bogus asylum seeker. The utopian longings of Mary Shelley's tale are replaced by the grossest form of sexual titillation: vampirism is described in the language of rape, and *Dracula* is in many ways close to what we would today call soft porn. But perhaps the most striking difference lies in the style. *Frankenstein* is written in the idiom of high Romanticism: its rhetorical eloquence is tempered by the elegance of the syntax. Mary Shelley is not Jane Austen, and the distance of irony is not one of her most striking characteristics, but she can write, which Bram Stoker, at least for most of his novel (if we except a number of set scenes like the miraculous arrival in Whitby harbour of the ghost ship in the midst of the wildest storm), cannot. His text bristles with the most trivial clichés and grossest rhetorical tropes. The following passage is a good example of Stoker at his worst. The scene is well-known: the count is vampirising Mina Harker on the marital bed, while Jonathan lies in a stupor; he is interrupted by a posse of vampire-haters, who burst in on an episode of what can only be described as fellatio. The speaker is Doctor Seward, the psychiatrist:

> The moonlight was so bright that through the thick yellow blind the room was light enough to see. On the bed beside the window lay Jonathan Harker, his face flushed and breathing as if in a stupor. Kneeling on the near edge of the bed facing outwards was the white-clad figure of his wife. By her side stood a tall, thin man, clad in black. His face was turned from me, but the instant we saw all recognized the Count – in every way, even to the scar on his forehead. With his left hand he held both Mrs Harker's hands, keeping them away with her arms at full tension; his right hand gripped her by the back of the neck, forcing her face down on his bosom. Her white dress was smeared with blood and a thin stream trickled down the man's bare breast which was shown by his torn-open dress. The attitude of the two had a terrible resemblance to a child forcing a kitten's nose into a saucer of milk to compel it to drink. As we burst into the room, the Count turned his face, and the hellish look that I had heard described seemed to leap into it.[22]

I spare you the rest of the scene. The piece is written in the typical style of a pornographic novel: the positions of the two bodies must be described with the utmost precision in order to titillate the reader and leave little to his imagination. But what interests me in this passage is the fine instance of bathos in the last but one sentence. This lurid description of rape ends on a comparison of surprising and mawkish innocence, involving a kitten and a child. If we forget the possibility of a pun *in absentia* on the word 'pussy', which only our cynicism may have suggested, we start wondering about the real object of the scene. And here a Deleuzian note creeps into the analysis and inclines us to read the novel as a whole in a slightly different way. The Count, we remember, has entered the marital chamber not as man or beast, but as a mist, which will remind us of the ghostly nature of the Deleuze event, hovering over the battlefield like a vapour. And we also remember that the count has the capacity not only to metamorphose into an animal, a black dog or a bat, but to attract animals, like the poor wolf in London zoo, which went berserk when it sensed the arrival of the vampire. So the animal comparison is not merely an instance of bathos (but of course it is also that, and a blatant one too): it illustrates a Deleuzian concept, which the vampire embodies, the becoming-animal of the human being. Two heterogeneous terms meet to form a single unit, through reciprocal deterritorialisation; an assemblage is created, new intensities emerge. The vampire is a becoming-animal of the human, the wolves who respond to the call of the vampire a becoming-human of the animal. And metamorphosis is the literary name of the becoming-animal. We know that Deleuze dislikes metaphor, that purely linguistic tropism, and prefers metamorphosis, which involves a machinic assemblage of desire as well as an assemblage of enunciation. And we also know his fascination with the work of Kafka, where Gregor Samsa is the very embodiment of a metaphor (what a cockroach that man is!) taken literally, that is, in the world of fiction, as metamorphosis (Gregor *is* a cockroach, and the tale develops the ineluctable consequences of this becoming insect). What I am suggesting is that the vampire too is a good literary incarnation of the becoming animal that potentially affects all of us.

Here, however, the slightest doubt creeps in. The metamorphoses of Count Dracula are temporary and instrumental: he turns into a black dog in Whitby to enter England unobserved; he turns into a mist in order to creep under the door of Mina's bedroom, and the assemblage of vampire and wolf is not so much a machine as an instrument. So in the case of the vampire, metamorphosis is not really a line of flight: the vampire is characterised by the stability of his identity over centuries (he does not grow older, he cannot die) rather than by the Heraclitean fluidity of becoming. The vampire has Being, not becoming, he has strong social identity (which will be the cause of his downfall, as he is too attached to Castle Dracula, his lair), and we saw that he had less difficulty filling in the passport application form than Frankenstein's monster. But there is another twist to the story. In their *Kafka*, where Deleuze and Guattari analyse forms of becoming-animal in Kafka's works, they define such a becoming in terms of deterritorialisation: becoming-animal is strongly contrasted with the fixity of the Oedipal structure, as fine an example of reterritorialisation as you can get, and territorial movements are clearly at the heart of *Dracula*.

The narrative structure of *Dracula* can be described in terms of a game of draughts or of a conventional cowboy film. In the first half of the novel, the villain invades the good characters' territory and tries to reach their base, the town of London. In the second half of the novel, the posse of goodies counter-attack, give chase to the villain who flees to his own base, and in a last battle succeed in destroying him in his lair. The vampire, therefore, is not quite a nomad (he is too deeply anchored in the territory of his ancestors, to the point of travelling with coffins filled with the consecrated earth of his local graveyard), but he is moved by the need to deterritorialise, to destabilise the pristine stability of his enemies' attachment to the glebe (remember Jonathan Harker's qualms when his employer decides to send him to Transylvania), and in order to do so he turns himself into a one-man, or rather a one-vampire, war machine, even if he is ultimately defeated by the regular army of the despotic state, in other words the assembled goodies. The problem of Count Dracula is not so different from Victor Frankenstein's monster: he may not betray the event he has provoked, but he does not take his lines of flight far enough, he is still, in the midst of his attempt at deterritorialisation, too attached to his ancestral grounds, he does not let himself be carried far enough by his becoming-animal, and this is the cause of his undoing. *Dracula*, a reactionary novel, pictures the ritual expulsion of the deterritorialising scapegoat: the vampire is ultimately vanquished, but in the few moments of his frantic undeath (the narrative covers a period of no more than a year), he has threatened to replace the striated space of the state with the smooth space of the nomad. It is significant that when the female vampire, Lucy, a recent convert, goes on the rampage in the night, the scene is described in the famous phrase: 'she walks'. If we go beyond the obvious sexual connotations of the phrase (the female vampire as streetwalker or vamp) we may decide that the vampire in fact subverts the established order because she is a rambler, literally and metaphorically. This is Rebecca Solnit, the historian of walking, on the century-old struggle between ramblers and landowners in the United Kingdom:

> The conflict is over two ways of imagining the landscape. Imagine the countryside as a vast body. Ownership pictures it divided in economic units like internal organs, or like a cow divided into cuts of meat, and certainly such division is one way to organize a food-producing landscape, but it doesn't explain why moors, mountains, and forests should be similarly fenced and divided. Walking focuses not on the boundary lines of ownership that break the land into pieces but on the path that functions as a kind of circulatory system connecting the whole organism. Walking is, in this way, the antithesis of owning. It postulates a mobile, empty-handed, shareable experience of the land. Nomads have often been disturbing to nationalism because their roving blurs and perforate the boundaries that define nations; walking does the same thing on the smaller scale of private property.[23]

The vampire is on the side of the body without organs, not of the order of the organism. He is concerned with biological as with spatial circulation, the circulation of the walking, but also of the bleeding body. His is a nomadic and therefore deeply subversive experience: he is ruined by his homing instinct, when the nomad yields to an ancestral yearning for his birthplace. Deleuze's geophilosophy is perhaps the best way to account for the myth of the vampire, and we begin to understand why *Frankenstein*'s superiority over *Dracula* as a literary text gives way to the equal importance, success and survival of the two stories considered as myths.

One of the literary inferiorities of *Dracula* is that the characters are flat, as flat as the playing cards in *Alice in Wonderland*, puppets rather than persons. But Deleuze's philosophy enables us to understand why this is not a liability but an asset. His is an aesthetic of affects and percepts: the task of the novelist is not to create person-like characters, but to extract blocks of affects and percepts from affections and perceptions. The difference between those similarly sounding pairs of terms (affect is a Spinozist term, which covers what is usually known as 'passion') is that affections (of the body) and perceptions are human, subjective and temporal, whereas affects and percepts are none of this: they are impersonal, objective, not affected by time. For Deleuze and Guattari in *What Is Philosophy?*, art has nothing to do with perception, and everything to do with sensation, a mixture of affects and percepts: the function of the work of art is to tear affect and percept from human perceptions and affections. Affect is defined as 'man's non-human becoming',[24] and the artist is a creator of unknown affects (the becoming-whale of Captain Achab, the violent affect that circulates between Catherine and Heathcliff in *Wuthering Heights*). Some animals can be described as the sites of a limited number of affects. Thus the tick evoked in *A Thousand Plateaus*:

> Von Uexküll, in defining animal worlds, looks for the active and passive affects of which the animal is capable in the individual assemblage of which it is part. For example the Tick, attracted by the light, hoists itself up to the tip of a branch; it is sensitive to the smell of mammals, and lets itself fall when one passes beneath the branch; it digs into its skin, at the least hairy place it can find. Just three affects; the rest of the time the Tick sleeps, sometimes for years on end, indifferent to all that goes on in the immense forest. Its degree of power is indeed bounded by two limits: the optimal limit of the feast after which it dies, and the pessimal limit of the fast as it waits.[25]

The tick sleeps: so does the vampire, a tick in human shape. The tick is characterised by, and limited to, three affects: so is the vampire, who is no longer a human being, but a machine that is sensitive to the presence of mammals, pounces when one passes by, and bites. He is however, slightly more active than the tick, in spite of his periods of passivity, sometimes for centuries on end, in that he actively seeks the mammals on which he will pounce. But we understand why Count Dracula is almost mute, why, unlike Ann Rice's vampire Lestat, he never tells us his side of the story: because there is no such thing as his side of the story, because he is reduced to three affects, within the optimal limits of the feast of blood after which he goes back to sleep and the pessimal limit of the fast to which his isolation in Transylvania condemns him. As such, the Count is a fine figure of a character in a novel, being the incarnation of the extraction of a block of affects.

There is another aspect of *Dracula* which strikes a sympathetic chord in the reader of Deleuze, the rather striking names the novel gives vampires: the Undead, an impossible name that turns them into walking paradoxes. This name may be taken as central to the novel. If we indulge in a Greimassian analysis in the shape of a semiotic square, we shall discover that the name involves a distribution of the characters, or roles, in the novel as well as the logical development of the narrative.[26] As we know, for Greimas the deep structure of a narrative is provided by the logical development of a semantic contrast, in the shape of a semiotic square. And since it will be readily granted that the *Dracula* myth deals with life and death, and the possibility of an in-between state, we may take the 'alive' versus 'dead' contrast as the basis of a semiotic square, which will have the following shape:

		2. The Haunted		
	A. Alive		B. Dead	
1. The Living				3. The Dead
	C. Not Dead		D. Not Alive	
		4. The Undead		

The semiotic square involves positions A to D. The relationship between A and B, C and D, is a relationship between contraries. This means that the contrast admits of a third term ('white' is the contrary of 'black' because there are third terms, both black and white, meaning 'grey', or neither black nor white, meaning 'red' or 'blue'), whereas A and D on the one hand and B and C on the other are contradictories, which means that no third term is possible ('white' and 'not white' cover the whole range of possibilities). So there may be a third term between 'alive' and 'dead', but not between 'alive' and 'not alive'. This provides the general semiotic framework of *Dracula*: some characters are alive, some die and some do not quite manage to die. In order to obtain a distribution of the characters into the functions or roles they play in the novel, all we have to do is take positions A to D in couples, thus obtaining four other positions numbered 1 to 4. Position 1 combines A and C, position 2 combines A and B, etc. The new positions are given names which define the characters that fill in those slots in the structure. Thus characters that are both alive and not dead are, trivially enough, called the Living. In the same vein, characters that are dead and not alive (position 3) are called the Dead. The interesting positions, however, are the two other possible combinations, 2 and 4. In position 2, characters are both alive and dead, a manifest impossibility in our world, but one exemplified in the novel by the victims of the vampire, no longer quite alive and yet not quite dead either: this is the state of Lucy in the last stages of her vampirisation. On the other hand in position 4, characters are neither alive nor dead but persist in a strange limbo, in other words they are undead. We can use these four positions to describe the narrative structure of the novel and the fate of the single characters. There is, for characters, a traditional path that goes from 1 to 3: in our normal world, we all proceed, at as slow a pace as possible, from life to death, from the realm of the Living to the realm of the Dead. Not so for everyone in *Dracula*, which is situated in an abnormal world. Quincey Morris, who dies a heroic death fighting the allies of the vampire, goes the normal path. But the vampire replaces the horizontal journey, from 1 to 3, with a vertical, unnatural journey from 2 to 4, from the position of the Haunted to the position of the Undead. This is what happened to Count Dracula long ago; this is what happens to Lucy in the course of the narrative. But the most interesting journey is that of Mina Harker, who is raped by the Count, but not enough for her to become a vampire, and who ultimately escapes a fate worse than death, namely undeath. She goes from position 1, where she is fully alive, to position 2, where she is haunted by the vampire (and indeed, when she is in that state, she remains in telepathic communication with her potential new Master, which allows the league of vampire hunters to track him down to his lair). In position 2 she is in great danger of moving to position 4, along the vertical path, but all is well in the end (the novel ends on the announcement, or annunciation, of the coming of a child to Mina and Jonathan Harker) and she is firmly and definitively shunted to the right path, in the direction of position 3.

But the name of the vampire, the Undead, is more than an instrument of narrative development, it is the point where the story as a whole takes its sense. My contention is that we must understand this process of taking or making sense in the acceptation in which Deleuze uses that term, the central concept in *The Logic of Sense*. The semiotic square charts the conventional aspect of a story with strong traditional elements (the vampire has always already been there, from the eighteenth century onwards): it defines the walks of life open to various characters; it evokes unnatural slippery paths only to use them as moral foils. Mina, not Lucy, is the heroine of this moral tale, in so far as she temporarily strays from the path of righteousness in order the better to find it again in the female fulfilment that motherhood (within holy matrimony) provides. But Lucy does not simply stray, she walks, and the impossible name, the unnatural coinage, that designates her and all her kin subverts that doxic order. In fact it precedes and underlies it in that, like Deleuzian sense of which it is the very inscription, it is impossible, a contradiction in terms, giving birth to monsters. (There has always been a link between the linguistic teratology of coinages, like Lewis Carroll's portmanteau words, and the natural teratology of the *lusus naturae*, the biological monster.) As we know, in his theory of sense, Deleuze plays on the two meanings of the French term, *sens*: direction and meaning.[27] Sense is the fourth element of the proposition, neither designation (by which a referent is pointed out), manifestation (in which a speaker expresses herself) nor signification (whereby God guarantees, with the help of the logical and grammatical structure of the proposition, that everything is as it should be and the world is a coherent whole), but something that precedes it, not so much in the chronological as in the logical sense in which the virtual enjoys precedence over the accident of its actualisation. In an as yet hazy and shapeless chaos of meaning in formation, sense develops in all possible directions, even opposite ones (as we saw, Deleuze is fond of quoting the dictum of the medieval philosopher Nicolas d'Hautrecourt, *contradictoria ad invicem idem significant*, contradictories enjoy the same sense), and provides the foundation on which the proposition will establish meaning, at the cost of freezing it into doxa, in the right direction of good sense, and the generally accepted meaning of common sense. The impossible name of the vampire, as fine an example of self-contradiction as there is, the only rational response to which is the flattest tautology (the dead are dead because they're no longer alive, death can't be undone, etc.) does not induce a conventional story of righted wrong that strays beyond the moral *doxa* the better to comfort it, but it is the matrix of a rambling beyond the bounds of meaning, a return into sense, to the moment when lines of flight (the vampire is a rambler) are not fixed into the striated space of the state with its conventional morality.

Becoming animal, deterritorialisation and reterritorialisation, the vampire as block of affect, a human tick, the impossible names as the very inscription of sense: only the concepts of Deleuze philosophy enable our reading of *Dracula* to go beyond a bad novel, steeped in misogyny and the most blatant form of xenophobia, written in the wooden style of cliché and adorned with the cheap titillation of purple passages, and emerge into the glory of a great myth, the worthy counterpart of the myth of *Frankenstein*.

Notes

1. R. Caillois, 'Le narval et la licorne', *Le Monde*, 24 December 1976, pp. 1, 11.
2. T. Todorov, *The Fantastic: A Structural Approach to a Literary Genre*, Ithaca, NY: Cornell University Press, 1975.
3. I. Calvino, *Il visconte dimezzato*, Turin: Einaudi, 1952.
4. R. Caillois, *Cohérences aventureuses*, Paris: Gallimard, 1965, p. 174.
5. A. Monterroso, 'El dinosauro', in *Œuvres complètes (et autres contes)*, Geneva: Patiño, 2000.
6. M. Shelley, *Frankenstein*, London: Penguin, 1985, p. 154.
7. On all this, see J.-J. Lecercle, *Frankenstein: mythe et philosophie*, Paris: PUF, 1988, ch. 3.
8. Shelley, op. cit.., p. 51.
9. Ibid., p. 53.
10. Ibid., p. 56.
11. Ibid.
12. A. Badiou, *Ethics*, London, Verso, 2001, pp. 64–5 (72–87).
13. S. Beckett, *The Beckett Trilogy*, London: Picador, 1979, p. 382.
14. A. Badiou, *Logic of Worlds*, London: Continuum, 2009, pp. 43–78 (51–99).
15. Ibid., p. 55 (64).
16. A. Badiou, 'Dialectiques de la fable', in E. During (ed.), *Matrix, machine philosophique*, Paris: Ellipses, 2003, pp. 120–9.
17. G. Deleuze and F. Guattari, *A Thousand Plateaus*, London: Athlone Press, 1988, pp. 171–2 (210).
18. J. Williams, 'If Not Here, Then Where? On the Location and Individuation of Events in Badiou and Deleuze', in *Deleuze Studies*, 3

(1), 2009, pp. 97–122. See also J.-J. Lecercle, *Deleuze and Language*, Basingstoke: Palgrave, 2002, pp. 108–18.
19. Williams, op. cit., p. 114.
20. G. Deleuze and F. Guattari, *What Is Philosophy?*, London: Verso, 1994, p. 156 (147–8) ; translation slightly modified.
21. A. Badiou, *Deleuze*, Minneapolis, MN: University of Minnesota Press, 1999, pp. 73–4 (111).
22. B. Stoker, *Dracula*, Oxford: Oxford University Press, 1996, pp. 281–2.
23. R. Solnit, *Wanderlust. A History of Walking*, London: Verso, 2001, p. 162.
24. Deleuze and Guattari, *What Is Philosophy?*, op. cit., p. 173 (163).
25. Deleuze and Guattari, *A Thousand Plateaus*, op. cit., p. 257 (314).
26. A. J. Greimas, *Sémantique structurale*, Paris: Larousse, 1966.
27. G. Deleuze, *The Logic of Sense*, London: Athlone Press, 1990; Lecercle, *Deleuze and Language*, op. cit., ch. 3.

Conclusion: Aesthetics or Inaesthetics?

The question that remains is: what exactly have I described in attempting to account for my two philosophers' mode of reading literature? Or, which is another way of asking the same question: what is the exact status of their 'strong readings' of literature? Or again, if we wish to generalise, what are the relationships between philosophy and literature that such a mode of reading involves?

Two philosophies of literature?

An immediate answer to my questions would be: I have described two philosophies of literature, conjoined and disjoined in disjunctive synthesis, as I suggested in theses two and three of my introduction: two similar and yet distinctive modes of reading literature philosophically, that is of applying to literary texts the techniques of reading and constructing concepts which are the usual province of philosophy. Yet such an answer, and such descriptions, would be indignantly rejected by Badiou and Deleuze: whatever they are doing when reading literary texts certainly does not amount to a philosophy of literature. The first reason for such rejection is cultural and contingent: the phrase 'philosophy of literature' is tarred with the brush of Anglo-Saxon and analytic philosophy, and it immediately suggests a philosophical agenda that has nothing to do with the way Deleuze and Badiou read literature. Such an agenda, with its specific set of themes, is exemplified in the work of Thomas Pavel:[1] the ontological status of characters of fiction (the object of a seminal essay by Searle); worlds of fiction that are, or fail to be, possible, consistent and complete; mimesis as make-believe (as in Kendall Walton); the status and workings of metaphor; the relations between author's intention and textual meaning, and between literature, truth and morality. In spite of the mention of the word 'truth', this has nothing to do with Badiou's concerns when he reads literature, even less with Deleuze's. To caricature: the analytic philosophy of literature is mostly preoccupied with the questions of whether Sherlock Holmes had a mole on his left buttock, and whether the blob of green slime that appears on the screen of a horror film and advances in a threatening fashion causes in me, as a member of the audience, genuine fear or only quasi-fear. Deleuze and Badiou would despise such *enfantillages*, such childish pursuits, unworthy of the seriousness with which they read literature.

More seriously, their objections might develop along the following two lines. First, the very name of a philosophy *of* literature presupposes a hierarchy, whereby philosophy thinks, and literature is thought, as an object for philosophical speculation – literature is merely yet another region over which philosophy exerts its jurisdiction, as a result of which, of course, the literary text is a mere pretext for the development of philosophical analyses that are independent of it, and for the illustration of philosophical concepts whose main field of relevance is located elsewhere. And this is exactly what Badiou and Deleuze, when they read literature, refuse to do: their strong readings are based on the idea that literature thinks on its own, that it is not one more object for philosophical theorising and that, therefore, the reading of literary texts by philosophers cannot be mere exploitation of the text for philosophical purposes. It is not certain, of course, that our philosophers' reading is *à la hauteur* of such exalted views, but if we wish to understand what they have to say about literature, we must begin by taking into account the high role they ascribe to literature in the realm of thought.

In Badiou, literature is one of the evental fields, one of the fields where procedures of truth occur, and, as we have seen, this implies a superiority of literature over philosophy, which does not produce independent truths, but only thinks, or 'compossibilises', truths produced in other fields. Compared to the artist, the philosopher, as Badiou reminds us in an interview for *Le Monde* newspaper, is reduced to the role of a *second couteau*, a sidekick.[2] Literature is one of the *conditions* for philosophy, it produces 'intraphilosophical effects', even if the strange term 'compossibilise', which defines the specific task of philosophy, may be deemed to reintroduce a form of transcendence (philosophy, if not as 'the science of generality', at least as a second-order form of thought, that thinks the thoughts other practices cannot, or cannot explicitly, think). In Deleuze too, art is one of the ways in which thought emerges, in its specific way: thought by way of percepts and affects, where philosophy is concerned with concepts, even if this separation involves more than a simple division of labour, as the thoughts of art, more often than not,

Conclusion: Aesthetics or Inaesthetics?

turn out to be similar to the thoughts of philosophy, or rather to be the very thoughts that philosophy had always already shaped into concepts. But both aspects of the paradox must be maintained: even if we have the impression that, in the end, philosophy will impose its agenda on the thoughts of literature, the claims of subservience (in Badiou) or (in Deleuze) strict equality between philosophy and literature must be taken seriously, and if the relationship between philosophy and art eventually turns out, once again, to be a form of exploitation, such exploitation, if I may say so, is less exploitative than the practice of the philosophy of literature, which treats literary texts as mere objects of analysis. To speak the language of Deleuze, what is wrong with the analytic philosophy of literature is that it belongs to the representative image of thought that it is the philosopher's task to overturn.

Perhaps the most striking difference between the strong readings that Deleuze and Badiou practise and the customary modes of analysis of literary texts is the depth of their engagement with the singular text and with literature in general, in terms both of quantity and of quality. It is an easily acknowledged fact that analytic philosophers rarely deal with literature in the sense of actually reading, that is closely reading, specific texts (Bouveresse on Musil is an exception): when they do deal with literature, it is in the most general terms, with little or no reference to text, form, plot or character (the truth or falsity of the proposition that Sherlock Holmes lives in Baker Street is usually enough), whereas Badiou and Deleuze not only read literature incessantly, as we saw, but, in a reversal that is no mere rhetorical trope, they are read by literature. In an important sense Artaud and Lewis Carroll read Deleuze, with their paradoxes and bodies without organs, as much as Mallarmé and Beckett read Badiou, as he himself acknowledges. The central concepts of their philosophies, truth and life respectively, are not concepts that emerge independently of literature: they are not merely illustrated by literary texts, they are produced by them. This is why, in the last months of his life, Deleuze engages with Dickens, and this is why Badiou, in his book on 'the communist hypothesis', a book which, he claims, is a book of philosophy, not merely a political pamphlet, establishes his hypothesis by quoting extensively from two of his own literary texts, the opera *L'Echarpe rouge* and his play *L'incident d'Antioche*.[3] There are truths that can only be formulated in the language of art – it is the task of philosophy to accommodate them, to do what it can with them; and there is a form of life which can only find expression in the work of art, before the philosopher starts constructing it into a concept. I have tried to formulate this engagement and this relationship between literature and philosophy through the Deleuzian concept of style: when the philosopher reads literature, he reads it for style.

Aesthetics?

Perhaps what I do not dare call a philosophy of language I might call an aesthetics. For Deleuze and Badiou do not merely read individual texts, they generalise, they talk about the relationship between philosophy and literature or art in general. And to be sure, one could maintain that there is a Deleuzian aesthetics. Mireille Buydens has devoted a book to the subject, prefaced by a letter by Deleuze himself: he appears to have given his blessing to the enterprise.[4]

Buydens's account of Deleuze's aesthetics is centred on the dialectic of form and deformation, in the opposition between the figurative and the 'figural', which can be expressed, as usual, in a correlation: figurative versus figural; optic versus haptic; striated versus smooth space; representation versus presentation. Only the second column, 'optic' versus 'haptic' needs an explanation: the contrast, which is traditional in art history and originally comes from Worringer, opposes *optic* contemplation of the painting to *haptic* grasping, where the painting is metaphorically touched upon by the spectator's gaze. In Deleuze, the contrast opposes optic distance, form and abstract line to haptic proximity, deformation and concrete line, the kind of line which delineates the figure in Bacon's paintings.

As we can see, the correlation, and indeed the whole dialectic of form and deformation (which places Deleuze in an old and venerable aesthetic tradition), concerns the art of painting, possibly the art of music, but not, or not directly, the art of literature. But it is entirely coherent with Deleuze's general philosophical agenda of overturning the representative image of thought, represented here by the chain of concepts, figurative – representation – narrative – perspective, hence a history of modern painting according to Deleuze, with its three moments of abstract art where form is dominant, informal art where form is dissolved and chaos reigns, and deformative art as exemplified by Deleuze's favourite painters, Bacon and Cézanne. There is one passage, however, where Buydens applies this analysis to Deleuze's reading of literature, namely his return to Proust, by quoting a passage from *A Thousand Plateaus*:

Conclusion: Aesthetics or Inaesthetics?

> Three moments in the story of Swann and Odette. First, a whole signifying mechanism is set up. [. . .] That is Swann's aestheticism, his amateurism: a thing must always recall something else, in a network of interpretations under the sign of the signifier. [. . .] This entire mechanism of signifiance, with its referral of interpretations, prepares the way for the second, passional subjective, moment, during which Swann's jealousy, querulous delusion, and erotomania develop. Now Odette's face races down a line hurtling toward a single black hole, that of Swann's Passion. The other lines, of landscapity, picturality, and musicality, also rush toward this catatonic hole and coil around it, bordering it several times.
>
> But in the third moment, at the end of his long passion, Swann attends a reception where he sees the faces of the servants and guests *disaggregate* into autonomous aesthetic traits, as if the line of picturality regained its independence, both beyond the wall and outside the black hole. Then Vinteuil's little phrase regains its transcendence and renews its connection with a still more intense, asignifying, and asubjective line of pure musicality.[5]

Buydens comments on this passage by suggesting that it is the most significant formulation, in a condensed form, of Deleuze's aesthetics. And it is clear that, in it, we find a number of key Deleuzian concepts: the limits of interpretation (its reign occurs in the 'first moment' of Swann's passion, soon to be superseded), the insistence on a-signifying semiotics, the account of the work of art in terms of lines of flight, together with the picturesque Deleuzian metaphors (the metaphorical nature of which is vigorously denied by Deleuze and Guattari) of faciality, black hole, with the added lexical monstrosity of 'landscapity' (*paysagéité*). But it is also clear that, if this passage does seem to support Buyden's general interpretation of Deleuze's aesthetics, and even if it concerns a literary text, it has very little to say about the specificity of the art of language, captured under the concept of style: this is about the pictoriality or musicality of Proust's texts, not about his *écriture*. Yet, as we know, there is at least an adumbration of a Deleuzian aesthetics of literature, or rather of a general aesthetics that would include literature as an integral part of its object.

The most likely place is undoubtedly the last chapter of *What Is Philosophy?*, entitled 'Percept, Affect, and Concept'.[6] In that chapter, a concept of art is constructed, in terms corresponding to the high modernist canon which is at the heart of Deleuze's understanding of art. We can formulate that aesthetics around a number of theses: 'art preserves, and it is the only thing in the world that is preserved'

(p. 163) – in other words the test of time, the eternity of aesthetic temporality, is the criterion for art; as a result of which each work of art is a monument (p. 167), even if Deleuze is careful to add that the temporality of such monumentality is not only the past but also the present and the future; the artistic monument is 'a bloc of sensations' (p. 164) and as such 'must stand up on its own' (p. 164); and the bloc of sensations that the work of art is, is a compound of affect and percept (p. 164). Affects and percepts must be distinguished from affections and perceptions (the contrast of affect and affection comes straight from Spinoza); in so far as they exist in the absence of man, they do not need a human subject as their bearer: affects are non-human becomings and percepts are non-human landscapes of nature (p. 169). The task of the artist is not to express her mediocre feelings and trite perceptions, but to extract from them blocs of sensation, to invent and present affects and percepts. This is why Deleuze devotes a significant part of the chapter to a critique of Merleau-Ponty's concept of 'flesh', that 'final avatar of phenomenology' (p. 178), which is too dependent on the lived human body to support affect and percept, since they are non-human, impersonal, pre-individual and non-subjective (in which they are like haecceities). The language of aesthetic grandiloquence can be heard in the summing up of the discussion of the inadequacy of the concept of flesh:

> The being of sensation is not the flesh but the compound of nonhuman forces of the cosmos, of man's nonhuman becomings, and of the ambiguous house that exchanges and adjusts them, makes them whirl around like winds. (p. 183)

Words and phrases like 'art preserves' (that the work of art should be *aere perennius* is no novelty), 'monument', 'aesthetic figures' (contrasted with 'conceptual personae' on p. 177), 'composition', do seem to formulate a kind of aesthetics, of a modernist kind.

As usual, this form of aesthetic grandiloquence (words like 'monument' are hardly innocent) in the discourse of a philosopher is associated with the need to ascribe strict limits to the field of art, and to see to it that it does not trespass on the precincts of philosophy. Aesthetic figures are not conceptual personae, affects and percepts are not concepts: the domain of art is circumscribed not only by the general title of the book (the question mark concerns philosophy before it does art) and by the very title of the chapter, which ends on the important word, 'concept'. Deleuze, of course, is not suggesting that art is a marginal and subordinate practice, and the claim he

Conclusion: Aesthetics or Inaesthetics?

makes for it has nothing to do with classical mimesis, adornment or entertainment. Art, like philosophy, like science, is one of the three varieties of thought, and 'art thinks' is a characteristically modernist thesis. But art thinks differently from philosophy or science, and the chapter ends on the typical figure of a Deleuzian correlation, the correlation of the three forms of thought. There is no hierarchy between them, but their difference must be carefully charted:

Art	*Science*	*Philosophy*
Plane of composition	Plane of coordinates	Plane of consistency
Sensations	Functions	Concepts
Monuments	States of affairs	Events

The function of thought is to draw a plane of immanence over chaos, but this plane is differentiated according to the type of thought. Thus science draws a plane of coordinates for its functions to construct and describe states of affairs, philosophy draws a plane of consistency for its concepts to capture events, or rather the one Event, and art draws a plane of composition ('composition is the sole definition of art', p. 191), extracting blocs of sensations and erecting monuments. Which means that art is not concerned with either concepts or events (and events in Deleuze, as we know, are closely associated with sense). No wonder the chapter ends on a thesis, the high modernist flavour of which will not escape us: the compounds of sensations that make up the work of art deterritorialise the system of opinion, or *doxa*, in other words the dominant perceptions and affections within a natural, historical and social situation (p.197).

What we have reached with the end of this argument is a concept of style, Deleuze's concept of style, where *doxa* is subverted by taking language to its limits, towards silence or towards images, through stuttering, rolling and pitching. There is, as we know, a Deleuzian literary gradient of language which moves from meaning or *doxa* to style through the stages (each associated with a representative of Deleuze's literary canon) of disequilibrium, continuous variation, vibration, minorisation, stuttering (the vital centre of the gradient), repetition, systematic digression, the sinuous line of syntax and rhythm.[7]

I have called this aesthetics 'grandiloquent'. Not a strictly positive word. It has received its philosophical elaboration in the work of Clément Rosset, another philosopher who mistrusts the powers of language: for him grandiloquence is the name of a disease of language, whereby words cease to have any reference to reality; they are foreign or indifferent to reality and create the fictitious world of which they appear to talk. In that sense, performative utterances, which claim to do things by saying them are the acme of grandiloquence.[8] No doubt Rosset would argue that calling a work of art a 'monument' is merely an example of the 'imperialism of language', calling for the reader's acquiescence by referring to a hoary tradition of value judgement. And no doubt Deleuze would respond that, far from using grandiloquent terms, he is constructing a number of concepts to capture the thought that art develops. This fictional controversy is meant to point out two questions raised by the aesthetics of *What Is Philosophy?*: Is it new, or a mere repetition of a modernist or perhaps even a Romantic aesthetics? And is it faithful to the specific thought of the work of art, or merely another case of the exploitation of art by philosophy?

Jacques Rancière has used the same chapter of *What Is Philosophy?*, supplemented by a passage from *The Logic of Sense*, to raise the first question, in an essay fittingly entitled 'Is There Such a Thing as a Deleuzian Aesthetics?'.[9] His conclusion is that 'Deleuze accomplishes the destiny of aesthetics, by ascribing the whole power of the work of art to *le sensible "pur"*, pure sensation.'[10] In other words, Deleuze is situated at the end of a tradition, or rather of what Rancière calls 'the aesthetic regime of art' which, in the last two centuries has replaced the representative regime of art, with its hierarchy in the distribution of the sensible (a hierarchy that implied the superiority of speech over the visible). With Deleuze, the work of art finds truth in sensation, in the blocs of sensation that it extracts – not the consensual or conventional sensations described or represented by *doxa*, the series of conventions whereby we interpret the world we live in, but dissensual sensation, beyond *doxa*, that is beyond common sensory experience. (We recognise here the difference between affection and affect.) That zone of sensation or affect separated from the ordinary realm of sensations and affections bears witness to the presence of another power, the power of spirit, of the idea, an idea, however, which is not transcendent as in the Platonist scheme, but immanent in the sensation the work of art extracts: it is the task of the figure, as in the work of Francis Bacon, in its disfiguring, to make the presence of the spirit in sensation manifest. All this, according to Rancière, defines an aesthetics which, if not new (Deleuze is a representative of the aesthetic

Conclusion: Aesthetics or Inaesthetics?

regime of art), is at least genuine, as it accounts for the work of art not in terms of *phusis* (its nature, different from the nature of ordinary objects, as it is the embodiment of a transcendent idea), not in terms of *techne* (the representative regime of art describes the work in the terms of the techniques used to give form to the raw material of sensation), but in terms of *aisthesis*, in terms of affects extracted from ordinary sensations, disfiguring our conventional representations, finding truth and thought in pure sensation as manifesting the presence of a spirit or idea that is immanent in it.

There remains the question of the relation between art and philosophy, between what Rancière calls 'a thought that does not think' (the spirit immanent in the bloc of sensation extracted by the artist) and the thought that thinks, the philosophical concept.[11] The separation between the two types of thought, which, as we have seen, is at the centre of Deleuze's chapter on aesthetics, still raises the question whether aesthetics is always, of necessity, a thought of the submission of art to philosophy, of the exploitation of art by philosophy – another form of the grandiloquence I have mentioned.

Inaesthetics?

This is what Badiou rejects – this is the rationale behind his adoption of the coinage 'inaesthetics'. I shall quote again the single paragraph by which he prefaces his *Handbook of Inaesthetics*:

> By 'inaesthetics' I understand a relation of philosophy to art that, maintaining that art is itself a producer of truths, makes no claim to turn art into an object for philosophy. Against aesthetic speculation, inaesthetics describes the strictly intraphilosophical effects produced by the independent existence of some works of art.[12]

The concept is not developed further in the text, except in the form of a practice of strong reading. But this paragraph is as dense as it is short and contains a number of theses. First, there is the idea, which Badiou shares with Deleuze and modernist thinkers, that art thinks – there is an independent thought of art, which cannot even be said to need philosophy to be made explicit or to be thought. Secondly, there is the rejection of any exploitation of art by philosophy: a work of art cannot be an object for philosophy, or a pretext for the rediscovery of philosophical concepts created independently of it – this implies an explicit rejection of any form of aesthetics. Thirdly, it appears that the relationship between art and philosophy, for relationship there is, contrary to what we might expect (the independence of art might be construed as implying that art has no need of other forms of thought, and so of philosophy) is inverted: far from being art that is in need of philosophy, it seems that it is philosophy that needs art, in the form of a kind of contamination (art induces 'intraphilosophical' effects within philosophy – an action from a distance, like a kind of radiation). For philosophy, as we know, does not produce independent truths, and therefore it needs the truths of art to reflect upon. But, fourthly, this reflection upon the truths of art and of other forms of thought, which, as we saw, takes the strange shape of a 'compossibilisation', is not a covert return to an aesthetics, as the last sentence makes it clear: it is the independent existence of 'a few works of art', and not of art in general, that sets philosophy thinking. So each work of art that belongs to the happy few of Badiou's artistic canon has the independent capacity to induce philosophical effects, which have nothing to do with the construction of a philosophical concept of art: this is what is meant when we suggest that Mallarmé or Beckett read Badiou, as much as Badiou reads Mallarmé or Beckett.

This attitude to art, at least according to Badiou, creates a sharp contrast between the ways our two philosophers read literature. This is what Badiou, in his *Deleuze*, has to say about Deleuze's method of reading (he is speaking of his attitude to the cinema, but this can easily be extended to his reading of literature):

> On the one hand, Deleuze singularly analyzes work after work, with the disconcerting erudition of a nonspecialist. Yet, on the other hand, what finally comes out of this is siphoned into the reservoir of concepts that, from the very beginning of his work, Deleuze has established and linked together.[13]

In other words, Deleuze exploits art, whether the cinema or literature, by finding in the works of art what he is bent on finding in them: the main concepts of his own philosophy. One has the impression that Proust or Lewis Carroll have read Deleuze and been influenced by him – a form of anticipatory plagiarism, as when Artaud, who 'translated' the poem *Jabberwocky*, accused Carroll of having plagiarised him in advance.[14] It would appear, therefore, that Deleuze's aesthetic position makes him a typical representative of what Badiou calls the *didactic schema*, one of the schemas under which one can think the *nouage*, the 'knot', the tying together (which Badiou calls suture) of philosophy and art. This schema is based on the thesis that art is incapable of truth, that truth is always exterior

Conclusion: Aesthetics or Inaesthetics?

to art, that the claims of art to truth are false claims, as art can only imitate truth. The definition of art according to this schema is: 'to be the charm of a semblance of truth'.[15] The result of this, which is the Platonist conception of art, is that art must remain under the careful watch of philosophy, and that its only function is didactic: art is 'a sensible didactic', the main interest of which is not the capture of truth but the effects that its charm, the charm of pure semblance, achieves. Badiou goes on to mention two other schemas for thinking art in its relation to philosophy, the *Romantic schema* whereby art is the sole source of truth, and the *classical schema*, represented by Aristotle, whereby art is incapable of truth and its essence is purely mimetic (in which this schema is similar to the didactic schema), but it does not matter, as art lays no claim to truth: its end is not cognitive but ethical – it is *catharsis*, the purgation and overcoming of passion.

The three schemas define the range of aesthetics, and Badiou contrasts them with a fourth schema, which characterises inaesthetics and may be called the *productive schema*. It is based on the following thesis: art is, in itself, a procedure of truth, a site in which truths emerge, with the twin characteristics of immanence (art is 'art is rigorously coextensive with the truths it generates')[16] and singularity (such truths can be found only in art). The consequence is that art is entirely separated from philosophy, which cannot claim to control it or express the thoughts that it produces better than it can think them itself. The only role of philosophy is one of monstration: simply to *show* the truths that art produces. There is no longer any exploitation of art by philosophy (as in the didactic schema) or any fusion between art and philosophy (as in the Romantic schema).

From these Badiouesque insights, Philippe Sabot has derived a systematic treatment of the relations between art and contemporary philosophy.[17] He seems to conflate the didactic and classical schemas under the didactic, and calls the Romantic schema a hermeneutic schema. He illustrates the didactic schema, which will not surprise us, by the readings of literature Deleuze practises: he insists on the indefinite variation in the readings of literary texts and the almost identical repetition of the contents of those readings (p. 37). The hermeneutic schema is illustrated by Ricœur's famous book on time and narrative.[18] But there is of course a third schema, illustrated by Vincent Descombes's reading of Proust[19] and by Badiou reading Mallarmé and Beckett, the productive schema, where the exploitative drive of philosophy or the contamination of philosophy by art are both avoided. In this schema only does the literary experience become an experience of thought.

The account of the supersession of aesthetics by inaesthetics, both in Badiou and in his disciple, creates a certain uneasiness. For it is clear that if Deleuze's method of strong reading can be charged with exploiting literature for the benefit of philosophy, because it finds in its analyses what it expects to find, namely the very concepts of Deleuze's philosophy, the charge can easily be reversed, as Badiou's strong reading seems to benefit from the same miracle and to find the very concepts of his ontology in Beckett and Mallarmé. It is not a case of Mallarmé and Beckett reading Badiou in the sense of producing literary truths that will help shape the philosophical concepts; it is rather a case of the two authors having read Badiou in anticipation and conforming their poetic practice to his philosophical constructions: another case of plagiarism in anticipation. Everything that Sabot says about Deleuze's didactic mode of dealing with literature can also be said about Badiou.

In his critical account of Badiou's inaesthetics, Rancière makes a similar point: he ascribes Badiou's version of the submission of poetic truth to philosophy to the deleterious influence of the philosophy of Althusser, an old enemy of his: 'Following good Althusserian logic, philosophy is [. . .] summoned in order to discover the truths encrypted in the poem, even if this means miraculously rediscovering its own, which it claims to have been divested of.' [20] That Rancière should be hostile to the idea of an inaesthetics is only to be expected, since, as we have seen, he analyses the modern attitude to art in the terms of an aesthetic regime of art. But his account of Badiou's inaesthetics is interesting to us as it confirms that Deleuze's and Badiou's attitudes to art are not as different as Badiou would claim. Rancière, unexpectedly, against the grain of received critical opinion (but then, there are as many definitions of modernism as there are critics), ascribes this to the fact that they are both modernist in their attitude to literature. That Deleuze is, almost explicitly, a modernist we have already noted. But for Rancière, Badiou too is a modernist, although a 'twisted' one: his modernism takes the form of an ultra-Platonism that situates him within the didactic schema in which he seeks to place Deleuze. Rancière firmly places Badiou's inaesthetics within the aesthetic regime of art that characterises modernity, and of which modernism is a product, as it shares with it the paradox of an affirmation of the specificity of art (what he calls 'the aesthetic identification of art') combined with the affirmation of the vanishing

Conclusion: Aesthetics or Inaesthetics?

of the differentiation between forms of art and forms of ordinary life (what he calls the 'disidentification of art'). In this context Badiou's inaesthetics is seen to share a number of characteristics with modernist aesthetics: a rejection of mimesis (art is free of any obligation to imitate external reality – this, as we saw, is a central tenet of Deleuze's aesthetics), the assertion that the truths of art are proper to it, and the separation between the various arts. But his modernism, being that strange monster, a Platonist modernism, is a twisted modernism, in so far, for instance, as he rejects what is thought to be the main characteristic of modernism, the idea that the specificity of art resides in its language: for him, as indeed for Deleuze, such specificity resides not in language but in ideas, hence his distancing not so much from *mimesis* as, Rancière claims, from *aisthesis*: the idea is pure subtraction, it involves the disappearance of the sensible.[21] Hence the two contradictory requirements of Badiou's inaesthetics:

> The knot [*nouage*] – or in Badiou's own vocabulary, the suture – through which philosophy is tied to the poem is then brought about through its very denial. The poem only says what philosophy needs it to say and what it pretends to discover in the surprise of the poem. This denial of the knot, this knotting carried out through denial, is not a matter of mere oversight. It is the only way of ensuring the necessary and impossible coincidence of two contradictory requirements: the Platonist/anti-Platonist requirement of a poem that teaches us about the courage of truth on the one hand, and the modernist requirement of the autonomy of art on the other.[22]

We shall take Rancière's strictures with the usual calm: what he is describing is what I have attempted to account for under the name of 'strong reading', which both Badiou and Deleuze practise with the same zest. The time, therefore, has come for a last comparison between their methods of reading literary texts, in the shape of a last correlation.

The final correlation

What I have described is two modes of writing about literature, two styles with strong similarities. Both philosophers share the modernist attitude towards literature, with the qualification that both mistrust language and therefore refuse to account for literary texts in terms of their autonomous language. And this is probably why both insist on a strict separation between literature and philosophy (thus distancing themselves from the Romantic schema): Sabot mentions an intuition of Derrida's, who claimed that the concept of literature had been invented by philosophers in order to fix the boundaries of their own discipline.[23] And both philosophers really engage with literature and its texts, which gives their readings an urgency and depth that are characteristics of a strong reading, at the cost of rediscovering in literature the concepts independently elaborated by their philosophies, but with the benefit of new insights into the literary texts thus 'exploited': the strong reading submits the literary text to the rule of the concept, but it does not kill it, it makes it alive – it reaches parts of the text that ordinary literary criticism cannot reach.

But such similarities are not the most important aspect of Badiou and Deleuze as readers of literature. Hence my final correlation, where their independent versions of a strong reading are contrasted and where two distinct concepts of literature emerge:

Badiou	*Deleuze*
Event	Life
Logos (truth)	Pathos (sensation)
Poem (restricted corpus)	Prose (extended corpus)
Contents (enigma)	Form (deformation: pictorial gesture, agrammaticality)
Syntactic machination	Intensive line of syntax (lines of flight)

The correlation pictures a Platonist whose modernism is duly twisted and a poststructuralist philosopher bent on overturning Platonism: from this point of view, the two columns are entirely coherent. We understand why Badiou's corpus has to be restricted: only the poem can be the site of the 'syntactic machination' (a characteristic, as we saw in Chapter 4, of Pessoa's poetry, but one that must be generalised), whereby the poem divests itself of its aura of pathos. And we also understand why Badiou's reading is always a reading in terms of contents (the poem takes the form of an 'enigma' in so far as its object is to inscribe the traces of the vanished event, or to anticipate the event that will come, or fail to come) whereas Deleuze's reading is closer to the traditional concerns of the literary critic, in so far as the text is read for its lines of flight, its deformations (both philosophers are 'modernists' in so far as they reject mimesis, or the representative image of thought as the characteristic of art), in other words for its style. We understand why, when Badiou analyses a picture (in *Logic of Worlds*), it is the figurative art of Hubert Robert, the eighteenth-century painter of ruins whereas Deleuze writes about the deformed figures of Francis Bacon. The main aspect of the correlation, however, contrasts Badiou's philosophy of the event and Deleuze's vitalism. This determines both their style of writing and their writing about style. For Badiou, style means the syntactic machination that informs and guarantees the emergence of the truth of art in its relation to the vanished event. For Deleuze, style lies in the deformation, small agrammaticalities and intensive line of syntax whereby literature becomes not the representation but the expression of life, not the individual or personal life of a character or an author, but *a* life, in its non-human, a-subjective and pre-personal development or becoming, an intensity on the plane of immanence which literature draws on chaos and constructs into a plane of composition. There is no better last word than Deleuze's own last words: immanence, a life.

Notes

1. T. Pavel, *Fictional Worlds*, Cambridge, MA: Harvard University Press, 1986; see also, for an introduction to the subject, C. New, *Philosophy of Literature*, London: Routledge, 1999.
2. A. Badiou, 'En tant que philosophe je ne peux rendre raison du roman, entretien avec Alain Badiou', in *Le Monde des livres*, 22 May 2009, p. 12.
3. A. Badiou, *L'Hypothèse communiste*, Paris: Lignes, 2009.
4. M. Buydens, *Sahara. L'esthétique de Gilles Deleuze.* Paris: Vrin, 1990.
5. Ibid., pp. 136–7. G. Deleuze and F. Guattari, *A Thousand Plateaus*, London: Athlone Press, 1988, pp. 185–6 (226–7).
6. G. Deleuze and F. Guattari, *What Is Philosophy?*, London: Verso, 1994, pp. 163–200.
7. On this, see J.-J. Lecercle, *Deleuze and Language* (Basingstoke: Palgrave, 2002), ch. 6.
8. C. Rosset, *Le réel, traité de l'idiotie*, Paris: Minuit, 1971, pp. 81–90.
9. J. Rancière, 'Existe-t-il une esthétique deleuzienne?', in E. Alliez (ed.), *Gilles Deleuze, une vie philosophique*, Paris: Les Empêcheurs de penser en rond, 1998, pp. 525–36.
10. Ibid., p. 536.
11. Ibid., p. 533.
12. A. Badiou, *Handbook of Inaesthetics*, Stanford, CA: Stanford University Press, 2005, p. 1 (7).
13. Badiou, *Deleuze*, p. 15 (27).

14. This fascinating subject has been treated by Pierre Bayard in *Le plagiat par anticipation*, Paris: Minuit, 2009.
15. Badiou, *Handbook of Inaesthetics*, op. cit., p. 2 (11).
16. Ibid., p. 9 (21)
17. P. Sabot, *Philosophie et littérature*, Paris: PUF, 2002.
18. P. Ricœur, *Time and Narrative*, three vols, Chicago: Chicago University Press, 1984–7.
19. V. Descombes, *Proust*, Paris: Minuit, 1987.
20. J. Rancière, 'Aesthetics, Inaesthetics, Anti-aesthetics', in P. Hallward (ed.), *Think Again*, London: Continuum, 2004, p. 227.
21. Ibid., p. 225.
22. Ibid., p. 228.
23. Sabot, op. cit., p. 30.

Bibliography

Works by Alain Badiou

NOVELS AND PLAYS

Almagestes, Paris: Seuil, 1964.
Portulans, Paris: Seuil, 1967.
L'Echarpe Rouge, Paris: Maspéro, 1979.
Ahmed le subtil, Arles: Actes Sud, 1994.
Calme bloc ici-bas, Paris: POL, 1997.

PHILOSOPHY

Le concept de modèle, Paris: Maspéro, 1972 (new edition, Paris: Fayard, 2007).
Théorie de la contradiction, Paris: Maspéro, 1975.
De l'idéologie, Paris: Maspéro, 1976 (with F. Balmes).
'Le flux et le parti', in *La situation actuelle sur le front de la philosophie*, Cahiers Yennan, 4, Paris: Maspéro, 1977.
Théorie du sujet, Paris: Seuil, 1982.
L'Etre et l'événement, Paris: Seuil, 1988 (*Being and Event*, trans. O. Feltham, London: Continuum, 2006).
Conditions, Paris: Seuil, 1992 (*Conditions*, trans. S. Corcoran, London: Continuum, 2008).
L'Ethique, Paris: Hatier, 1993 (*Ethics*, trans. P. Hallward, London: Verso, 2001).
Beckett: L'increvable désir, Paris: Hachette, 1995 (*On Beckett*, trans A. Toscano and N. Power, Manchester: Clinamen Press, 2003).
Gilles Deleuze: 'La Clameur de l'Etre', Paris: Hachette, 1997 (*Deleuze: The Clamor of Being*, trans. L. Burchill, Minneapolis, MN: University of Minnesota Press, 2000).
Saint Paul et la fondation de l'universalisme, Paris: PUF, 1997 (*Saint Paul: The Foundation of Universalism*, trans. R. Brassier, Stanford, CA: Stanford University Press, 2003).
Court traité d'ontologie transitoire, Paris: Seuil, 1998 (*Briefings on Existence*, trans. N. Madarasz, Albany, NY: State University of New York Press, 2003).

Petit manuel d'inesthétique, Paris: Seuil, 1998 (*Handbook of Inaesthetics*, trans. A. Toscano, Stanford, CA: Stanford University Press, 2005).
Infinite Thought: Truth and the Return to Philosophy, eds J. Clemens and O. Feltham, London: Continuum, 2003.
Circonstances 1, Paris: Lignes, 2003 (part 1 of *Polemics*, trans. S. Corcoran, London: Verso, 2006).
'Dialectiques de la fable', in E. During (ed.), *Matrix, machine philosophique*, Paris: Ellipses, 2003.
Circonstances 2, Paris: Lignes, 2004 (part 2 of *Polemics*, trans. S. Corcoran, London: Verso, 2006).
'Afterword', in P. Hallward (ed.), *Think Again*, London: Continuum, 2004.
Badiou: Theoretical Writings, eds A. Toscano and R. Brassier, London: Continuum, 2004.
'The Adventure of French Philosophy', *New Left Review*, 35, 2005.
Le Siècle, Paris: Seuil, 2005 (*The Century*, trans. A. Toscano, London: Polity, 2007).
Logique des mondes, Paris: Seuil, 2006 (*Logic of Worlds*, trans. A. Toscano, London: Continuum, 2009).
De quoi Sarkozy est-il le nom? Paris: Lignes, 2007 (*The Meaning of Sarkozy*, trans. D. Fernbach, London: Verso, 2008).
Petit Panthéon portatif, Paris: La Fabrique, 2008 (*Pocket Pantheon*, trans. D. Macey, London: Verso, 2009).
L'hypothèse communiste, Paris: Lignes, 2009.
L'antiphilosophie de Wittgenstein, Caen: Nous, 2009.
'En tant que philosophe, je ne peux rendre raison du roman, entretien avec Alain Badiou', in *Le Monde des Livres*, 22 May 2009, p. 12.

Works by Gilles Deleuze

Empirisme et subjectivité: Essai sur la nature humaine selon Hume, Paris: PUF, 1953 (*Empiricism and Subjectivity: An Essay on Hume's Theory of Human Nature*, trans. C. Boundas, New York: Columbia University Press, 1991).
Proust et les signes, Paris: PUF, 1964, 2nd edn, 1972 (*Proust and Signs*, trans. R. Howard, London: Continuum, 2008).
Différence et repetition, Paris: PUF, 1968 (*Difference and Repetition*, trans. P. Patton, London: Continuum, 2004).
Spinoza et le problème de l'expression, Paris: Minuit, 1968 (*Expressionism in Philosophy: Spinoza*, trans. M. Joughin, New York: Zone Books, 1990).
Logique du sens, Paris: Minuit, 1969 (*The Logic of Sense*, trans. M. Lester and C. Stivale, New York: Columbia University Press, 1990).
and Félix Guattari, 'La synthèse disjonctive', in *L'Arc*, 43, 1970, pp. 54–62.

and Félix Guattari, *L'Anti-Oedipe*, Paris: Minuit, 1972 (*Anti-Oedipus*, trans. R. Hurley, M. Seem and H. Lane, London: Athlone Press, 1984).

and Félix Guattari, *Kafka*, Paris: Minuit, 1975 (*Kafka*, trans. D. Polan, Minneapolis, MN: University of Minnesota Press, 1986).

and Claire Parnet, *Dialogues*, Paris: Flammarion, 1977 (*Dialogues*, trans. H. Tomlinson and B. Habberjam, New York: Columbia University Press, 1987).

and Félix Guattari, *Mille plateaux*, Paris: Minuit, 1980 (*A Thousand Plateaus*, trans. B. Massumi, London: Athlone Press, 1988).

Francis Bacon: Logique de la sensation, Paris: Editions de la Différence, 1981 (*Francis Bacon: the Logic of Sensation*, trans. D. Smith, Minneapolis, MN: University of Minnesota Press, 2003).

Cinema 1: L'image-mouvement, Paris: Minuit, 1983 (*Cinema 1: The Movement-Image*, trans. H. Tomlinson and B. Habberjam, London: Continuum, 1987).

Cinema 2: L'image-temps, Paris: Minuit, 1985 (*Cinema 2: The Time-Image*, trans. H. Tomlinson and R. Galeta, London: Athlone Press, 1989).

Foucault, Paris: Minuit, 1986 (*Foucault*, trans. S. Hand, London: Athlone Press, 1988).

Le Pli: Leibniz et le baroque, Paris: Minuit, 1988 (*The Fold: Leibniz and the Baroque*, trans. T. Conley, London: Continuum, 2001).

Pourparlers 1972–1990, Paris: Minuit, 1990 (*Negotiations, 1972–1990*, trans. M. Joughin, New York, Columbia University Press, 1995).

and Félix Guattari, *Qu'est-ce que la philosophie?*, Paris: Minuit, 1991 (*What Is Philosophy?*, trans. H. Tomlinson and G. Burchill, London: Verso, 1994).

Critique et clinique, Paris: Minuit, 1993 (*Essays Critical and Clinical*, trans. D. Smith and A. Greco, London: Verso, 1998).

and Claire Parnet, *L'Abécédaire de Gilles Deleuze*, Paris: Editions du Montparnasse, 1997.

L'Ile déserte et autres textes, 1953–1974, Paris: Minuit, 2002 (*Desert Islands and Other Texts*, trans. M. Taormina, New York: Semiotext(e), 2003).

Deux regimes de fous, textes et entretiens 1975–1995, Paris: Minuit, 2003 (*Two Regimes of Madness*, trans. A. Hodges and M. Taormina, New York: Semiotext(e), 2007).

Other works cited

Alliez, Eric (ed.), *Gilles Deleuze, une vie philosophique*, Paris: Les Empêcheurs de penser en rond, 1998.

Althusser, Louis, *Positions*, Paris: Editions Sociales, 1976.

Antonioli, Manola, *Géophilosophie de Deleuze et Guattari*, Paris: L'Harmattan, 2003.

Austin, J. L., *Philosophical Papers*, Oxford: Clarendon Press, 1970.
Bayard, Pierre, *Le plagiat par anticipation*, Paris: Minuit, 2009.
Beckett, Samuel, *Murphy*, London: John Calder, 1963 (1938).
Beckett, Samuel, *The Beckett Trilogy*, London: Picador, 1979.
Beckett, Samuel, *Ill Seen Ill Said*, London: John Calder, 1981.
Beckett, Samuel, *The Complete Dramatic Works*, London: Faber, 1986.
Beckett, Samuel, *Quad, suivi de L'Epuisé, par Gilles Deleuze*, Paris: Minuit, 1992.
Bergen, Véronique, *L'ontologie de Gilles Deleuze*, Paris: L'Harmattan, 2001.
Boundas, Constantin and Dorothea Olkowski (eds), *Gilles Deleuze and the Theater of Philosophy*, London: Routledge, 1994.
Bouveresse, Jacques, *La connaissance de l'écrivain*, Paris: Agone, 2007.
Buchanan, Ian and Marks, John (eds), *Deleuze and Literature*, Edinburgh: Edinburgh University Press, 2000.
Buydens, Mireille, *Sahara. L'esthétique de Gilles Deleuze*, Paris: Vrin, 1990.
Caillois, Roger, *Cohérences aventureuses*, Paris: Gallimard, 1965.
Caillois, Roger, 'Le narval et la licorne', in *Le Monde*, 24 December 1976, pp. 1 and 11.
Calvino, Italo, *Il visconte dimezzato*, Turin: Einaudi, 1952.
Carroll, Lewis, *The Annotated Snark*, ed. M. Gardner, Harmondsworth: Penguin, 1967.
Carroll, Lewis, *Alice's Adventures in Wonderland*, Harmondsworth: Penguin, 1994.
Cressole, Michel, *Deleuze*, Paris: Editions Universitaires, 1973.
Cusset, François, *La décennie. Le grand cauchemar des années 1980*, Paris: La Découverte, 2006.
Descombes, Vincent, *Proust*, Paris: Minuit, 1987.
Descombes, Vincent, *Le platonisme*, Paris: PUF, 2007 (1971).
Dickens, Charles, *Our Mutual Friend*, Harmondsworth: Penguin, 1971 (1864–5).
Dosse, François, *Gilles Deleuze Félix Guattari*, Paris: La Découverte, 2007.
Dowd, Garin, *Abstract Machines*, Amsterdam: Rodopi, 2007.
Feltham, Oliver, *Alain Badiou, Live Theory*, London: Continuum, 2008.
Foucault, Michel, *Les mots et les choses*, Paris: Gallimard, 1966.
Gelas, B. and Micolet, H. (eds), *Deleuze et les écrivains*, Nantes: Cécile Defaut, 2007.
Gibson, Andrew, *Beckett and Badiou*, Oxford: Oxford University Press, 2006.
Grice, H. P., *Studies in the Way of Words*, Cambridge, MA: Harvard University Press, 1989.
Greimas, Algirdas Julien, *Sémantique structurale*, Paris: Larousse, 1966.

Bibliography

Guattari, Félix, *Psychanalyse et transversalité*, Paris: Maspéro, 1972.
Guattari, Félix, *Molecular Revolution*, Harmondsworth: Penguin, 1984.
Hallward, Peter (ed.), *Think Again: Alain Badiou and the Future of Philosophy*, London: Continuum, 2004.
Hallward, Peter, *Out of This World. Deleuze and the Philosophy of Creation*, London: Verso, 2006.
James, Henry, *Selected Literary Criticism*, Harmondsworth: Penguin, 1968.
Jameson, Fredric, *A Singular Modernity*, London: Verso, 2002.
Lakoff, George and Johnson, Mark, *Metaphors We Live By*, Chicago: Chicago University Press, 1980.
Lecercle, Jean-Jacques, *Interpretation as Pragmatics*, Basingstoke: Macmillan, 1999.
Lecercle, Jean-Jacques, *Deleuze and Language*, Basingstoke: Palgrave, 2002.
Leclaire, Serge, *Psychanalyser*, Paris: Seuil, 1968.
Lyotard, Jean-François, *Discours, figure*, Paris: Klincksieck, 1971.
Lyotard, Jean-François, *The Differend*, Manchester: Manchester University Press, 1988 (1983).
Lunn, Eugene, *Marxism and Modernism*, London: Verso, 1985.
Macherey, Pierre, *Marx 1845*, Paris: Amsterdam, 2008.
Mallarmé, Stéphane, *Œuvres Complètes*, Paris: Gallimard (Bibliothèque de la Pléiade), 1945.
Milner, Jan-Claude, *Constats*, Paris: Gallimard, 1999.
Montebello, Pierre, *Deleuze*, Paris: Vrin, 2008.
Monterroso, Augusto, *Œuvres complètes (et autres contes)*, Geneva, Patiño, 2000.
New, Christopher, *Philosophy of Literature*, London: Routledge, 1999.
Olkowski, Dorothea, *Gilles Deleuze and the Ruin of Representation*, Berkeley, CA: University of California Press, 1998.
Ortony, Andrew (ed.), *Metaphor and Thought*, Cambridge: Cambridge University Press, 1979.
Panaccio, Claude, *Le discours intérieur*, Paris: Seuil, 1999.
Pavel, Thomas, *Fictional Worlds*, Cambridge, MA: Harvard University Press, 1986.
Ramond, Charles (ed.), *Alain Badiou. Penser le multiple*, Paris: L'Harmattan, 2002.
Rancière, Jacques, *Mallarmé, la politique de la sirène*, Paris: Hachette, 1966.
Rancière, Jacques, *Politique de la littérature*, Paris: Galilée, 2007.
Ricœur, Paul, *Time and Narrative*, three vols, Chicago: Chicago University Press, 1984–7.
Rinzler, Simone, *La Passion du discours*, forthcoming.
Ross, Kristin, *The Emergence of Social Space*, London: Verso, 2008.

Rosset, Clément, *Le réel, traité de l'idiotie*, Paris: Minuit, 1971.
Ryle, Gilbert, *The Concept of Mind*, Harmondsworth, Penguin, 1963 (1949).
Sabot, Pierre, *Philosophie et littérature*, Paris: PUF, 2002.
Saint-Girons, Baldine, *L'acte esthétique*, Paris: Klincksieck, 2007.
Sauvagnargues, Anne, *Deleuze et l'art*, Paris: PUF, 2005.
Shelley, Mary, *Frankenstein*, London: Penguin, 1985.
Simondon, Gilbert, *L'individu et sa genèse physico-biologique*, Paris: PUF, 1964.
Solnit, Rebecca, *Wanderlust. A History of Walking*, London: Verso, 2001.
Stivale, Charles (ed.), *Gilles Deleuze, Key Concepts*, Stocksfield: Acumen, 2005.
Stoker, Bram, *Dracula*, Oxford: Oxford University Press, 1996.
Strawson, P. F., *The Bounds of Sense*, London: Methuen, 1966.
Todorov, Tzvetan, *The Fantastic: A Structural Approach to a Literary Genre*, Ithaca, NY: Cornell University Press, 1975.
Williams, James, 'If Not Here, Then Where? On the Location and Individuation of Events in Badiou and Deleuze', in *Deleuze Studies*, 3 (1), 2009, pp. 97–123.
Žižek, Slavoj, *Organs Without Bodies*, London: Routledge, 2004.

Index

Althusser, L., 12, 49, 132, 200
Aristotle, 106
Artaud, A., 153, 198
assemblage, 46, 60, 129, 145, 146–7, 180–1

Bacon, F., 71, 73, 81, 138, 192, 196, 203
Badiou, A.
  Badiou sentence, 54–5
  inaesthetics, 3, 42, 108, 197–9, 201
  language, 107–8, 110, 137, 139–41
  matheme, 47–8, 49
  metaphor/metonymy, 94–5, 100
  mode of reading, 53–4
  paradoxes, 102–13
  philosophical importance, 1–5
  poetics, 97–102, 108
  reading Deleuze, 22–31
  relationship with Deleuze, 6–9
Balibar, E., 16
Beckett, S., 103, 120, 129–39, 139–42, 143–54, 171
Bergson, H., 33, 129
Boldini, A., 87–9
Bosteels, B., 47
Bouveresse, J., 191
Brecht, B., 106
Burchill, L., 53
Buydens, M., 192

Caillois, R., 158–60, 166
canon, 41, 57–8, 105, 111, 113, 114, 119–22, 127, 129, 143, 147, 151, 153, 154, 193
Carroll, L., 17, 99, 128, 158, 198
Céline, L. F., 153
Chomsky, N., 74, 128, 144, 151
compossibilisation, 3, 93, 137, 166, 190
Conley, T., 48
continental philosophy, 10–14
correlation, 32, 49, 50, 51–2, 56–7, 82, 85, 192, 195, 201–2
Crane, S., 158, 176, 178
Cressole, M., 43–4
Cusset, F., 33

Descombes, V., 199
Deleuze, G.
  aesthetics, 60, 192–7
  cinema, 70–2
  Deleuze sentence, 55–6
  language, 73–4, 143, 147–50, 152
  metaphor/metamorphosis, 86–7, 123, 125–6, 181
  paradox, 102–13
  philosophical importance, 1–5
  reading Badiou, 22
  relationship with Badiou, 6–9
Dickens, C., 61–4
disjunctive synthesis, 2, 16–26, 30, 34, 42, 46, 50, 52, 146–7, 152, 154, 189

Dowd, G., 144, 146
Dracula, 162–3, 174, 179–87

Eisenstein, S., 71
essence, 47, 81–7, 88, 89, 90
event, 78, 114, 130, 135–6, 138, 141, 142, 164–6, 167–8, 173–4, 176–8

fantastique, 159–61, 163–4, 166–75, 178–9
Feltham, O., 102–3, 112
Foucault, M., 121–2, 126
Frankenstein, 161–3, 173–4, 175, 179

Gibson, A., 130, 132–3, 135–6, 138, 142, 165
Greimas, A. J., 184–5
Grice, H. P., 10, 80
Guattari, F., 21, 29–30, 74

Hallward, P., 22, 27, 57

interpretation, 3, 42, 45, 61, 63, 69, 77–87, 90, 100–2, 107–9, 116, 134, 140, 193

Jakobson, R., 51
James, H., 63–4
Jameson, F., 120–2, 126–7

Kafka, F., 59–61, 160, 181
Kant, I., 143, 144

Lacan, J., 8, 14, 38, 39, 43, 46, 47, 51, 53–4, 90, 94–5, 100, 104, 163, 176
Lalouette, J.-F., 59–60
Leclaire, S., 19
logos endiathetos, 71–2
Luca, G., 58, 147, 153
Lunn, E., 127–9

Mallarmé, S., 92–7, 101, 108–9, 110, 113, 138, 141, 165
Mandelstam, O., 58–9
Maoism, 6–7, 39–40, 46
marvellous, 159–61, 178–9
Masoch, S., 50
Melville, H., 143, 153, 158
Metz, C., 70, 73
Monterroso, A., 161
Milner, J.-C., 100–1
Milosz, C., 108
modernism, 120–2, 127–9, 130

Parmenides, 105
Pasolini, P. P., 70
passion, 38–41
passport application form, 161–3
Péguy, C., 153
Pessoa, F., 97, 102, 108
philosophy of literature, 189–90, 191
Platonism, 25–6, 28, 29, 42, 84–5, 104, 106
Power, N. & A. Toscano, 130, 138, 139–40
problem, 27, 31, 41, 46, 53, 68, 69, 72–3, 76–7, 89–90, 107, 115–16, 148
Proust, M., 68–90

Rancière, J., 33, 42, 130, 136–7, 196–7, 200–1
representation, 19, 25, 33, 40, 48, 53, 71, 74, 78, 81, 83, 85, 87, 88, 113, 121–7, 142, 165, 192
Rimbaud, A., 110, 113–14, 141, 165
Ross, K., 113–14
Rosset, C., 196
Roussel, R., 153

Sabot, P., 199–200, 201
Saint-Girons, B., 42
Sartre, J.-P., 112, 131

Index

Saussure, F. de, 73, 74, 75, 78, 82, 151
Sauvagnargues, A., 16, 58
sense v. meaning, 20–1, 45, 90, 128–9, 151–2, 176–7, 186–7, 195
sign, 72, 75–6, 78–84, 87
Simont, J., 53–4
Sophist, 30–1, 104–5
Stoics, 75
strong reading, 26–31, 38, 43–6, 68–70, 89, 90, 113, 115–16, 133, 138–9
style, 42, 46–8, 54, 70, 89–90, 147, 150–3, 154, 195
subject, 19–20, 26, 32, 39, 43, 45, 48–9, 61, 81, 83–7, 96, 102, 114–24, 129–30, 133, 138, 140, 145, 164–5, 168–74

syntax, 64–5, 97–101, 103, 108, 112–13, 141, 143,150–1, 152–3, 195, 202–3

Thirouin, M.-O., 60
tick, 181–2
Todorov, T. 159, 163
truth, 3, 14, 16, 29, 32, 45, 48, 58, 79–82, 92, 93, 101, 106–7, 110, 112, 114–15

Vincennes, 7–8

Williams, J., 176
Wittgenstein, L., 11, 51, 81, 105
Woolf, V., 81

Žižek, S., 22

BADIOU AND DELEUZE READ LITERATURE
is part of
PLATEAUS: NEW DIRECTIONS IN DELEUZE STUDIES

Other Titles from this Series

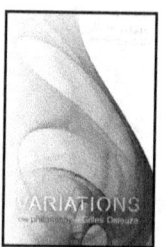

VARIATIONS: THE PHILOSOPHY OF GILLES DELEUZE
By *Jean-Clet Martin*
Translated by Constantin V. Boundas & Susan Dyrkton
Publication: April 2010, ISBN: 978 0 7486 3882 6

An insightful reading of Deleuze, from a fellow philosopher with whom Deleuze himself corresponded about his work.

POSTCOLONIAL AGENCY: CRITIQUE AND CONSTRUCTIVISM
by Simone Bignall
Publication: May 2010, ISBN: 978 0 7486 3943 4

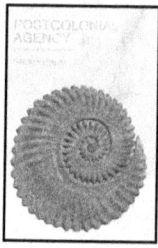

Uses Deleuzian thought to come to a significantly new understanding of the struggles faced by many societies in the aftermath of empire.

IMMANENCE – DELEUZE AND PHILOSOPHY
By *Miguel de Beistegui*
Publication: June 2010, ISBN: 978 0 7486 3830 7

Identifies the original impetus and the driving force behind Deleuze's philosophy as a whole and the many concepts it creates.

DELEUZIAN FABULATION AND THE SCARS OF HISTORY
By *Ronald Bogue*
Publication: July 2010, ISBN: 978 0 7486 4131 4

Proposes a newly formulated theory of fabulation as the guiding principle of a Deleuzian approach to literary narrative.

SEE THE FULL SERIES AT WWW.EUPPUBLISHING.COM/SERIES/PLAT

EUP JOURNALS ONLINE
Deleuze Studies

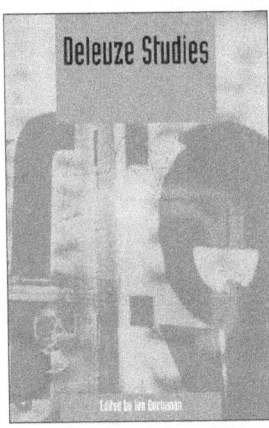

Now three issues per year

Editor
Ian Buchanan, *Cardiff University*
Executive Editor
David Savat, *University of Western Australia*
Reviews Editor
John Marks, *University of Nottingham*
Co-editors
Claire Colebrook, Penn State
Tom Conley, Harvard University
Gary Genosko, Lakehead University
Christian Kerslake, Middlesex University
Gregg Lambert, Syracuse University

Deleuze Studies is the first paper based journal to focus exclusively on the work of Gilles Deleuze. Published triannually, and edited by a team of highly respected Deleuze scholars, *Deleuze Studies* is a forum for new work on the writings of Gilles Deleuze.

Deleuze Studies is a bold journal that challenges orthodoxies, encourages debate, invites controversy, seeks new applications, proposes new interpretations, and above all make new connections between scholars and ideas in the field. The journal publishes a wide variety of scholarly work on Gilles Deleuze, including articles that focus directly on his work, but also critical reviews of the field, as well as new translations and annotated bibliographies. It does not limit itself to any one field: it is neither a philosophy journal, nor a literature journal, nor a cultural studies journal, but all three and more.

A 2010 subscription will include a free supplementary issue of the journal, *Deleuze and Political Activism*, guest-edited by Marcelo Svirsky.

ISSN 1750-2241   eISSN 1755-1684   Three issues per year

Register to receive Table of Contents Alerts at www.eupjournals.com

EU representative:
Easy Access System Europe
Mustamäe tee 50, 10621 Tallinn, Estonia
Gpsr.requests@easproject.com

www.ingramcontent.com/pod-product-compliance
Lightning Source LLC
Chambersburg PA
CBHW061713300426
44115CB00014B/2669